The World of Shipping

Studies in Transport History

Series Editor: John Armstrong

Coastal and Short Sea Shipping
John Armstrong

Railways (volume I)
Terry Gourvish

Railways (volume II)
Geoffrey Channon

Road Transport in the Horse-Drawn Era
Dorian Gerhold

Air Transport
Peter J. Lyth

Canals and Inland Navigation
Gerald Crompton

Motor Transport
Margaret Walsh

The World of Shipping
David M. Williams

The World of Shipping

Edited by

DAVID M. WILLIAMS

Routledge
Taylor & Francis Group

LONDON AND NEW YORK

First published 1997 by Ashgate Publishing

Reissued 2018 by Routledge
2 Park Square, Milton Park, Abingdon, Oxon, OX14 4RN
52 Vanderbilt Avenue, New York, NY 10017

Routledge is an imprint of the Taylor & Francis Group, an informa business

Publisher's Note
The publisher has gone to great lengths to ensure the quality of this reprint but points
out that some imperfections in the original copies may be apparent.

Disclaimer
The publisher has made every effort to trace copyright holders and welcomes
correspondence from those they have been unable to contact.

A Library of Congress record exists under LC control number:

ISBN 13: 978-1-138-36783-8 (hbk)
ISBN 13: 978-1-138-36784-5 (pbk)
ISBN 13: 978-0-429-42960-6 (ebk)

Contents

Studies in Transport History

Series Editor's Preface

The idea for this series originated in a meeting of the Editorial Board of *The Journal of Transport History*. As part of the celebrations to mark the fortieth anniversary of the founding of the journal, a classified index of the articles appearing in each of the series was compiled by Julie Stevenson and published in the September 1993 number of the journal. This exercise revealed the wealth of material that lay in the journal but which was largely forgotten and relatively inaccessible, unless a full run of the journal was close to hand. The index took the first step in making it simpler to determine what was in the journal. The Editorial Board decided it should continue this process by making the best of the essays more readily available.

Hence it is proposed to issue a series of volumes, each containing a number of articles reprinted from *The Journal of Transport History*, dealing with a particular mode of transport. As initially planned there are eight volumes in this series, each covering one form of transport and edited by a different member of the Editorial Board. Each volume contains about ten articles, reprinted from *The Journal of Transport History*. The articles have been selected because they were seminal at the date of their publication and have stood the test of time. Hence they are still important contributions to the state of our knowledge on the topic.

Each volume also contains an introduction by the editor of the volume, which seeks to contextualise the articles selected; that is, to show how each contribution fitted into the state of knowledge at the time of its publication, to explain its importance, to indicate any more-recent literature on the topic that might moderate its findings, and suggest how the debate has moved since the initial publication. Each article retains its original pagination, as in the journal. This will allow citations to be made to the original source.

Thus this series aims to make easily available the most important essays which have appeared in *The Journal of Transport History* over the last forty years, collected together on a thematic basis. It is hoped that this will encourage and provoke further research into transport history, in order to carry the debates into the twenty-first century.

John Armstrong
1996

Thames Valley University

Introduction: the world of shipping

DAVID M. WILLIAMS

Of all modes of transport, shipping can claim to be the most international. It was unique in its ability to link countries and continents across the world until the 1920s when commercial aviation breached this monopoly. That challenge was of little import before the 1950s and thereafter was only of significance in the carriage of passengers, mail and light freight. The transport of bulk commodities, the crucial elements of world trade and development - foods, raw materials and, in the last two centuries, the essential fuels of coal and petroleum - has always been, and will continue to be, the preserve of maritime transport.

Of course, not all shipping business was international or long distance, the majority of vessels operated over lesser routes in coastal and short sea trades.[1] Such traffic was part of commercial systems feeding into networks of maritime transport which served an international and, sometimes, world-wide function. The beginnings of this world of shipping lie in the great voyages of discovery of the late fifteenth century. These ushered in three centuries of European exploration, colonisation and the establishment of trading links embracing both hemispheres, with European shipping often integrating with existing regional networks, notably in the Indian Ocean and Far East. Through such expansion, particularly from the mid-nineteenth century when steam power brought enhanced speed and efficiency, shipping came to assume a global character.

The concept of a world of shipping, however, has a dimension beyond that of being the form of transport which served all countries and all continents. More subtly, there was a 'world' of shipping in another sense. By its very nature shipping possessed characteristics different from other transport modes which led to special structures of ownership, finance, management and operation. These structures were unique in their form and their internationality. In shipping, the factors of capital and labour were internationally mobile; ships - according to their size and type - could be operated in many, or all, waters and ownership and the vessel itself could be easily transferred. Likewise, labour could be hired, or choose to offer itself for hire, at ports all over the world.[2] More particularly, operating between countries, especially in trans-oceanic trades, involved skills, techniques and facilities beyond those demanded in any land-based enterprise. Languages, laws, customs, commodities and markets were all different from those encountered in internal trade and, moreover, transactions were undertaken 'at distance' where the crucial dimension was that of time rather than any linear measurement. Only perhaps in finance did a degree of a similar international involvement emerge (and then closely linked with trade and shipping). While finance may have matched shipping in terms of sophisticated organisation, it did not involve the manipulation of physical capital such as ships. Nor did it assume a world-wide coverage so early. Shipping served the world and it evolved its own peculiar pattern of international and ultimately, in the late twentieth century, global operation. A further feature peculiar to shipping was government action. From time immemorial governments involved themselves with shipping for strategic, commercial and financial reasons; moreover, mercantile marines were viewed as naval reserves. Shipowners and merchants had to take special account of policy and possible changes in it when conducting their operations.[3]

These two worlds of shipping which most certainly had begun to emerge by 1700 underwent dramatic change in the nineteenth and twentieth centuries. The forces underlying such change were many. Industrialisation, the huge expansion of world trade and new methods of transferring information all had a massive impact but, primarily, the stimulus was technological change in the vehicle and power of maritime transport. It is quite remarkable that the great maritime developments of the sixteenth through to the nineteenth centuries, while owing much to new skills in navigation, hydrography and cartography, had nevertheless been achieved within conditions of a relatively static technological framework in terms of sail power and tonnage.

The nineteenth century saw a transformation. Steam and iron, the key components of nineteenth-century industrialisation, were the prime factors. Steam's most basic impact lay in its ability to reduce shipping's subservience to wind and tide, thus permitting an unprecedented level of speed and regularity in service. Iron, and later steel, overcame the problem of timber shortage and enabled the construction of much larger vessels. These new qualities together with the capital requirements of steamship construction and operation had an effect on all aspects of the world of shipping. Vessels, labour, finance, port facilities and operating practices were all to undergo huge changes. Steamships, being more costly, required continuous operation and thus more efficient management; maritime labour, in the sense of the nature of work and the make-up of the labour force, was transformed with the appearance of a below deck engine-room staff, and the finance of shipping took on an increased dimension. Ports were directly and indirectly, influenced by steam. Steamships required berths and more efficient cargo handling, while steam technology, in the form of the railway, expanded hinterlands and promoted business and competition.

The triumph of the steamship, though in the long run of history remarkably rapid, took over seventy years. Steam shipping, a novelty in the 1820s, did not relegate sail to insignificance until around 1900. The long transition was in part due to the limits of early technology; initially the low efficiency of paddle wheels and heavy coal consumption (entailing the sacrifice of much cargo space) checked steam's progress.[4] It was only from the mid-nineteenth century that the screw propellor and, more so, the compound engine brought a level of fuel efficiency sufficient to curtail excessive bunker space. However, in the mid-nineteenth century, ironically at the very time when steam commenced its challenge, the sailing ship, after centuries of static technology, underwent its own revolution. In size of vessels, hull design, sail power and labour productivity, progress in sail was remarkable. The world's sailing fleet reached it maximum tonnage in the 1870s. For all its advance, sail could not compete; steam captured in turn, though never quite exclusively in the nineteenth century, coastal, short sea, oceanic and ultimately world trade routes.[5] In the twentieth century coal, and in the maritime context, steam shipping, underwent its own challenge from petroleum fuels and oil-fired shipping. Both the general and specific challenge were highly significant; the transporting of oil proved more important than the coal trade and, in turn, oil-powered shipping deposed steam more rapidly than steam had replaced sail. Nevertheless, in the two hundred years or so from the commencement of industrialisation, the crucial transformation was that of steam power and materials, iron and steel. It was these which made the vital breakthroughs in the old bottlenecks of natural limitations, weather, wind, tide and wood. In the twentieth century, oil power and larger vessels served to enhance that seminal advance.

As the world of shipping, in the sense of the market, was expanding and being transformed by new technologies so, too, was that other world of shipping, the world of special skills, contacts and operating practices. Extended shipping routes, the growing variety and volume of cargoes handled, and the expansion of passenger traffic, particularly emigrants, required new and more sophisticated business practices often resulting in greater specialisation of function and greater needs for commercial links and networks of information. The complexities of this world of shipping took on a new character as, for the first time, commercial information could travel faster than goods. The speed and reliability of steam vessels was one aspect of the more rapid transit of commercial intelligence though, interestingly, the notion of special, fast passage-making vessels was pioneered in the age of sail, first by post office packets and from the 1820s by commercial operated American trans-Atlantic packets. Of greater importance were new technologies. The optical telegraph of the late eighteenth century is the first such example; more significant was the electric telegraph and, even more so, the laying of submarine cables after 1850. Around 1900 wireless telegraphy introduced another dimension by permitting communication between land and vessels at sea. All such information imparted a new aspect to commercial relationships and decision-taking leading to markets for maritime services, capital and labour becoming more specialised, more comprehensive and fully international. The new ability to transmit commercial information more rapidly than the transport of goods, like steam power's positive challenge to the constraints of nature, represented, quite literally, a sea change in the world of shipping.

The articles in this volume reflect the changing world of shipping from the late eighteenth century to that of the mid-twentieth century. All develop some of the themes outlined above. All papers too have an international dimension although many, particularly those set before 1914, possess a British focus. As such they reflect the character of the world of shipping. For over a century from the 1830s Britain dominated the maritime world. At no time has one nation been so powerful in a crucial economic sector. Britain's supremacy in shipping was assured when a potential challenge from the United States fell away after 1850 through a slower response to steam and the tribulations of civil war.[6] Around 1900 Britain carried half the world's trade by volume and value; her merchant fleet represented over 40 per cent of world tonnage and she built over 60 per cent of the world's ships. The First World War hastened a decline from this exalted position but Britain remained a major player in world shipping until the 1960s. Thus, along with massive market expansion, revolutionary technical change and new

sophisticated organisation, the world of shipping in the nineteenth and twentieth centuries
was characterised by the rise, and latterly the decline, of British maritime power.

The earliest paper, in terms of period is that of Simon Ville embracing the years 1775-
1830. Its focus is on sail but while set in the age before crucial technical advance, the
study is very much concerned with economic progress. Utilising the papers of the London
shipowners Michael and Joseph Henley, Ville argues that the period saw significant shifts
towards higher productivity in shipping operations. This was achieved by greater
flexibility in the deployment of vessels, in different trades rather than only one trade, and
by aiming at continuous employment throughout the year. A trend towards the better use
of resources was to be ongoing in an age of new technology and expanding markets.[7]

Its central theme of greater efficiency apart, Ville's article raises other features which
characterised the new world of shipping. One such was the development of new trades.
The success of the Henleys lay in their movement into trades not merely new to them but,
in great measure, to British shipping. In the early nineteenth century new trades emerged
in North and South America, in both instances due to political and strategic factors. In
South America, Spanish and Portugues colonies threw off imperial rule while French
economic warfare and military success in Scandinavia led to the promotion of the North
American timber trade. The latter triggered phenomenal expansion and set in train the rise
of the British North American colonies to a prominent place among shipowning nations
in the 1870s, albeit with a sailing ship fleet.[8] The nineteenth century saw a succession of
new or expanding regions of trade, notably in the Far East and Pacific.[9]

Henleys initially operated as coal merchants and shipowners, but later concentrated on
shipowning. The trend towards separation and specialisation of function was to occur in
many aspects of maritime activity. Ville has developed this analysis and the operations of
specialist shipowners has become a major focus of research.[10] The context of the market
confronting the Henleys represents a further important theme. The period 1775 to 1830
was characterised by fluctuating fortunes as naval actions, privateering and economic
warfare distorted trading patterns. More particularly, the post-1815 depression was an
early indicator of the cycle of boom and slump which came to characterise shipping
business. While the secular trend of shipping business was upward, swiftly reacting to, or
better still anticipating, these shorter-term movements was often the key factor
determining the success of maritime operators.

The articles of Wilde and Harcourt which follow chronologically after that of Ville are
both concerned with policy. Traditionally governments sought to promote and protect
their shipping industries and this was true of most countries in the nineteenth century and
certainly after the First World War when international shipping fell on hard times. The
apparent exception to this was Britain which in 1849 swept away two centuries of
protection with the repeal of the Navigation Laws.[11] Yet while repeal is rightly viewed as
the application of free trade principles to shipping and while British economic policy
generally is characterised as non-interventionist and *laissez faire*, at the very time when
government was rejecting old policies it introduced two measures which were to have a
significant impact on shipping, British and international.

Wilde examines the creation of the Marine Department tracing its origins to the Select

Committee on Shipwrecks of 1836. That Committee marked the start of a new era of regulation for it implied a new responsibility for government, that of ensuring the safety of life and property at sea. High among the Committee's recommendations was the establishment of a single department to handle matters relating to the merchant marine. An early duty of that department was to improve standards of seamanship with compulsory examinations for masters and mates. Neither government nor shipowners favoured such proposals but following further official enquiries, against the backdrop of fierce controversy over the Navigation Laws, the Merchant Shipping Act was passed in 1850. The Act, embodying 120 clauses, codified maritime law, established a centralised agency in the Board of Trade to oversee shipping matters and introduced the certification of masters and mates.[12] In the years after 1851 many further obligations were placed on the Marine Department, notably in the areas of safety (dangerous cargoes, load lines and unseaworthy vessels) and that of seaman's welfare covering aspects such as the payment of wages, accommodation, diet and health. These policies had a significance far beyond the British setting: the Marine Department served as a model for other nations; some British standards came to cover foreign shipping through the insistence that British standards be applied to all vessels entering British ports and, finally, some British regulations were adopted as international conventions. In the forty years since Wilde's pioneering article, the work of the Marine Department has been a widely researched field.[13]

Harcourt's paper reviews the issue of mail contracts. Steamships which offered speedy passages and relative reliability of voyage times were, from their beginning, attractive to government. The prospect of rapid communications induced governments to offer contracts as an incentive to the establishment of steamship services on important routes. Britain as an international and imperial power, and the leader in steam, pioneered such a policy in the 1830s. In 1837 the Peninsular Steam Navigation Company (subsequently P&O) gained a contract for the carriage of mail to Gibraltar, Portugal and Spain, which was followed in 1840 by a further contract when the service was extended to India. In 1839 came the Cunard contract for Canadian and northern United States mail; 1840 saw Pacific Steam contracted to serve central and South American ports and in 1842 Royal Mail gained a contract for Caribbean services. Harcourt views these long-distance contracts as 'momentous for British maritime history'. The subsequent history of mail contracts is complicated with periodic official commissions and vigorous discussion at the time of expiry and renewal of contracts. Contracts continued down to 1914, although total payments fell from 1875.

No government policy has given rise to such debate as that of mail contracts, moreover the controversy is as alive today as it was to contemporary commentators. Essentially that controversy revolved around the basic question of whether mail contracts represented commercial payments or subsidies? Important subsidiary questions are: did the recipient companies gain commercial, and perhaps monopolistic advantage over other British companies? Was British steam shipping subsidised, unfairly aided and given a head start? This last question has invariably been answered in the affirmative by foreign observers and equally strongly rejected by most British writers. The fierce, often bitter debate has been clouded by the different interpretations of such terms as 'bounty', 'subsidy', 'subvention' and 'commercial transaction'. Harcourt in her seminal article charts a clear course through the maze of charge and counter-argument. She accepts that payments did embody a measure of subsidy but she views British mail contracts as a 'multi-functional mechanism' aimed at the expansion of trade, the capture of major routes, promoting shipbuilding and particularly as a spur to the new technology of steam navigation. She perceives the mail contract system as falling into two phases, the periods before and after the 1860s. In the first, the heavy start-up investment in ships, coal and repair depots, necessary to ensure a reliable service, would have been too risky to have been undertaken by private capital alone. Hence the need for assured returns through mail contracts. In the second period, conditions changed. Improved technology, notably the compound engine, facilitated the activities of other companies and promoted fierce competition involving British and foreign operators some subsidised by their governments, but the same contractors continued to receive subsidies, albeit under increasing scrutiny and at reduced levels. Measured as such conclusions are, the debate is ongoing. A recent study of the Royal Mail Company again considers contract payments. Though noting that the Royal Mail group did not set up a company until assured of the contract it concludes that payments 'allowed returns broadly appropriate to the risks involved' and that before 1914 contracts represented 'due consideration for the performance of a valuable public service' rather than 'contractors' bounties' or 'excess returns'.[14]

Companies receiving mail contracts feature directly or indirectly in the articles of Broeze, Cooper and Jones but, more particularly, these articles all examine steam shipping in eastern trades. European trade with the Indies and beyond has a long history: it was the motivation for exploration in the fifteenth century and underlay the establishment and operations of East India companies in many European countries in the seventeenth and eighteenth centuries. Important as such developments were, the great growth of European and American involvement with eastern markets came in the nineteenth century. Various influences brought this about: for the India and East Indies trade, the loss of monopoly or collapse of the chartered East India companies was one factor; further east, the forced opening of China and Japan was another; so, too, was the discovery of Australia. Yet all these attractive markets were distant and, in terms of wide participation, new trades, thus embodying additional risks. In the later nineteenth century, the time element of such risks was reduced by steam shipping and the construction of the Suez Canal The canal by its restriction to steamships assured the supremacy of new technology.

The title of Broeze's article, 'Distance tamed' is a succinct summary of the ultimate triumph of steamshipping. The takeover of steam was gradual for its advantages were offset by the costs of fuel and bunker space. This supply-side equation influenced the traffic carried and the length of route operated. Hence steam soon captured the mail, high-value freight and cabin passenger trades (bulk cargo emigrants were a different matter!), and rapidly penetrated coastal and short sea trades. The conquest of the busy trans-Atlantic routes, relatively short in comparison with other oceanic trades, was not far behind. More problematical, and consequently a later process, was steam's introduction into the longer, relatively less developed trades to the East. However, Broeze stresses that while the process, of steam navigation to Australia and New Zealand was the product of market forces, it was also influenced by entrepreneurial activity, technological and political factors.

In the introduction of steam to Australasian routes the policy of mail contracts was highly significant. The extension of P&O's contract to India (using the overland route via Egypt) gave the company great commercial advantage and a monopoly of steam services to the East. This the company jealously guarded. Hence, early schemes for services to Australia came to nought and when, from 1852, contracts were awarded to P&O and other companies, P&O with its resources and established network saw off all rivals. Although P&O now provided a modern link in no way did the steamship dominate Australasian trades; P&O vessels served only some ports and only the top of the freight market. Until the 1870s, sailing vessels still carried the bulk of imports and exports, most passengers and all immigrants. The costs of distance still prevailed. The Suez Canal and more so the compound and later the triple expansion engine dramatically changed the market. Now both the P&O and those segments of the market where sail dominated were open to challenge but still, given the long voyage, if viable steam shipping companies were to be established, entrepreneurial talent and financial resources were essential.[15]

In the attainment of these requirements, Broeze stresses the 'pivotal functional and organisational role played by the established shipbrokers'.[16] Their experience of sailing ship traffic and special knowledge of the Australian market together with ability to raise finance for steamships and to act for owners was vital. The Orient Steam Navigation Company was the creation, in 1878, of two of London's most prominent shipbroking companies in the Australian trade, Andersons and Green. Unlike P&O, the Orient Line aimed at providing a complete range of passenger and cargo services. The line's success demonstrated that sail could be replaced in both the mass emigrant and commodity trades, and led to a wave of investment in steam and new company formation. In most of these formations, brokers were directly involved. By the mid-1880s steam tonnage was sufficient to provide for all the immigrant business and the expanding new dairy and meat exports. Yet strangely brokers were also responsible for the persistance of sail in certain trades. For most of the year the pattern of Australian trade was that of imports (including migrants) exceeding exports but during the wool exporting season this imbalance was reversed. It thus made sense to use sailing vessels to freight the extra cargoes which steam could not handle. Broker/shipowners recognised this and therefore retained some sail capacity years after steam had effectively triumphed.

The final major theme of Broeze's study is that of the conference system. Shipping conferences were a crucial feature of the new world of shipping and therefore merit general consideration.[17] Conferences arose directly out of the nature of steamship line operation. Establishing lines and maintaining regular services was costly, particularly if trade flows were seasonal or unbalanced on outward and inward voyage legs. These conditions prevailed in most trades. Operators of steamship lines were thus anxious to limit competition with other lines, deter newcomers and prevent non-liner ships, tramps, from securing cargo on an opportunistic basis. Conferences, agreements between liner companies to share trade or pool receipts, were the system which evolved to control competition. Besides agreement between suppliers it was necessary to secure customer loyalty, this was achieved through the device of the deferred rebate which was paid only to those who remained faithful to the liner company's services. It was once believed that the conference system first appeared in the 1870s but it is now recognised that there were agreements between British coastal steamship operators in the 1830s and that, internationally, the celebrated rivalry between the Cunard and Collins Lines of the early 1850s masked a receipt pooling agreement.[18] However, it was from the 1870s that conferences became widespread.

Broeze notes that a conference was established in the Australian trade in 1876 at the instigation of eight leading London shipping brokers. Its operation proved difficult due to the imbalance in trade, market fluctuations and the ability of colonial governments and large exporters in Australia to play off members of the conference.[19] At the same time Australasian trade expanded particularly in the new field of refrigerated exports. New shipping lines were set up, many existing ones expanded and the period from the 1890s was characterised, as in other sectors of world shipping and the world economy generally, by concentration and control of ownership. Large groups came to dominate, so that in the Australasian trades steam ultimately prevailed and organisational structures became more complex. On the eve of the First World War, many of the shipping companies operating in the Australasian sector were linked and sometimes integrated within the complex business and financial structure of world shipping.

Stephanie Jones's article has a narrower focus than Broeze's continental survey but the same themes of an expanding market, steam's penetration and the role of specialist functionaries are reflected in her examination of the activities of George Benjamin Dodwell, a shipping agent active in the Far Eastern trades from 1872 to 1908. The opening of China and Japan offered new trading opportunities and while sail and steam vessels participated, steam soon gained prominence. In part this was through the cost advantages of Suez and compound engines but also because silk and tea, the key products in the Far Eastern trade were of high value and low bulk. Jones reviews the development of shipping routes to China and Japan and the role of the shipping agent. One firm which quickly entered the new market was W. R. Adamson and Co., registered in 1858, (later, Adamson, Bell and Co.). In 1872 the firm appointed George Dodwell as full-time shipping clerk in Shanghai. Dodwell's function was that of managing a general shipping agency acting in the matters of securing cargoes, clearances, insurance and other business. In that the concern of the agency was consigning and dispatching vessels and it did not engage in the buying and selling of vessels or crewing and provisioning, its function was specialised but within its field it was general as Dodwell acted for a variety of operators and not just one fleet. The firm acted as agents for sail and steam vessels (principally tramps) but also liner companies; the latter involving dealings with the first major shipping conference in the Far East trade from 1879.

Dodwell's activities expanded the firm's business which in the late 1870s established branches in Japan. Dodwell recognised the strong participation of American interests in Japanese trade. He personally pioneered steamship links between Canada and Far Eastern ports and was instrumental in the establishment of the Canadian Pacific Railway's trans-Pacific service which he gained the contract to manage. His initiatives were threatened in the late 1880s when weak leadership and increased competition seriously weakened the position of Adamson Bell. Bankruptcy threatened in 1890. Aware of the potential of some facets of the business and his own agency, Dodwell with another manager engineered the takeover of the parent company by their new firm, Dodwell Carlill and Co., cleverly concealing their plans so that the new company emerged 'overnight' with all its old contracts in place. The new company focused on agency work; it was instrumental in forming the Northern Pacific Steamship Company and took advantage of market opportunities such as those associated with the Alaskan gold rush and the Sino-Japanese, Spanish-American and Russo-Japanese wars. Reorganised as a limited liability company in 1899, the company was highly successful and survives as an international marketing and shipping organisation today. Dodwell's ability to thrive in a highly competitive environment, lay in his expertise as a specialist shipping agent; Jones observes that 'as a constant middleman he was not tied to a particular company, port or commodity, and could spread his risks widely'. He was thus able to act on opportunities where and when they arose; in this an informed understanding of markets was crucial and no doubt assisted by the extension of European telegraph and cable services to east and south east Asia in the early 1870s.[20]

The shipping market of the Far East is also the setting for Malcolm Cooper's study of McGregor Gow and the Glen Line. The firm of McGregor Gow was formed to run a steamer service in the carriage of tea from China. In the tea trade, the premium for speed and reliability was of the highest and until the late 1860s sailing clippers raced to provide the seasons's earliest deliveries. In the 1870s this competitive trade transferred to steam. McGregor Gow by 1880 had a fleet of twelve vessels in the trade. Large firms like Alfred Holt's Blue Funnel Line, P&O, the French Messageries Maritimes (with a government contract) and the smaller Shire and Castle Lines were also active. Such competition led to John Swire, Holt's agent in the Far East, forming the Far East Shipping Conference in 1879.[21] McGregor Gow, a small operator running a high quality service, had much to fear from rate cutting and was an early and enthusiastic conference member.

The Glen Line enjoyed expansion and good returns in the 1870s. In the 1880s problems arose; voyage profits fell and the company could not match the fleet expansion of its larger rivals. Its problems were those of a narrowly based business and a failure of management to respond to the market. Glen had concentrated on the homeward China tea trade. While highly profitable in the 1870s the trade had inherent problems; outward cargoes were always hard to find and, outside the tea season, remunerative homeward freights were also scarce. These problematical features loomed much larger in the 1880s when the China tea trade fell away in the face of Indian tea. Such problems faced all operators; responses however varied. The Holts' Blue Funnel Line, utilising smaller and more economical vessels than Glen, managed to sustain regular services and to lower its rates when required. It maintained a good share of the market and, with conservative dividend policies, accumulated reserves which allowed expansion in the later 1890s. Holts also extended their operations in trans-Pacific, Japanese and Australian trades. The

Glen Line showed scant initiative; the firm remained a one-route line, moreover large sums were taken from the business to maintain the family's expensive lifestyles. The death of the founder, McGregor, in 1896 changed little. By 1904 Glen was operating only six ships on an irregular service. Eventually, in 1910, financial reconstruction was undertaken with the formation of Glen Line but the new company merely served to facilitate its sale to Owen Philipps's Royal Mail group. Even after merger the line failed to prosper and ultimately it was sold to Blue Funnel in 1935.

Glen Line's experience was the outcome of poor management and scant response to market changes. The shipping market was extraordinarily complex. So many factors were at work: its international character, its composition of various commodity and regional trades, seasonal factors, the imbalance of inward and outward cargoes on many routes, the competition between sail and steam and, within steam, that between liners and tramps, is to mention but a few. However, at the most basic level, the fortunes of world shipping depended on the relationship between available carrying capacity and the volume of world trade. This was seldom in balance. As Aldcroft observes, early in his article, 'few industries have been subject to such violent fluctuations in fortune as the shipping industry'. Aldcroft's study is of the depression in British shipping between 1901 and 1911 but, although focusing on one national mercantile marine, it nevertheless points to many of the determining influences on the world of shipping in the modern period. Worth noting also are some of the problems of analysis. Not the least is that of interpreting freight rate data given the differences in inward and outward and liner and tramp rates, and the fact that freight rates were falling almost continuously in the nineteenth century as technological advance lowered transport costs.[22] Company accounts are a further problem.[23]

Aldcroft's study highlights features of the new world of shipping, notably the nature of fluctuations, the challenge to British dominance and a trend towards concentration of ownership. He stresses that the depression was international; fluctuations in shipping inevitably were for obvious reasons. While fluctuations arose out of inequilibrium in the market through changes in supply and demand, it was regularly the case that supply-side behaviour in a boom period contributed to, and deepened, the following slump. Prospects of high freights led to over-orders for new vessels which were only delivered once the boom had peaked with the outcome that at a time when demand was falling back there was now more tonnage than ever and, moreover, more efficient tonnage as new vessels were built to the latest standards. This pattern underlay most slumps in shipping as it did the depression of 1901-11. Then over-orders occasioned by huge government chartering in the Boer War caused the British mercantile marine to grow faster than British trade. The same was true of world shipping; the period saw Germany and Japan building up their own fleets and commencing a challenge to British shipping.[24]

Depressed conditions had the effect of accentuating trends already set by the nature of steamship operation, those of attempts to restrict competition and concentration of ownership. Attempts at co-operation met with no success in the tramp shipping sector because of the multitude of small operators, but in liner trades there was a strengthening of conference systems. Interestingly, in 1907 the British government appointed a Royal

Commission on Shipping Rings and although scant action resulted, the evidence presented is still the starting point for the debate over conferences and the balance between supplier and consumer interests. In the two decades before the war, as noted by Broeze, combinations or mergers proceeded apace. Such developments occurred on a massive scale in European shipping. The activities of Owen Philipps of Royal Mail and Albert Ballin of Hamburg-Amerika represent the most spectacular examples of the concentration of power.[25]

The century before the First World War had seen the world of shipping undergoing revolutionary change. After 1914, economic growth and technological advance continued to be the key influences and the long-term trend of shipping was upward. Yet there were many contrasts with the previous century. Shipping, pre-war, had suffered fluctuations but these were minor compared with what was to come. The First and Second World Wars disrupted and distorted their respective contemporary 'normal' trading patterns as had no previous conflicts. New technology had revolutionised destructive as well as productive capability: war losses and consequent huge wartime building programmes together with over-optimistic post-war replacement characterised both conflicts. Nor did peace bring respite, the collapse of world trade in the great slump of the 1930s brought unprecedented depression to shipping. Furthermore, after 1945 the desire of capitalist and communist blocs and newly independent countries to provide their own shipping services further distorted the market as did a subsequent series of crises in the Middle East. Despite all such stresses, trade and shipping continued to expand but with significant changes. Most notable were the huge growth of traffic in petroleum and the decline of passenger traffic. Both commenced before the Second World War; the turning point in the passenger trade was the United States' decision to curtail immigration in the 1920s; post-1945, the triumph of oil and the coming of age of air transport confirmed these shifts. While technological change in the twentieth century could never compare with the seminal impact of steam, oil-powered ships quickly replaced steamships. As steam had transformed the operation, finance and organisational structure of shipping and port development, so oil-powered shipping together with a huge increase in vessel size, consequent on advances in shipbuilding design, brought massive change in its wake.[26]

Another contrast was in the international balance of power. Before 1914 Britain had been supreme. This dominance could not be maintained and a German challenge was apparent before the war. Germany's defeat and the punitive conditions of Versailles extinguished this threat, but the war damaged British shipping and shipbuilding, and provided opportunities for other nations notably the United States, Norway and Japan. The inter-war depression in shipping effected Britain more than most; the decline of her exports, particularly coal, was crucial and a slow response to new oil technology weakened British maritime power still further. The Second World War, though effecting all shipping nations, saw Britain suffer most, ironically at the expense of lesser participants and, indeed, defeated parties.

Such trends in patterns of trade, new oil technology and Britain's role had their bearing on the world of shipping in the business and organisational sense. The changing international balance of power brought new companies to the fore, while the slump hit many prestigious British companies causing demise or painful restructuring. Access to finance became ever more crucial to shipping, as did government intervention, for as nations sought to protect or promote their shipping sectors policy influenced decision-taking and patterns of organisation. Yet some operators saw their best opportunities outside traditional national frameworks, the practice of flagging out which from the 1970s turned traditional ownership, finance and management on its head, had its roots in the 1920s when some United States owners sought Panamanian registration.[27]

The four articles in this collection which are set primarily in the post-1914 era deal with some of these facets. Two articles, those of Barsness and Olokoju cover the crucial aspect of port development, only indirectly covered in earlier papers. Olokuju's study of Lagos is yet another example of new and expanding markets. West African trade, especially in palm oil and, later, cocoa, grew rapidly in the nineteenth century encouraged by steamshipping which assisted in the assembly of cargoes from small estuarial ports.[28] Lagos, 'the Liverpool of West Africa' was by far the biggest port in the region. The problems it faced between 1892 and 1946 were those which have been encountered by all ports in the modern era, and because growth and technological change are ongoing, such problems have been effectively ever present. Ports have to meet the challenge of increased vessel size, growing traffic volumes and the need to improve handling facilities and hinterland communications. The ability to respond determines a port's prosperity and future. Lagos deepened its harbour, constructed moles to facilitate port approaches and built wharves which reduced the need to tranship cargoes. Simultaneously, inland rail and road links were improved. Yet for all these efforts, facilities did not keep pace with growing trade resulting in inefficiencies and slow vessel turnaround. In Lagos, the course of improvement was troubled because of the varying interests of expatriate businesses, the colonial government and the conflicting priorities of merchant and shipping groups - whether the Lagos or Apapa side of the harbour should be developed was a crucial issue. In these respects Lagos's experience typifies the problems of ports as they constantly grapple with changes in trade and shipping, the restraints of inter-related capital and the pressures of competing interests.

Port problems are even more apparent in Barsness's wider review of port development in the United States since 1900. United States' shipping has the special features of an extensive, long-distance coastal traffic and inter-coastal traffic through the Panama Canal but Barsness's examination of traffic, technological change and port competition bears on the experience of ports internationally. Traffic patterns changed as passenger traffic declined and petroleum grew, although after 1945 the United States changed from an exporter to an importer of oil. Trade with the East, particularly Japan increased especially after 1945, indicative of the general shift in the world economy and shipping from Atlantic to Pacific. Traffic levels generally were influenced by wars and fluctuations, and coastal traffic was hit by rail, truck and pipeline competition. Technological changes were primarily those of huge increases in vessel size, growing vessel specialisation and moves to more capital-intensive cargo handling techniques. In the latter context, containerisation, introduced in the late 1950s in the United States' 'offshore' coastal trades, was ultimately to revolutionise shipping and port business. Besides such factors, the relative strength of individual ports was also influenced by uneven regional economic development, the opening of the St Lawrence seaway which transformed several Great Lake ports into ocean ports and by the policy of port authorities which were variously controlled by railway interests, state or local governments or private corporations. The sum of all these factors was to reduce the historic superiority of New York on the Atlantic, New Orleans on the Gulf and San Francisco on the Pacific coast. Barsness's article, written in 1974, deplored the neglect of studies of port development. Since then, partly perhaps because of the high publicity given to the move of port terminals downriver, the decay and re-development of old dock areas and the massive impact of containerisation, research into port history has considerably increased.[29]

The shift from coal to oil as the principal fuel of industry and transport had major implications for shipping. Fletcher examines the effects on British shipping. The impact was profound; most obviously it meant the loss of Britain's coal-bunkering trade. While world shipping depended on coal, British shipping enjoyed the inestimable advantage of a ready outward cargo[30] The loss of the coal trade seriously affected the balance of British trade volumes reversing the excess of outward over inward cargoes. The effect was a rise in inbound freights. The loss of the coal trade undermined the economic basis of Britain's tramp shipping which declined in tonnage by over half between 1913 and 1933. Of course, oil propulsion brought enormous advantages; it was more efficient, of lighter weight, cleaner in use and allowed quicker and more convenient bunkering. Before 1914, doubts as to the costs and supply of oil restricted its use to less than 3 per cent of the world's merchant fleet, though fighting navies, less concerned with tight financial economies, made a much quicker transfer. Thereafter, partly as a result of wartime experience and American initiatives (as a major producer the United States recognised the economic and strategic advantages of oil) the shift was rapid. By 1935 around half the world merchant fleet was oil fuelled and the transition was virtually complete by 1950. Within Europe, Scandinavian countries adopted diesel propulsion most rapidly and most fully. Wedded to steam, British shipowners and shipbuilders lagged; conservatism, an interest in initial cost rather than long-run economies, the combination of group structure and the conference interests which caused inflexibility, and the difficulty of raising finance in a depressed climate all contributed to a limited response[31]. Nor did Britain, despite a pioneering involvement in the carriage of oil, move rapidly enough into tankers.[32] The outcome of these varied failures was a dramatic decline in Britain's role in world shipowning and shipbuilding.[33]

Less favourable trading circumstances, changes in patterns of resource advantage and a failure to respond to new challenges are but one side of Britain's decline. The changing balance of power in world shipping owed as much to the rise of other mercantile marines. The United States, Scandinavian countries and Japan had gained heavily from Britain's pre-occupation with the First World War and they fared relatively better between the wars. The Second World War virtually eliminated Japan's shipping industry; yet by 1980, Japan had become the second largest maritime nation in the world. Tomohei Chida examines this remarkable transformation. In 1945, not merely was Japan's merchant fleet effectively non-existent but the Allied settlement imposed restrictions on total tonnage levels, anti-trust policies which handicapped major companies, and regulations which prevented shipping companies from managing or operating their own vessels. Not until the peace treaty of 1952 was Japanese shipping freed from all restraints. Chida attributes the subsequent rapid rise to the quality of entrepreneurship and company rivalry, the flexible attitude of organised labour towards new technology, the great growth of the Japanese economy but, especially, to government shipping policy. Japan's post-war shipping policy had a protective character and was embodied in two principal measures. The 'Interest Subsidy for Shipping Finance' subsidised interest payments on loans taken to acquire new vessels. Far more important was the 'Programmed Shipbuilding Scheme' under which the government decided the tonnage to be constructed each year and made loans to companies wishing to build vessels. Loans were only for part of the cost and in operating the scheme government took account of the world market and the type of vessels being proposed. Chida sees the success of the scheme less in terms of supplying cheap finance but more in its flexible application. Shocks like the closure of the Suez Canal and the first oil crisis of 1973 were met and Japanese companies were to the fore in the development of giant carriers and containerisation. More so, perhaps, than in other sectors, success in shipping breeds competition; as Chida observes 'innovation enjoys but a short monopoly'. Japan's shipping was to face competition and its own challenges of mounting labour costs and an appreciating yen. Along with other national shipping industries it reacted in ways which dramatically changed the business world of shipping.[34]

The articles in this volume cover a period in which the world of shipping underwent a crucial transformation in response to economic growth and technical change. During the nineteenth century almost all facets of the old world disappeared and the new formats which had appeared in the 1830s were, by 1900, common to all sectors. However, the new world of shipping that had emerged was short lived. Arguably, it lasted only until the 1960s, then commenced changes which were to make the 'new world of shipping' of this volume a thing of the past. The growth of carriers and bulk tankers of monstrous size transformed a major section of the freight market.[35] Even more momentous was the spread of containerisation which in its impact on shipping, port development, the relative roles of capital and labour and the integration of sea and land transport represents a genuine revolution. In both the operation of gigantic vessels and containerisation, advances in computer technology were an essential element. Such technology impacted also on information flows, providing instant access which transformed the existing sophisticated pattern of shipping business.[36] That business, however, was more changed by the shift of shipowners into 'flags of convenience' which destroyed the age old concept of national fleets. Flagging out, the move towards basing managerial functions overseas and the recruitment of labour on a world-wide, or Third World-wide, basis has globalised the conduct of operations in the world of shipping.[37] The recent formation in container operation of trans-national consortia under such names as Global Alliance and Worldwide Alliance is the clearest evidence that the world of shipping which emerged with industrialisation and steam has been superseded practically and conceptually by the global market of shipping.

Notes

1 The notes to this introduction are inevitably selective. As a general rule references relate only to work appearing after the original publication date of the individual papers. On short sea trades see the companion volume in this series, J. Armstrong (ed.), *Coastal and Short Sea Shipping* (Aldershot, 1996).

2 L. R. Fischer, 'International maritime labour, 1863-1900: wages and trends', *The Great Circle*, vol. X, (1988); C. P. Kindleberger, *Mariners and Markets* (New York, 1992); L. R. Fischer (ed.), *The Market for Seamen in the Age of Sail* (St John's, 1994).

3 On the early development of this other world of shipping see F. Mauro, 'Merchant communities 1350-1750', in J. D. Tracy (ed.), *The Rise of Merchant Empires. Long-distance Trade in the Early Modern World (1350-1750)* (Cambridge, 1990). The complexities of this world in the late nineteenth century are apparent in G. Boyce, *Information, Mediation and Institutional Development: the Rise of Large-scale Enterprise in British Shipping, 1870-1919* (Manchester, 1995).

4 S. Palmer, 'Experience, experiment and economics: factors in the construction of early merchant steamships', in K. Matthews and G. Panting (eds), *Ships and Shipbuilding in the North Atlantic Region* (St John's, 1978).

5 An important international survey of the transition from sail to steam is L. R. Fischer and G. E. Panting (eds.), *Change and Adaptation in Maritime History: the North Atlantic Fleets in the Nineteenth Century* (St John's, 1984).

6 J. J. Safford, 'The decline of the American merchant marine 1850-1914', in Fischer and Panting, *Change and Adaptation*.

7 S. Ville, 'Total factor productivity in the English shipping industry: the north-east coal trade, 1700-1850', *Economic History Review*, 2nd series, vol. XXXIX (1986).

8 E. W. Sager with G. E. Panting, *Maritime Capital. The Shipping Industry in Atlantic Canada, 1820-1914* (Montreal, 1990).

9 F. E. Hyde, *The Far Eastern Trade, 1860-1914* (London, 1973).

10 See S. P. Ville, *English Shipowning during the Industrial Revolution* (Manchester, 1987); D. J. Starkey, 'Ownership structures in the British shipping industry: the case of Hull, 1820-1916', *International Journal of Maritime History*, vol. VIII (1996); Boyce, *Information, Mediation and Institutional Development*.

11 S. Palmer, *Politics, Shipping and the Repeal of the Navigation Laws* (Manchester, 1990).

12 C. Jeans, 'The first statutory qualifications for seafarers', *Transport History*, vol. VI (1973); V. Burton, 'The making of a nineteenth century profession: shipmasters and the British shipping industry', *Journal of the Canadian Historical Association*, new series, vol. I (1990).

13 See for example D. M. Williams, 'State regulation of merchant shipping 1839-1914: the bulk carrying trades', in S. B. Palmer and G. Williams (eds), *Charted and Uncharted Waters* (London, 1982); C. Dixon, 'Pound and pint: diet in the merchant service 1750-1980', in Palmer and Williams, *Charted and Uncharted*; G. Alderman, 'Joseph

Chamberlain's attempted reform of the British mercantile marine', *The Journal of Transport History*, new series, vol. 1 (1972).

14 A. J. Arnold and R. G. Greenhill, 'Contractors' bounties or due consideration? Evidence on the commercial nature of the Royal Mail Steam Packet Company's mail contracts, 1842-1905', in S. P. Ville and D. M. Williams (eds), *Management, Finance and Industrial Relations in Maritime Industries: Essays in International Maritime and Business History* (St John's, 1994).

15 A full survey of the Australian trade in the mid-nineteenth century is provided in F. Broeze, *Mr Brooks and the Australian Trade. Imperial Business in the Nineteenth Century* (Melbourne, 1993).

16 Only in recent years have historians begun to research the activities of shipbrokers. See L. R. Fischer and H. W. Nordvik, 'The growth of Norwegian shipbroking: the practices of Fearnley and Eger as a case study, 1869-1914', in L. R. Fischer and W. E. Minchinton, *Peoples of the Northern Seas* (St John's, 1992); L. R. Fischer and A. M. Fon, 'The making of a maritime firm; the rise of Fearnley and Eger, 1869-1917', in L. R. Fischer (ed.), *From Wheel House to Counting House* (St John's, 1991).

17 B. M. Deakin and T. Seward, *Shipping Conferences: a Study of their Development and Economic Practices* (Cambridge, 1973); G. K. Sletmo and L. V. W. Ernest, *Liner Conferences in the Liner Age* (London, 1981); F. Broeze, 'Albert Ballin, the Hamburg-Bremen rivalry and the dynamics of the conference system', *International Journal of Maritime History*, vol. III (1991).

18 E. W. Sloan, 'Collins versus Cunard: the realities of a North Atlantic steamship rivalry, 1850-1858', *International Journal of Maritime History*, vol. IV (1992).

19 F. Broeze, 'Merchants from sail to steam: the West Australian Shipping Association and the evolution of the conference system', in L. R. Fischer (ed.), *From Wheel House*.

20 For a fuller account of the market in which Dodwell operated see S. Jones, *Two Centuries of Trading: the Inchcape Group* (London, 1986); idem, *Trade and Shipping, Lord Inchcape* (Manchester, 1992).

21 S. Marriner and F. E. Hyde, *The Senior: John Samuel Swire, 1825-98* (Liverpool, 1967).

22 C. K. Harley, 'Ocean freight rates and productivity, 1740-1913; the primacy of mechanical invention reaffirmed', *Journal of Economic History*, vol. LX (1988).

23 A. J. Arnold, 'Privacy or concealment? The accounting practices of liner shipping companies, 1914-1924', *International Journal of Maritime History*, vol. VIII (1996).

24 D. H. Aldcroft, 'The mercantile marine', in D. H. Aldcroft (ed.), *The Development of British Industry and Foreign Competition, 1875-1914* (London, 1968).

25 Boyce, *Information, Mediation and Institutional Development.* The complex character of business relationships, combinations and mergers is examined in many company histories. See for example F. E. Hyde, *Blue Funnel* (Liverpool, 1957); idem, *Cunard* (London, 1975); Marriner and Hyde, *The Senior;* P. N. Davies, *The Trade Makers: Elder Dempster in West Africa, 1852-1972* (London, 1973); idem, *Sir Alfred Jones, Shipping Entrepreneur par Excellence* (London, 1978); A. Muir and M. Davies, *A Victorian*

Shipowner: a Portrait of Sir Charles Cayzer (London, 1978); J. Orbell, E. Green and M. Moss, *From Cape to Cape: the History of Lyle Shipping Co.* (Edinburgh, 1978); A. Porter, *Victorian Shipping, Business and Imperial Policy: Donald Currie, the Castle Line and Southern Africa* (Woodbridge, Suffolk, 1986); E. Green and M. Moss, *A Business of National Importance; the Royal Mail Shipping Group, 1902-37* (London, 1982); M. Falkus, *The Blue Funnel Legend: a History of the Ocean Steam Ship Company* (Basingstoke, 1990); Jones, *Trade and Shipping.*

26 E. Corlett, *The Revolution in Merchant Shipping 1950-1980* (London, 1981).

27 R. P. Carlisle, *Sovereignty for Sale: the Origins and Evolution of the Panamanian and Liberian Flags of Convenience* (Annapolis, 1981); A. Cafruny, *Ruling the Waves: the Political Economy of International Shipping* (Berkeley, 1987).

28 Davies, *The Trade Makers.* For a bibliographical survey of shipping to Africa see J. Forbes Munro, 'African shipping: reflections on the maritime history of Africa south of the Sahara, 1800-1914', *International Journal of Maritime History*, vol. II (1990).

29 See for example G. Jackson, *The History and Archaeology of Ports* (Kingswood, Surrey, 1983); F. Broeze, P. Reeves and K. McPherson, 'Imperial ports and the modern world economy: the case of the Indian ocean', *The Journal of Transport History*, 3rd series, vol. VII (1986); F. Broeze (ed.), *Brides of the Sea: Port Cities of Asia from the 16th-20th Centuries* (Honolulu, 1989); P. Holm and J. Edwards (eds), *North Sea Ports and Harbours - Adaptations to Change* (Esbjerg, 1992); M. Tull, 'American technology and the mechanisation of Australian ports, 1942-58', *The Journal of Transport History*, 3rd series, vol. VI (1985); M. Tull, 'The development of port administration in Australia: the case of Freemantle', *The Journal of Transport History*, 3rd series, vol. X (1989); L. R. Fischer and H. Nordvik, 'The evolution of the Norwegian ports', in L. U. Scholl and J. Edwards (eds), *The North Sea; Resources and Seaway* (Aberdeen, 1996).

30 C. K. Harley, 'Coal exports and British shipping, 1850-1913', *Explorations in Economic History*, vol. XXVI (1989).

31 For a somewhat different analysis see A. J. Robertson, 'Backward British businessmen and the motor ship, 1918-39: the critique reviewed', *The Journal of Transport History*, 3rd series, vol. IX (1988); G. Boyce, 'Union Steam Ship Company of New Zealand and the adoption of oil propulsion: learning-by-using effects', *The Journal of Transport History*, 3rd series, vol. XVIII (1997), pp. 134-55.

32 M. Radcliffe, *Liquid Gold Ships. A History of the Tanker* (London, 1985).

33 Still by far the best analysis of decline is S. G. Sturmey, *British Shipping and World Competition* (London, 1962).

34 On Japanese shipping and policy see R. Miwa, 'Maritime policy in Japan, 1868-1937', and K. Nakagawa, 'Japanese shipping', both in T. Yui and K. Nakagawa (eds), *Business History of Shipping Strategy and Structure* (Tokyo, 1985); T. Chida and P. N. Davies, *The Japanese Shipping and Shipbuilding Industries* (London, 1990); Y. Yamashita, 'Responding to the global market in boom and recession: Japanese shipping and shipbuilding industries, 1945-1980', in Ville and Williams, *Management, Finance and Industrial Relations.*

35 A. Couper (ed.), *The Shipping Revolution, the Modern Merchant Ship* (London, 1992).
36 To gain an appreciation of the complexities of modern shipping business see M. Stopford, *Maritime Economics* (London, 1988).
37 T. Lane, 'Flags of convenience and the globalisation of the seafaring labour market', in Scholl and Edwards, *The North Sea.*

1 The deployment of English merchant shipping: Michael and Joseph Henley of Wapping, ship owners, 1775–1830

SIMON VILLE

Ralph Davis has argued that in the eighteenth century most merchant vessels operated continually in the same trade.[1] A consensus exists that most vessels were laid up during winter. This article argues that both views are false; the characteristics of the deployment of vessels in the late eighteenth and early nineteenth centuries are flexibility and intensity. The implication is higher profits and therefore, through the multiplier effect, a significant contribution by the shipping industry to the industrialisation of Britain. Moreover, high productivity in the shipping industry, facilitating the more efficient movement of goods, implies a notable social saving and the smoother functioning of the economy. The French wars of 1793–1815 greatly increased the demand for shipping, and, with supply remaining relatively inelastic in the short run, freight rates and profits rose to very high levels. Naturally, in these conditions, ship owners would keep their vessels regularly employed and send them wherever a profitable freight offered. In the post-war depression excess shipping capacity existed and the level of deployment fell but its flexibility continued.

Very little has been written on this important subject, largely as a result of the inadequacy of shipping sources for the period. Most of this material, largely statistical, is of a vague and macro-economic nature. For example, little information can be gained about the flexibility and productivity of individual vessels over a reasonable length of time. This situation has radically changed with the recent discovery of the Henley collection,[2] now housed at the National Maritime Museum. Michael and Joseph Henley were London ship owners based at Wapping in the period 1775–1830. During this period they owned a total of around 120 vessels, sometimes over twenty simultaneously. From this substantial collection a much clearer view of the deployment of shipping can be gained. In addition, it gives important information respecting changes in the areas of deployment. This is significant, since deployment patterns changed rapidly under the impact of war and it is instructive to see how quickly the Henleys responded to political developments and new trading opportunities.

Ralph Davis saw the main obstacles to flexible deployment as being 'timidity', 'conservatism' and 'a rigidity of mind which saw a vessel committed to one function'.[3] He does say there were a few exceptional ship owners who sent vessels to many parts. However, this does not mean the Henleys were in a small minority. The work done on the Liverpool registers by Robin Craig and Rupert Jarvis[4] confirms that the Henleys were just one of a number of similar shipping businesses. Ralph Davis has also looked at shipping flows in his study of the seamen's sixpences.[5] However, this concentrates on the aggregate productivity of British shipping and says little about the areas of deployment and nothing about the performance of individual vessels. W. J. Hausman has written about the deployment of collier vessels in the eighteenth century.[6] However, by concentrating largely on the collector's returns for the orphans' duty, which recorded all coal-laden vessels entering London, he was unable to show their accompanying deployment in other trades and so also underestimated their productivity. C. E. Fayle does talk briefly of 'the flexibility of shipping' and 'the impossibility of drawing hard-and-fast lines between the ships engaged in various trades'.[7] Aside from these few, most other related studies have concentrated on the trades themselves rather than the shipping that was involved, though sometimes making rather too brief allusions to the latter.[8] This is to be expected, given that most national sources reflect the value of goods traded rather than the volume of shipping that carried them — though in recent years there has been a greater acceptance of the importance of shipping volumes.[9]

Records exist for entrances and clearances for British ports in the period 1786 — 1807.[10] In addition, a survey of deployment was carried out in 1833.[11] The latter illustrated the importance of the coastal trade, which represented nearly half of all the vessels analysed. Local directories, such as those for London, often indicate some of the shipping of the area, though they are neither comprehensive nor consistent.[12] In general, these statistics suffer from a number of shortcomings. They say nothing about the flexibility or productivity of vessels. Nor do they tell us anything about the type of vessels involved. These are important, though highly complex problems that only a micro-economic study of individual vessels can solve. Moreover the existence of a large amount of literary evidence in the Henley collection also helps to explain the reasons why vessels were so deployed. Even the macro-economic question of trade and shipping flows is not dealt with comprehensively by national statistics, owing to gaps in these figures. In particular, the size of the coasting trade has been underrated. For example, the coasting trade of London is largely unrecorded.[13] If anything, it was virtually too large to quantify. The extent of the Henleys' involvement in coasting reaffirms this point. Similarly, estuarial and river shipping has gone unrecorded by national statistics. A large number of watermen were employed on many rivers around Britain.[14]

Michael Henley began work as a London waterman. By the early 1770s he was also involved in coal merchanting. In 1775 he bought his first vessel, the *Henley*. The Henley business expanded from this point, reaching a peak of at least twenty vessels owned simultaneously in the first decade of the nineteenth century. The merchanting side of the business became less important and ceased about 1800. Interestingly, though, the Henleys, like many other ship owners, continued to be regarded as merchants.[15] Only partial information about the business survives before about 1790. The deployment of some vessels is unknown or uncertain. As a result, statistical analysis of deployment is taken from 1790. From what is known about the fifteen years before 1790 it seems that most Henley vessels were deployed on the coal trade, with occasional ventures into the Transport Service. The *Henley*, for example, was employed in the coal trade from 1775 to 1781. She was then in the Transport Service for the next year or two[16] before returning to the coal trade for the rest of the decade. Similarly, the *Polly* was deployed in the coal trade during her four years of ownership by the Henleys from 1776 to 1779. The *Pitt*, on the other hand, was in the coal trade in 1784 and 1785 but in the next few years also made voyages to Amsterdam and Gibraltar with coal for the Royal Navy. On leaving Gibraltar in September 1788, she went under charter to New York to load a cargo of staves for Lynn. At 242 tons she was larger than most vessels owned by the Henleys at this early stage of the business, and this may have been indicative of future trends within the firm. However, in these fifteen years most Henley vessels were employed in the coal trade, reflecting the importance accorded to the coal merchanting side of his business by Michael Henley. After about 1790, possibly through the active influence of Michael's son, Joseph, the business became largely orientated towards ship-owning.

In discussing deployment, ten main geographical areas are used, namely coasting, Northern Europe (including the North Sea and the Baltic), France, the Mediterranean (including Spain and Portugal), the East, British North America, the United States, Central America, the West Indies and South America. Central America deals solely with the mahogany trade from Honduras, whilst deployment in the East was at the Cape of Good Hope, India and Ceylon. Naturally, there will occasionally be only a fine distinction between these areas. Canada and the United States of America obviously border on to each other. However, the length and navigation of a voyage to Quebec are clearly very different from one to Virginia. Moreover, it is the commodity traded as well as the length and direction of the voyage which is important. Shipping two different commodities from a similar geographical area requires flexibility from the ship owner, to gain a foothold in both trades. Again, shipping different goods requires flexibility from the vessel herself. In this light the mahogany trade of Central America can clearly be differentiated from the West Indies trade in sugar, rum and coffee.

It has already been shown that Ralph Davis argued for the specialisation of vessels in particular trades. The following results show that, on the contrary, Henley vessels were employed very flexibly in many trades. Since a number of Henley vessels were owned for only a year or two, it would obviously be wrong to use vessels owned for such a short period in a study of deployment flexibility. Taking vessels owned for three years or more, however, the results shown in table 1 emerge. It can be clearly seen that half the vessels were involved in four trades or more at some time during their ownership by the Henleys. However, since ten main areas of deployment have been identified, three years is still insufficient time for a vessel to show maximum flexibility. To allow for that, vessels owned for five years or more have been separately analysed, from which the pattern in table 2 emerges. This time as many as 70 per cent of vessels are deployed in four or more trades sometime during their ownership by the firm. Finally, the pattern in table 3 is revealed by an analysis of the twelve Henley vessels which were owned for ten years or more. The proportion of vessels deployed in four trades or more rises to 75 per cent.

It may be asserted that the operations of the Transport Service caused an unnatural amount of flexibility in shipping deployment, since vessels might be ordered to many different areas with troops, horses, stores and so forth. For example, a voyage in the Service to the West Indies would not involve carrying the valuable produce from that area. Therefore, if the ten-year table is reassembled omitting all Transport Service voyages, the results are as in table 4. Average flexibility falls, although 41 per cent of shipping is still involved in four trades or more. However, this is an inadequate representation, since in many cases it records only about half a vessel's deployment. Moreover the war, at the same time, also restricted

Table 1 *Number of trades in which each vessel was deployed*

No. of trades	No. of vessels	% of total No. of vessels
1	2	4
2	5	10
3	18	37
4	13	27
5	7	14
6	1	2
7	2	4
8	1	2

Table 2 *Number of trades in which principal vessels were deployed*

No. of trades	No. of vessels	% of total No. of vessels
1	0	0
2	0	0
3	8	29·5
4	8	29·5
5	7	26
6	1	4
7	2	7
8	1	4

Table 3 *Number of trades in which main 12 vessels were deployed*

No. of trades	No. of vessels	% of No. of vessels
1	0	0
2	0	0
3	3	25
4	3	25
5	3	25
6	0	0
7	2	17
8	1	8

Table 4 *Number of trades in which main 12 vessels were deployed, excluding transport service work*

No. of trades	No. of vessels	% of No. of vessels
1	0	0
2	5	42
3	2	17
4	1	8
5	3	25
6	0	0
7	1	8

the areas of deployment — for example, to America and sometimes to the Baltic and France. In addition, to be hired by the Transport Service required a degree of flexibility in itself and often meant a major refit of the vessel. Most of the Transport Service operations were in the Mediterranean, so there was little commercial trading there. After 1815 vessels continued to show considerable flexibility in their deployment.

It is now appropriate to focus more closely on the twelve Henley vessels which were owned for at least ten years to discover whether there was anything especially characteristic about them and in exactly which trades they were deployed. (Table 5.) The outstanding characteristic of all these vessels is their size. With two marginal exceptions they are all of a 'handy' medium size between 200 and 400 tons.[17] Henley falls slightly below this figure and as the first vessel purchased was likely to be a smaller capital investment. Significantly, *Henley* spent a much larger proportion of her time in the coastal coal trade than any of the other vessels. *Trusty* was somewhat larger than the rest and made only one coastal coal voyage during her eleven years in the possession of the Henleys. She was also the only one not built on the east coast of England. She was built at Liverpool. The rest of the vessels reflect

The deployment of English merchant shipping 21

Table 5 *Trades in which main 12 vessels were deployed*

Name of vessel	Tonnage	Coasting trade	Northern Europe	Mediterranean	W. Indies	Central America	S. America	British North America	France	USA	East
Ann	243	x	x	x					x		
Cornwall	368	x	x		x	x		x			
Freedom	317	x	x	x	x	x	x	x			
Friendship	225	x	x	X							
Heart of Oak	324	x	x	X					X		
Henley	181	x	x							x	
Lady Juliana	379	x	x	X	X	x		x	X		
Lord Nelson	319	x	x	X	x	x	X	x			X
Norfolk	319	x	x	X							
Pitt	291	x	x	X					x		
Polly	285	x	x	X			X	x			
Trusty	465	x	x		x	x		x			

Capital X denotes employment in Transport Service only.

what are believed to be the characteristics of vessels built on the east coast — well and sturdily built, with a flat bottom and a large cargo capacity.[18] Four of the vessels were newly built for the Henleys, *Lord Nelson* (1799–1824), *Pitt* (1791–1802), *Ann* (1792–1802) and *Freedom*[19] (1791–1830). Of the total of about 120 vessels the Henleys owned, these are the only ones that were bought new. *Freedom*, the longest surviving Henley vessel, was built according to their specifications.

These findings show that there is little or nothing to be gained from breaking down the Henley deployment evidence into average ship sizes for different trades. The general conclusion can be accepted that although small vessels up to about 150 tons were found predominantly in the coasting trade and that large vessels of about 500 tons and above were found largely in the long-haul trades, especially to the East Indies, there was a large range of medium-sized vessels which could be employed to advantage in a great many trades.[20] On the other hand, the condition of a vessel could affect her deployment. Old, leaky bottoms could not be employed in high-value commodity trades. In 1815 Joseph Henley wrote to his Shields agent, James Kirton, pointing out the dangers:

Mr Ward the mast maker of this place sent the ship, Queen, for a cargo of cotton . . . put into a port homewards on Survy was Condem'd the cargo the merchant sues & recovers £25 000 — damages — ship proved defective.

A great many more such cases . . . why cannot you be content in the coal and Baltic Trade you understand that the cargoes are not valuable . . . some owners will take any freight wether there vessels is fit or not.

However, relatively old vessels could carry valuable cargoes if the ship had been well maintained. This seems to have been the Henleys' policy. For example, *Freedom* was still in the West Indies trade when she was twenty-four years old, whilst *Star* was sent to the West Indies when she was fifteen years of age. As long as ship masters carried one of the many guides to stowage there was no reason why many vessels could not carry a wide range of goods.[21] Indeed, the existence of such guides, with their freight rate conversion tables from one cargo to another, suggests that many different cargoes were carried on the same vessels. *Freedom*, for example, carried a wide range of cargoes, from valuable colonial produce like sugar, rum and coffee through government stores and troops, furnishing and constructional timber, to coal.

The capitalised observations in table 5 show when a vessel was deployed only as a transport in that particular area. The results show the predominance of transports in the Mediterranean. Predictably, this reduces the vessel's apparent flexibility, although that is only to be expected, since vessels such as the *Lady Juliana* and *Lord Nelson* spent a substantial proportion of their time in the service. Clearly, the Henleys saw advantages in diversifying by employing some vessels in the Transport Service and some on commercial ventures. One of the chief advantages of the service was a guaranteed income in return for very little day-to-day management by the owner. This left him more time to try and break into new trading areas such as in the West Indies or Central America which also involved higher risk. However, the salient point resulting from table 5 is that vessels could be deployed in a very flexible manner if the policy of the company so required.

Far from there being ship specialisation in particular trades, it was the master who, if anything, was committed to a particular area. He would be able to familiarise himself with the navigational problems of a particular voyage and build up contacts with merchants and brokers. When the master was also the owner, or when there were a great number of passive investors involved in the enterprise, the same master would remain in charge of a vessel over a number of years. This fact helps to explain why some vessels stayed in the same trade constantly over a period of time, which suggested ship specialisation. Similarly, the vertical integration of merchant and ship owner would explain the preference of some owners for a particular trade. This explains why the Henleys deployed most of their vessels in the coal trade in the early years, when they were primarily merchants rather than ship owners. Vertical integration was very evident in the coal trade, many factors, fitters, mine owners and merchants owning vessels.[22] But even they, if successful in the long run, would diversify and send their vessels into other trades, especially as a means of spreading risks if the coal trade was depressed. Robert Gardner is an example of a Henley master who specialised. During a nine-year period he was employed in three different Henley vessels and always took them to the West Indies. His experience in this trade enabled him to load full cargoes in the immediate post-war years when there was

severe over-capacity, especially in the West Indies trade. Gardner came from Liverpool, which explains his competence in this trade. It is true that the coasting trade
was surely within the capability of all masters.[23] It was in the more difficult though
rewarding long-haul trades that specialisation occurred.

The regular as well as flexible nature of deployment is illustrated by the small
amount of time that Henley vessels were laid up. The extent of laying up is largely
governed by the demand for shipping in any one year in relation to its supply.
During the French wars demand was very high, and so Henley vessels were rarely
laid up for more than ten per cent of the time.[24] This is a very different picture
from the view that vessels were laid up for three months each winter. It is true that
in the post-war years and in the 1820s the proportion of laying up by Henley vessels
rose. However, these were particularly difficult years for the shipping industry, and
since Joseph Henley was by then getting old it seems likely that the business was
being run in a less efficient manner than previously. However, these figures can take
little account of underemployment. This occurred in the form of vessels waiting in a
foreign port for a likely return freight. It will be shown later that this was a problem
only in the immediate post-war years. During the war Henley vessels almost invariably
voyaged under charter. The suggestion that the 'division between tramp and liner
which is fundamental to the shipping industry of today has very little relevance to
the eighteenth . . . century'[25] is clearly untrue. There are numerous examples of
Henley masters complaining that freights were low and scarce as a result of the
presence of a large number of 'constant traders' in a foreign port. Ship owners like
the Henleys would send their vessels out 'seeking' when prearranged freights were
difficult to find.

It is evident, then, that vessels were more intensive and flexible in their deployment than has for long been assumed. The diversified use of a ship did not have to
be more profitable than its continuous employment in one trade. However, unless
a static situation is assumed, there were surely many occasions when it made sense
to transfer a vessel from one trade to another because of changes of fortune between
them. In other words, the ability to diversify increased the potential profits of the
ship. More intensive deployment also implied higher profits. It is true that a more
active vessel could be making losses and therefore, conversely, would increase her
losses. However, it was the promise of higher profits, as a result of rising freight
rates, that induced owners like Henley to keep their vessels at sea. With the exception
of a couple of years of optimistic experimentation in various trades at the end of the
war, the Henleys acted conservatively by laying up their vessels, or trying to sell
them, if they were unlikely to yield profits. These high profits are clearly indicated
in the accounts of many Henley vessels. It was not unusual to earn a return on the
fixed capital of the ship of over 50 per cent in one year. Even allowing for such
elements as the overhead costs of the company, this was still an impressive result.
For the economy as a whole, high profits represented a large injection of demand,
whilst good productivity suggested a substantial social saving.

It is now necessary to look at the deployment of the Henley fleet as a whole in order to show how trading patterns changed over time and what the main influences on them were. The deployment of each vessel was separated into the number of months in a year that she was used in different trades. For example, in 1790 the *Valiant* spent one month coasting, nine in the Central American trade, and was laid up for the remaining two months. By analysing the trades to which the whole fleet was committed it is possible to see what proportions were deployed in which regions over a forty-year period. The figures from the mid-1820s are of less validity, since they deal with such a small sample as the business contracted. There were a few vessels that the Henleys bought for immediate resale, sometimes after being repaired, and these have not been included, since they were never intended for long-term employment.

A series of interesting and important points arise from table 6. Throughout most of the period of the French wars the very high demand for shipping meant that Henley vessels were rarely laid up. Not until 1803, with the temporary peace, were they laid up for more than ten per cent of the time. The figure remained low until 1812, when Henley vessels were laid up for 18 per cent of the time. This was a reflection of the reduced demand for government transports.[26] Captain Blues of the *Valiant* wrote in April that year, 'the times are so unfavble to shipping'. 1813 and 1814 were better, but by 1815 the reduced demand for vessels in peacetime meant that a large proportion of shipping remained idle. The situation deteriorated further in the early 1820s and, despite a temporary recovery in 1824–25, the prospects for shipping remained bad until beyond 1830.[27]

A significant feature of these figures is the proportion of active employment (not laying up time) spent in the Transport Service, over 60 to 70 per cent at the peak. The first boom in Transport Service activity was in the mid-1790s as a result of the campaign in the West Indies. Attention shifted to the Mediterranean in the early 1800s. Heavy involvement in the service in 1805 and 1806 came as a result of operations in the Baltic and the Mediterranean. During the next couple of years transports were also deployed in South America, as a result of conflict with Argentina, at the Cape of Good Hope and in India. Between 1809 and 1811 the Henleys' transports were once again concentrated in the Mediterranean. In the final years of war fewer Henley vessels were employed by the government as the demand for transports fell. Henley vessels were also employed by the government to deliver coal to dockyards in England such as Portsmouth, Plymouth and Woolwich. In such cases the firm normally bought the coal at Newcastle and was paid on delivery at the dockyard. In other words it merchanted the coal as well as shipping it. In addition, the Henleys sometimes freighted vessels belonging to other owners to deliver coal cargoes at the dockyards. This was normally done if Henley vessels were more profitably employed elsewhere or if only small amounts of coal were required and their own vessels were too large to do the job efficiently. After about 1803 fewer Henley vessels were employed delivering coal to the dockyards, owing to a scandal

The deployment of English merchant shipping

Table 6 *Distribution of deployment, 1790–1830 (%)*

Year	Laid up	Coast	Baltic	Med	W Inds	Can	Hond	S Am	France	US	East	Total Ship Yrs	Proportion of active Employment in Trans. Ser. (%)
1790	7	56	6	7	16	0	8	0	0	0	0	9	32
1791	2	72	16	0	0	0	8	0	2	0	0	8·3	12
1792	3	54	38	5	0	0	0	0	0	0	0	8·6	18
1793	0	70	21	4	5	0	0	0	0	0	0	8·3	29
1794	0	45	27	14	14	0	0	0	0	0	0	10·4	38
1795	0	49	15	11	14	0	0	0	11	0	0	8·6	68
1796	9	47	18	18	8	0	0	0	0	0	0	10·8	53
1797	5	41	5	49	0	0	0	0	0	0	0	9·6	76
1798	2	51	0	47	0	0	0	0	0	0	0	7·8	73
1799	2	35	16	47	0	0	0	0	0	0	0	9·5	74
1800	3	58	11	26	0	0	0	0	2	0	0	9·5	76
1801	3	44	9	35	9	0	0	0	0	0	0	9·8	54
1802	2	49	6	22	8	0	13	0	0	0	0	10·8	37
1803	14	45	14	2	21	0	4	0	0	0	0	10·9	11
1804	6	66	13	2	5	0	8	0	0	0	0	14·4	4
1805	3	31	32	27	0	0	7	0	0	0	0	15·0	51
1806	2	40	20	14	0	0	14	6	0	0	4	14·5	31
1807	2	13	24	7	0	0	21	33	0	0	0	13·3	41
1808	6	14	14	35	0	9	12	3	1	0	6	14·5	64
1809	2	17	18	51	0	0	12	0	0	0	0	17·7	71
1810	3	24	5	43	10	10	4	1	0	0	0	19·3	63
1811	9	8	1	63	9	2	5	3	0	0	0	17·2	60
1812	18	8	4	29	8	9	11	13	0	0	0	17·5	25
1813	9	13	13	22	12	7	13	11	0	0	0	14·3	26
1814	5	5	16	25	26	9	8	7	0	0	0	11·2	32
1815	14	12	10	14	22	10	11	0	0	7	0	9·3	15
1816	20	30	35	0	7	0	8	0	0	0	0	9·3	0
1817	27	11	23	0	8	24	7	0	0	0	0	12·0	0
1818	21	13	31	0	9	26	0	0	0	0	0	11·7	3
1819	37	13	11	0	3	28	8	0	0	0	0	10·1	12
1820	26	21	14	5	0	26	0	0	0	0	9	8·8	11
1821	28	14	14	7	0	31	0	0	0	0	5	8·1	17
1822	28	13	10	5	0	44	0	0	0	0	0	7·0	7
1823	19	9	33	0	0	39	0	0	0	0	0	6·8	0
1824	21	11	21	0	0	47	0	0	0	0	0	3·2	0
1825	8	19	73	0	0	0	0	0	0	0	0	2·2	0
1826	41	21	17	0	0	21	0	0	0	0	0	2·0	0
1827	21	25	54	0	0	0	0	0	0	0	0	2·0	0
1828	33	25	17	0	0	25	0	0	0	0	0	2·0	0
1829	25	8	67	0	0	0	0	0	0	0	0	2·0	0
1830	18	18	64	0	0	0	0	0	0	0	0	1·4	0

over Henley vessels which was revealed in a report by the Commissioners of the Navy in that year.[28] It was shown that the vessels were delivering a larger volume of coal to the dockyard at Plymouth than the size of the ships would have suggested. This was a consequence of masters bribing meters and clerks of the yard, with the result that the Henleys were paid for more coal than they actually delivered. Not surprisingly, the government was reluctant to offer contracts to the Henleys in subsequent years. Finally, Henley vessels sometimes carried small amounts of government stores outwards when they were going on a commercial voyage to the West Indies, though these obviously have not been classified as transports. The domination of transport activity in some years is partly explained by the great length of some transport voyages. For example, the *Polly* was employed as a transport in the Mediterranean throughout the period 1809—15. Often transports remained in the same port for months on end; although they apparently remained idle for such long periods, they were still earning money for the owner and were fulfilling a vital back-up role for land and sea campaigns.

The coasting trade[29] was the most important area of deployment for much of this period. It implies, assuming that other owners devoted a similar amount of resources to it, that London possessed a large volume of coastal traffic. Ninety-five per cent of the Henleys' coastal deployment was accounted for by the coal trade[30] from Newcastle to London or the dockyards at Woolwich, Chatham, Sheerness, Portsmouth and Plymouth. There were a few voyages to Ireland, mainly for the Transport Service, but several unfortunate experiences in the early years of the business may have discouraged the Henleys from sending their vessels to Ireland. In 1787—88 Captain Dann of the *Polly* reported that he found the Irish prone to greed, cheating and drunkenness, whilst in May 1793 Captain Maw of the *Ann* wrote to the Henleys, 'I thank you for your hints of the Irish Merchts & am fearfull I shall have some trouble.' The high demand for coal meant that the coal trade remained very prosperous throughout most of the war, with high prices being paid. In particular the demand from the naval dockyards increased dramatically. For example, Captain Cummins of the *Freedom* reported of Portsmouth dockyard in June 1798, '. . . a great maney more coals expended last year than any year before'. By 1800 nearly 60 per cent of deployment time was spent in the coal trade, and in March that year the *Friendship* sold a cargo of coal at London for the very high price of 61s 9d per chaldron. From 1807 to 1813 the coal trade was used less, despite the persistence of high prices, reflecting an increased interest in the Transport Service and the expansion of the Honduras mahogany trade. However, there is evidence of a growing depression in the coal trade by the end of 1813 as London prices began to fall whilst the purchase price in the north-east remained high. In December 1813 Joseph Henley observed, 'I do not intend to have any thing to do with colliers for some time to come.' The coal trade remained unprofitable for some years; in 1822 James Kirton noted, '. . . to go in the coal trade it's dowing worse than nothing'.

Most of the shipping in the Baltic was concerned with timber and other ship-building materials such as flax and hemp, plus a small amount of re-exported West Indian produce. The large demand for new ships during the French wars explains the importance of this trade. However, its obvious strategic importance made it highly susceptible to the political course of the war. The Continental blockade certainly had an adverse effect. This helps to explain the changes in the incidence of Baltic deployment. The imposition of timber duties in 1806 and 1811,[31] along with the blockade and the emergence of the Canadian timber trade, reduced the demand for shipping in the Baltic. Moreover, with peace approaching, the demand for new ships fell. It is surprising, therefore, to find that in the years 1816—18 an average of 30 per cent of deployment time was spent in the Baltic. This was because there was concealed underemployment. In the depressed post-war years, rather than lay their vessels up, the Henleys sent them into the Baltic to look for freights. Many other owners decided to do the same, hence freights were low and scarce. In June 1816 Captain Darley of the *Star* reported that many vessels were leaving St Petersburg in ballast. By 1819, however, the post-war optimism about the future of the Baltic timber trade had collapsed.[32] The narrowing of the duty differential between Canadian and Baltic timber in 1821, along with improved trading conditions, may help to explain the high proportion of deployment in the Baltic in the mid-1820s.[33]

The growth of the Canadian timber trade is one of the main features of the period. No Henley vessels traded with Canada until 1808, and it did not become a central feature of Henley deployment until 1817, when it replaced the fruitless post-war ventures into the Baltic. Unpromising experience in Quebec and Miramichi in 1813−15 may have discouraged the Henleys from moving into the Canadian trade at that time. In 1813 Captain Darley of the *Lady Juliana* made a voyage to Quebec and found that currency and provisions were scarce, the discount and commission on bills high. In 1815 the same master found that at Miramichi there was rarely sufficient water to load the vessel, and many vessels had to wait six or seven weeks for a good enough tide. James Kirton had commented perceptively in relation to the Quebec trade in February 1808, 'I downot see there will be any other traid for larger ships.' Once these larger vessels had been discharged from the Transport Service at the end of the war and had spent several unprofitable years in the Baltic, the natural alternative was the Canadian timber trade. Although timber merchants were forced into the uneconomic policy of importing timber from Canada rather than the Baltic, ship owners benefited from the resultant demand for shipping, and the freight rate appears to have been sufficiently remunerative.

The mahogany trade with Honduras does not enter into the competition discussed above, since the wood was used for furnishing rather than ship construction. The Henleys' main period of deployment in this trade was from 1802 to 1819, reaching a peak in 1807. Ralph Davis,[34] on the other hand, points out that whilst furnishing timber, principally mahogany, represented 20 per cent of all timber imports in the 1780s, the proportion fell away during the war years, since its price was rising and as a luxury its demand fell. As the demand for shipbuilding rose during the French wars, the proportion of furnishing timber would be expected to fall. However, since it was a highly fashionable luxury of the rich the demand might be expected to have been price-inelastic. Moreover, the high price might confirm a buoyant demand. Its appeal to the Henleys lay in the steep rise in its freight rate during the war. In 1790 mahogany was imported into London from Honduras for £3 5s per ton. By 1803 the Henleys were receiving twelve guineas per ton. This was the reward for the high risk involved. Such was the nature of the risk that after a few voyages the Henleys had a clause entered into charter parties that vessels were to load only at

Belize and not at a place about seventy miles away called 'Golden Stream', since it was considered too close to Spanish settlements and would require extra insurance. In these years the Henleys were operating a large fleet and probably wanted to combine the deployment of vessels in low-risk trades offering less profitable though stable returns with high-risk investments in Honduras and the West Indies offering potentially very good returns. The trading accounts of the vessels confirm that they could sometimes make very good profits. Nor were the Spanish the only risk in the Honduras trade. In 1819 the *Trusty* took four months in Honduras to load a cargo of mahogany. There had been no rain until as late as the end of July, and hence no stream to float the wood down for loading. Although demurrage was paid it might not repay the full extent of lost earnings. In addition, it meant a winter passage back to England which would be longer and more dangerous than a summer one and might make the vessel too late for a West Indian voyage the following year; by contrast, in 1812 the *Cornwall* had been delayed because there was a shortage of labour required to 'manufacture' the wood. By 1816 the freight rate for mahogany had fallen back to £5, thus removing the rewards of the war years. At the same time the mahogany trade of Honduras was probably impaired by attempts to develop furnishing woods elsewhere, such as in Africa, Jamaica, British Guiana and New Zealand. In addition, Indian teak began to play an important role from about 1812.[35]

Most of the Henleys' deployment in the Mediterranean was for the Transport Service. Not surprisingly, then, the Mediterranean features most heavily during the fiercest years of the war and disappears almost totally after 1815 except for a single Transport voyage by the *Star* in 1820–22. Most of these voyages were therefore to Gibraltar and Port Mahon, though in 1801 three vessels spent most of the year supporting the campaigns in Egypt and Turkey. However, in the later years of the war, about 1811–14, the Henleys were also sending vessels out on commercial ventures into the Mediterranean. A worsening situation in the coal trade, along with obstacles to trade in the Baltic and a reduction of military activity in the Mediterranean, encouraged them to send vessels to the Mediterranean in search of freights. However, freights were low and scarce. This is another example of concealed underemployment, with vessels obliged to make many passages in ballast. In November 1811 Captain Carr of the *Aurora* informed the Henleys that shipping was unprofitable throughout the Mediterranean and that if he could not get a freight there he would sail to Tenerife or Madeira, and failing that to Surinam, Demerara or Barbados. In February 1812 Captain Armstrong wrote from Oporto to explain why freights were so low and scarce: '. . . their has so many fish ships arrived from Newfoundland that makes freights so bad to be got their is one vessel that has offered to take wine at tow pounds per ton to Plymouth which they onley want as Ballast.' Competition from Canada and the United States, as well as the Mediterranean itself, certainly contributed to the problems of over-capacity in this area.

The Henleys first began to show an interest in the West Indies from 1801. Some involvement from 1794 to 1796 at Martinique was for the Transport Service. How-

ever, in April 1795, during one of these voyages to Martinique, Captain Robson of
the *Concord* wrote to the Henleys saying that freights of coffee and sugar to England
were 6s per cwt and that as much money could be made from a freight home as
could be earned in twelve months in the Transport Service. This may have influenced
their decision to stop merchanting coal in London and start sending vessels to the
West Indies. Generally, the West Indies trade was expanding at this time. Its dangers
in wartime offered potentially high rewards. In addition, political expansion led to
a growth of trade. By 1814 St Lucia, Trinidad, Tobago, Martinique, Guadeloupe,
St Thomas, St Eustatius and Curaçao, along with the mainland colonies of Surinam,
Berbice, Demerara and Essequibo, had all been captured from the French.[36] Except
for a short period in 1795, the existing British islands in the West Indies remained
safe. Although there were occasional visits to these new possessions, Henley vessels
generally went to St Vincent, Jamaica and St Kitts. On the South American mainland, however, they were quick to 'follow the flag', voyaging to Surinam, Berbice
and Demerara. Trade with South America lasted only from 1806 to 1814. There was
also employment in the Transport Service during the conflict with Argentina, which
helps to explain the large figure for 1807. R. G. Albion has pointed out that a series
of revolutions in Latin America had left, by 1806, 'a maritime and commercial
vacuum' which Britain was best equipped to fill.[37] From 1805 to 1809 the Henleys
deployed no vessels in the West Indies, perhaps on account of interest in South
America. Alternatively, it may have been due to the problems of re-exporting
colonial produce to the Baltic as a result of the Continental blockade, although
this did not quite reach a crisis until 1811, which would have reduced the demand
for shipping in the West Indies.

Indeed, the Henleys had made it clear to one of their masters in 1805 that they
were not interested in the West Indies trade at the time. The largest proportion of
deployment in the West Indies by Henley vessels occurred at the end of the war.
Freight rates remained high until peace was declared. In 1809 the freight rate of
sugar and coffee from St Vincent to England was 9s 6d per cwt, by 1817 it had
fallen to 4s or 5s. Certainly the size of the crop influenced the freight rate. Captain
Chapman wrote from St Kitts in March 1815, '. . . it is quite different with good
& bad crops last year was plenty, but not the case this'. The coffee freight stood at
8s that year. The larger fall after 1815 was due to the increased supply of shipping
as a result of the peace. In the short run, the level of freight rates had only a slight
influence on the number of vessels deployed in the trade. This was due to the fact
that most if not all vessels had to sail from England before the state of the crop for
that year was known. As a result the trade suffered from gross over-capacity for
several years after the war. On a voyage to St Vincent in 1817 Captain Gardner of
the *Star* observed, '. . . ships have been offering large premiums . . . as much as
£400 . . . the ships are undercutting each other in such a shameful manner.' Gardner
himself managed to procure a freight by offering to take a cargo for 6d per cwt
less than the prevailing rate.

There were very few voyages to France or the United States, mainly because of the war. The only occasion between 1790 and 1830 when a Henley vessel went to the United States was in 1815, when the *Mary Ann* took some American prisoners back to New York. The vessel went on to Virginia to look for a return freight. Captain Carr found that goods were expensive and freights rare, and commented, 'There is not a freight worth takeing in any port of the U.S.' The only deployment in the East was for the Transport Service.

The problem remains how far the Henley experience was typical of the shipping industry as a whole. Certainly there were many vessels too small to demonstrate such flexibility as the Henleys'. Moreover the idea of the individual specialised ship owner, as distinct from the merchant-owner or a collective of owners, was still fluid at the end of the eighteenth century. However, work by Sarah Palmer, along with that of Craig and Jarvis, indicates that the Henleys were not exceptional. Occasional evidence in the collection hints at the existence of other London ship owners of a similar nature. A good deal of work is required in such records as the London shipping registers in order to quantify the ship owner. The expansion in many trades, especially the long hauls, partly under the impact of the French wars, fostered the growth of the ship owner in this period. The fact that owners of vessels were willing and able to deploy them flexibly when the opportunities arose, as they did during the war, is surely one of the key reasons for the emergence of the ship owner at this time.[38] How far entrepreneurs took a positive decision to become ship owners or were forced into it by the market is difficult to say. The experience of the Henleys suggests that the process was a gradual one. In particular, the war acted as a catalyst. The American war led them to buy vessels and suggested their wider use. The French wars converted the Henleys into ship owners as such. The wars increased the demand for shipping and encouraged its diverse use. Moreover the Transport Service forced many merchant ship owners to act solely as ship owners, often for several consecutive years. However, this process of development was not inevitable. Michael Henley was also interested in other related occupations and was originally a waterman. Men of his type were 'general merchants' in the true sense of the word and would deal in one product or another as the market directed. Finally, was this movement into ship-owning as a profession unique to the period or did it happen earlier on a smaller scale, even as a temporary phenomenon? If this period was unique it was probably the intensity and sheer length of an essentially maritime war at the beginning of the nineteenth century which allowed men like the Henleys to accumulate sufficient capital to become ship owners.[39]

Neither the 'teething' problems of being a 'new' ship owner nor the accompanying policy of diversification sufficiently explain the decline of the company. Clearly the coal trade, as backbone, played a valuable stabilising role in the earlier years and steadied it during its years of expansion. But the period of diversification was only temporary and after the war the company based its operations on three reliable trades — Canada, the Baltic and coastal coal, with the first of these more of a backbone. This was a low-risk operation and reflected the less dynamic attitude taken by the Henleys as Joseph approached old age. Moreover, it is necessary to address the question of how far the company was forced into decline by misconceived policies and a shipping depression or, alternatively, whether it was more a case of deliberate, even controlled, contraction. From being probably the best source of investment in the first decade of the nineteenth century, shipping became one of the worst by the third. The Henleys gradually withdrew their money as they became convinced that the downturn was more than a temporary one. Furthermore, personal factors must have weighed heavily in a private firm like theirs. There was the problem of continuity from generation to generation. The undoubted entrepreneurial flair of Michael and his son Joseph was not necessarily vested in the latter's son, Joseph Warner Henley. Joseph Warner showed only a passing interest in the company and there is no evidence of his active involvement. Instead he was brought up as a gentleman, educated at Oxford, and became actively involved in local politics. From Oxford he went on to a seat in Parliament and became President of the Board of Trade in the Conservative administrations of 1852 and 1858.[40] In addition, if personal factors are applied to the evolution of the firm, it can be seen that it was Michael who was most interested in the coal trade. He retired about 1806, and this may help to explain why the firm increasingly moved away from that activity. Joseph, on the other hand, was probably the prime force in directing the business in the Atlantic trades in the first decade of the new century.

In retrospect, it can be said that merchant vessels in the late eighteenth and early nineteenth centuries showed considerable flexibility and productivity in the nature of their deployment. The evidence has been taken from the papers of Michael Henley & Son, and there seems little reason to doubt that there were other similar ship owners of the period. In particular, medium-sized vessels built in the reputable yards of the east coast could be deployed in most trades. The demand for shipping during the war years may have encouraged the diverse use of Henley vessels. Nonetheless, there was nothing to prevent a ship owner deploying his vessels in a variety of trades in other years. This is confirmed by the trends before 1793 and after 1815. High utilisation is shown by the small proportion of laying-up time during the war. Demand fell during the final years of the war, and this is confirmed by underemployment as the Henleys sent their vessels out, sometimes abortively, in search of freights. In the post-war years there was a depression in the shipping industry due to over-supply, and the amount of laying-up time increased. Finally, we have examined the changes of deployment over time. The rise of the Canadian timber trade and the temporary boom in the West Indies and South America, and the Henleys' response, have been shown. The apparent absence of wide trading opportunities in the Mediterranean in this period is similarly striking. Furthermore the large size of the coasting trade seems to be confirmed. Above all, it can be seen that the productive and flexible nature of shipping caused it to play a key role in the British economy, through high profits and a substantial social saving, in these critical years for industrialisation.

Notes

1 R. Davis, *The Rise of the English Shipping Industry in the Seventeenth and Eighteenth Centuries*, (1962), pp. 194—5.

2 The condition and extent of the papers has necessitated a large cataloguing process which is now nearing completion. Therefore reference numbers of specific evidence cannot yet be given. I would like to thank Dr Roger Knight and Mrs Ann Currie for their assistance and co-operation in allowing me to work on the collection at this early stage. Equally, I would like to thank Mr Robin Craig, who initially directed me towards the Henley papers and has continually offered advice and encouragement.

3 Davis, *English Shipping*, pp. 194—5.

4 R. S. Craig and R. C. Jarvis, *Liverpool Registry of Merchant Ships* (Manchester, 1967).

5 R. Davis, 'Seamen's sixpences, an index of commercial activity, 1697—1828', *Economica*, XXIII (1956), pp. 328—43.

6 W. J. Hausman, 'Size and profitability of English colliers in the eighteenth century', *Business History Review*, LI (1977), pp. 460—73.

7 C. E. Fayle, 'The employment of British shipping', in C. N. Parkinson (ed.), *The Trade Winds* (1948), p. 78.

8 For example, see Parkinson, *Trade Winds*, chapters 7—12.

9 See D. Alexander and R. Ommer, *Volumes not Values* (Newfoundland, 1979).

10 Public Record Office, Customs 17/7—30, Customs 36/5.

11 J. Marshall, *Digest of all Accounts* (1833), p. 235.

12 *The Universal British Directory* (1791), pp. 621—32.

13 Custom 17/1—9 gives the size of the foreign and coastal trades of British ports, 1772—85. However, the shipping of London is falsely recorded as being entirely in the foreign trades. S. R. Palmer, 'The Character and Organisation of the Shipping Industry of the Port of London, 1815—49', unpublished Ph.D. thesis, University of London (1979), p. 8, points out that the main coasting series for entrances and clearances begins in 1835. Also see pp. 82—3 for the deployment of a minor London ship owner, John Long. Between 1815 and 1828 Long owned, wholly or partly, ten vessels. They included the *Little Sally*, which travelled widely to such places as northern Europe, Trieste, Havana, Lisbon, Buenos Aires, Malta and Smyrna.

14 For example, on the Tyne keelmen see D. J. Rowe, 'The decline of the Tyneside keelmen in the nineteenth century', *Northern History*, IV (1969), pp. 58—75, and J. M. Fewster, 'The last struggles of the Tyneside keelmen', *Durham University Journal*, new series, XIV (1937), pp. 5—15.

15 See their ship registrations in the Public Record Office, Board of Trade 107/1—60.

16 Public Record Office, Admiralty 108/1C, 12 April 1782, shows the *Henley* in the service at Charlestown.

17 These are their registered tonnages, taken from P.R.O., BT 107/1—60 (as above). The size of several of these vessels changes owing to structural repairs, but never by more than ten or twenty tons.

18 Davis, *English Shipping*, pp. 61—2.

19 For the full year-to-year deployment of *Freedom* over its forty-year life span see S. Ville, 'Wages, prices and profitability in the shipping industry during the Napoleonic Wars', *Journal of Transport History*, third series, II (1981), pp. 39—52.

20 L. F. Horsfall, 'The West Indian trade', in Parkinson, *Trade Winds*, p. 180, says that vessels in the West Indies trade varied from 200 to 500 tons and were not built specifically for that trade.

21 For example, see *The Shipowners' Manual and Sea-faring Man's Assistant* (Newcastle, 1804) and G. Harrison, *The Freighters' Guide and Corn Merchant's Assistant* (Newcastle, 1834).

22 See P. M. Sweezy, *Monopoly and Competition in the English Coal Trade, 1550—1850* (Cambridge, Mass., 1938).

23 Though Captain Ross of the *General Elliot* had remarked about taking a captaincy in the coal trade, '. . . no man is eaqual to but those bread up in it from their youth'.

24 N. Atcheson, *A Letter addressed to Rowland Burdon Esquire, M.P., on the Present State of the Carrying Part of the Coal Trade* (1802), p. 10, shows that the number of ships delivering coal at London in 1800 and 1801 was relatively constant from month to month, suggesting very little laying-up.

25 Davis, *English Shipping*, p. 196.

26 On the Transport Service see M. Condon, 'The Administration of the Transport Service during the War against Revolutionary France 1793—1802', unpublished Ph.D. thesis, University of London (1968), and D. Syrett, *Shipping and the American War, 1775—83* (1970).

27 On the depressed state of shipping in the 1820s see *Select Committee on Manufactures, Commerce and Shipping*, Parliamentary Papers, VI, 1833.

28 *The Eighth Report of the Commissioners of Naval Enquiry. His Majesty's Victualling Department at Plymouth*, P.P., III, 1803—04.

29 See T. S. Willan, *The English Coasting Trade, 1600—1750* (Manchester, 1938).

30 On the coal trade see Sweezy, *Monopoly and Competition*; R. Smith, *Sea coal for London* (1961); T. S. Ashton and J. Sykes, *The Coal Industry of the Eighteenth Century* (Manchester, 1929). Although not officially part of the coastal trade until October 1823, trade with Ireland has been included under this section for simplicity. At any rate there were very few voyages to Ireland by Henley vessels after 1790.

31 J. Potter, 'The British timber duties', *Economica*,

The deployment of English merchant shipping   33

new series, XXII (1955), pp. 122—36.

32 R. G. Albion, *Forests and Sea Power: the Timber Problem of the Royal Navy, 1652—1862* Cambridge, Mass., 1926), p. 355, points out that the timber magnates argued that the end of the Napoleonic wars would cause a reversion to the Baltic.

33 On the shipping boom of 1824—25 see D. Williams, 'Bulk carriers and timber imports: the British North American trade and the shipping boom of 1824—5', *Mariner's Mirror*, LIV (1968), pp. 373—82.

34 Davis, *The Industrial Revolution and British Overseas Trade* (Leicester, 1979), pp. 46—7.

35 Albion, *Forests and Sea Power*, p. 365.

36 L. F. Horsfall, in Parkinson, *Trade Winds*, p. 158.

37 R. G. Albion, 'British shipping and Latin America, 1806—1914', *Journal of Economic History*, 11 (1951), pp. 361—74.

38 Conversely, it might be argued that diversification and flexibility had become possible because professional shipowners were beginning to appear. However, it seems clear that before the 1790s the Henleys were essentially merchants who were expanding their business by the process of vertical integration into shipping. It was from the end of the century, with the wartime expansion of shipping, that the merchanting side of the business was replaced by a concentration into shipowning. Indeed, it is clear that the Henleys had frequently arranged the future deployment of a vessel before buying it rather than simply purchasing extra vessels as a means of expanding the enterprise and then, subsequently, looking around for suitable employment. Joseph Henley appears to have held influence in the London mercantile community which enabled him to secure diverse employment for a large fleet.

39 On the emergence of the ship owner, G. Jackson, *Hull in the Eighteenth Century* (Oxford, 1972), pp. 140—4.

40 See entry in the *Dictionary of National Biography*.

2 The creation of the Marine Department of the Board of Trade

J. H. WILDE

THAT the compulsory examination of masters and mates in the merchant fleet would be an unwarranted intrusion upon the interests of shipowners was one of the primary arguments advanced in 1837 by the President of the Board of Trade, Charles Poulett Thomson, in opposing a Bill to establish a marine board to regulate the merchant service.[1] However, in little over a decade following the defeat of this Bill, the British government was forced to recognize that the question of the competence of the seamen who manned her merchant ships was of prime importance if her maritime supremacy were to be maintained. Even before the repeal of the Navigation Acts and the consequent exposure of British shipping to the full force of world competition made the problem urgent, it became obvious that it was imperative for the government to turn its attention towards setting standards for masters and seamen and that this type of legislation, designed to secure the greater safety of life and property at sea, was of more importance than an over-tender concern for the rights of shipowners. The defeat in 1837 of the Bill based upon the plan for the regulation and improvement of the mercantile marine outlined in the report of a Select Committee in the previous year indicated that centralized administration would not be easily secured. In the years that followed, the issue of compulsory examination of merchant service officers became linked with that of centralized administration of merchant shipping law, and proved the means whereby Britain secured for the first time a central agency with the sole responsibility for supervising the merchant service. The growing concern of Britain in the 1840s with the condition of her seamen, the investigations in 1843 and 1847 of the Foreign Office, a department not ordinarily concerned with merchant shipping, the evidence before Select Committees in 1843 and 1847-8, and finally the repeal of the Navigation Acts, all were elements which forced the government to pass the first piece of merchant shipping legislation which marked a distinct change in approach from previous enactments. The Mercantile Marine Act of 1850 "for improving the Condition of Masters, Mates, and Seamen, and for maintaining Discipline in the Merchant Service", which established the Marine Department of the Board of Trade, may well be considered to mark the beginning of a new era in the regulation of British shipping, recognizing as it did that the state had some responsibilities for securing the safety of life and property by sea as well as on land.

In 1836 the problem of safety at sea had first been placed before Parliament and the nation by the Select Committee on shipwrecks. The credit for securing the appointment of the Committee as well as for the reforms suggested in its report belongs to James Silk Buckingham, who was the first spokesman in Parliament for the cause of marine reform.[2] Most of Buckingham's early life was spent in the merchant navy. He went to sea as a boy of ten, and at the end of his seafaring career he commanded a ship in the West India trade. From the time he left the sea about 1817 until his election to Parliament in 1832, he was occupied as a journalist, traveller, and lecturer. His first journalistic venture, the *Calcutta Journal*, begun in 1818, ended in 1823 with a severe financial loss when Buckingham was expelled from India and the publication suppressed by the Governor-General for his outspoken criticisms of the Government of India. For the next decade he was occupied with other journalistic ventures in England. With a background of seafaring, and an interest in social reform, it is not strange that, after his election to Parliament, he sought to remedy the conditions faced by seamen. After making a strong effort to force the government to abolish impressment, Buckingham turned his attention to the causes of shipwreck. In the report of the Select Committee of 1836, which presented a comprehensive plan for the professionalization of the merchant service, Buckingham enumerated the causes of maritime disaster that were then costing the nation the lives of some 900 seamen and an estimated £2,836,000 in property annually. It was neither humane nor financially sound to allow the continuance of these losses arising from the poor construction of ships; from the use of unseaworthy vessels; from the incompetence of masters and mates too young or too poorly educated for their responsibilities; from drunkenness among officers and seamen; and from the system of marine insurance which led owners to neglect ordinary precautions for safety.[3] Before steps could be taken to improve conditions under which seamen worked and to ensure greater safety at sea, two pre-requisites had to be met. The first and more essential was to vest in a single department of government the sole responsibility for the enforcement of statutes regulating the merchant service. The second, the compilation of a code of maritime law, or at least a consolidation of existing enactments, some of them dating to the days of Elizabeth I, was to be one of the first duties of the proposed board, which was to consist of experienced officers from the Royal Navy and the merchant fleet, shipowners, and shipbuilders elected by the Admiralty, shipowners, and Trinity House.[4] The board was to establish standards of qualification for seamanship. All who desired to hold responsible position on board ship were to pass examinations designed to test their competence. Government offices were to be established in the ports at which captains were to sign on their crews, thus eliminating the evils arising from dependence upon boarding-house keepers and crimps. Nautical schools were to be established. The new board was to be financed by fees charged for the registration of ships and for granting certificates to masters and mates. These steps, Buckingham was convinced, would greatly improve the merchant marine, making it the safest and most efficient in the world.

In 1837, Buckingham attempted to secure the passage of a measure embodying the plan which he had outlined in the report. He thought it paradoxical that, although maritime supremacy was the national pride, Parliament had felt no need to legislate to secure safety at sea, but rather allowed maritime disasters to continue "without appearing to do more than lament the catastrophes when they are reported to us", and doing nothing to prevent their recurrence. Buckingham's arguments, eloquent and strongly humanitarian with overtones of the huge financial loss to the nation, had little effect.[5] The debates on the Bill show that not only the shipowners but also the government were opposed to the measure, which was admittedly badly drafted. The President of the Board of Trade, Charles Poulett Thomson, feared that the Bill would create an arbitrary power that would destroy the merchant service. He objected particularly, as has been stated, to the clause requiring the compulsory examination of merchant-service officers, terming it "an unjust interference with the rights of the shipping interest".[6] Although admitting that such tests would be beneficial, he maintained that they should be administered on a voluntary basis only. Buckingham insisted upon dividing the House on the second reading; he could muster only 28 votes against 176 opposed.[7] Thus the world's leading maritime power failed to secure a central agency to regulate the merchant navy and Britain continued to lag behind many nations, such as Sweden, Norway, Holland, and Prussia, with far smaller merchant fleets, which had comprehensive codes of law safeguarding the rights of their seamen and the safety of the ships in which they served.

Although at this point Buckingham withdrew from the fight for marine reform, subsequent events proved that his suggestions could not be forgotten nor could the question of the competence of the merchant service continue to be overlooked by the government. The belief was growing slowly but steadily that the large number of maritime casualties were not the necessary accompaniment of the merchant service and that precautions for security at sea could not be left entirely to self-interest. But the reforms which Buckingham had sought to achieve in one comprehensive measure were now to be enacted piecemeal as the need for one reform and then another became urgent. In the following decade, the examination of the competence of masters and mates was regarded as the solution most likely to stop unnecessary maritime casualties.

The one sizeable area in which examinations of competence had been required came to an end with the disappearance of the East India Company's Marine. This is not to say that many individual owners did not demand proof of the abilities of those who commanded their ships. One London firm attributed its success and freedom from wrecks for a quarter of a century entirely to the qualifying examinations required of its officers. The fleet of R. H. Green achieved its pre-eminent position in the British merchant navy by careful attention not only to the quality of its ships, but also to the training given to those who were to command the vessels. Other owners also conducted their own examinations, most of them thoroughly convinced that they were competent enough in nautical science accurately to determine the abilities of those they employed. This was true enough for owners who had themselves spent many years at sea, but an increasing number of persons were investing in ships who had no sea experience and insufficient knowledge to assess the competence of their officers.[8] Individual action of this sort thus had many weaknesses. There was no uniformity in the examinations which might be given; no guarantees that uniform standards of competence were insisted upon. The results were thus always open to charges of favouritism and partiality. Above all, there was nothing to require or to show that any examination at all had been given. Some owners, however, realized the need for group action, particularly in the northern ports of Sunderland, South Shields, and Newcastle. In 1837, Sunderland owners and masters set up a system of qualifying examinations administered by a local board, thus undertaking to enforce the sort of regulations their representatives in Parliament had refused to enact.[9] However, the charges of favouritism and of the lack of competent examiners lodged against the Sunderland board illustrated the weaknesses of private action by means of a body not responsible to public authority.

Several years elapsed before the government took any further action on the question. The agitation for examining boards continued, particularly at Glasgow and the northern ports, and an increasing number of memorials were submitted to the Board of Trade requesting tests of competence. In 1841, this movement found a leader in Captain Robert Fitzroy of the Royal Navy, who had been elected to Parliament for Durham. Fitzroy had commanded the Beagle from 1828 to 1836 on the survey of the Straits of Magellan, the expedition to which Charles Darwin was attached as a naturalist. After his retirement from active duty in 1850, Fitzroy rendered further service to seafarers through his work as secretary of the Lifeboat Association and particularly after 1854 when he was appointed to head the new Meteorological Department of the Board of Trade. In this capacity he instituted a system of storm warnings which evolved into the present system of daily forecasts. In March 1842 a deputation of members of Parliament and shipowners headed by Fitzroy conferred with the President of the Board of Trade on a proposed measure to establish boards in various ports of the United Kingdom to conduct examinations into the qualifications of masters and mates. The President of the Board, the Earl of Ripon, seemed to favour the suggestion, but indicated that he wished for further proof of the necessity of the measure.[10] On 29 July 1842 Fitzroy moved for leave to introduce a Bill to require examinations for officers of merchants vessels, hoping that the proposals could be studied between sessions and acted upon early in the following session. Fitzroy's plan was to vest responsibility for the entire system in a chief examiner at London, to be assisted by Trinity House in practical nautical matters, but to be under the direct control of the Board of Trade. This marked one of the first times that it was suggested that the Board have control of this sort over any area of merchant shipping. The examiners of the district boards to be set up in the ten chief ports were to be chosen by the local ship-owners, and the entire system was to be financed by the fees charged for the issuance of certificates to successful candidates.[11] In replying for the government, William Ewart Gladstone, the Vice-President of the Board of Trade, showed that no conclusions had yet been reached on the best method for dealing with the issue. Although he agreed that a strong sentiment existed for legislation, he stated that consideration would have to be given to the great disagreement among shipowners as to the method to be employed in these examinations.[12] Fitzroy, however, was unable personally to carry through his efforts to secure legislation. Early in the 1843 session, the government stated that action on the question would have to await the report of the Select Committee on shipwrecks which was then hearing evidence.[13] Shortly thereafter, Fitzroy was appointed Governor of New Zealand, thus removing from Parliament the leader of the movement. The government refused to take over Fitzroy's Bill as a ministerial measure.

Any hopes that might have been entertained for immediate legislation following the report of the Select Committee proved over-sanguine. The testimony before the Committee was on many points contradictory, particularly on the question of compulsory examinations. The chairman of the Shipowners Society considered Fitzroy's Bill an undue interference with the rights of the owners. Others thought the examinations would be of little use since masters would be able to gain the requisite knowledge to pass after twenty-four hours of cramming the standard nautical texts. Still others felt that they had themselves enough knowledge to test the competence of the masters they employed.[14] Opinion was equally divided upon the question of local boards or a central authority to supervise the system if established. Some of the strongest testimony in favour of compulsory examinations and a central board came from one of the patriarchs of Liverpool shipping, John Gladstone. The elder Gladstone, who aided Fitzroy in the drafting of the Bill, did not feel this type of legislation would in any way restrict his freedom as a shipowner and employer, nor that it would be detrimental to the merchant service to require that none but qualified men be placed in positions of command.[15] Opposed to this, however, there was a strong current of *laissez-faire* thinking among members of the shipping interest which found expression in the belief that it was wrong to legislate for the protection of seamen, adults who should be well able to look after their own welfare. This view was well summed up by the *Economist* in an article advocating voluntary examinations. The practice of interfering between the employer and the employed was "fraught with mischief", and the *Economist* felt that the practice should not be extended, "for its extension brings with it a train of evils, being in fact the total degradation of the people, to which death itself, in its thousand forms, is greatly preferable".[16]

In view of these conflicting opinions, it is not surprising that the report of the Select Committee as originally drafted contained no recommendation for compulsory examinations. However, by a vote of six to five, the draft report was amended to recommend the establishment of local boards to "examine the ability, conduct, and character, of all who wish to qualify as Masters and Mates in the Merchant Service".[17] Because of this divergence of opinion, as well as the strong opposition of the shipping interest, no immediate action was forthcoming from the government, which continued to regard voluntary examinations as the practical expedient. However, it was becoming apparent that the shipping interest could not expect to continue relatively free from regulation. There was increasing comment upon the poor condition of the merchant navy in contrast to foreign merchant fleets, much of it coming from men who had commanded British merchant vessels.[18] There was a growing belief that the shipping interest could itself do much to diminish maritime casualties. The *Westminster Review* characterized the protected shipping interest as "the nation's spoiled child" which "is come to maturity half instructed and reckless". Declaring that the number of unavoidable maritime disasters was greatly overestimated, it charged that a large amount of this loss "must be laid to the sheer default of the shipowner and his servants".[19]

It was at this same time that an investigation into the condition of the British merchant service was undertaken, strangely enough, by the Foreign Office. The results of this inquiry are of the greatest importance, for it gave a strong impulse to the movement to centralize the administration of the laws relating to the merchant service. The credit for instituting the investigation must go to James Murray, a minor but extremely able civil servant at the Foreign Office who rose through the ranks to become, in 1858, Assistant Under-Secretary of State. Murray's acquaintance with Captain Fitzroy and others connected with the merchant service had brought to his attention the condition in which many British ships sailed the seas. This, together with the failure to enact any reforming legislation, had convinced Murray that the government was not fully aware of the great damage being done the shipping interest by the lack of regulation. On 1 July 1843 Murray, on his own initiative, sent a letter to various British consuls requesting information on the condition of the merchant service. This letter, when finally published in 1848 with the reports of the consuls, aroused a storm of protest from the shipping interest, which could quite fairly claim that the letter was couched in terms practically inviting adverse criticism. Murray had written:

> "I am particularly desirous of gaining information in regard to instances which have come under your observation of the incompetency of British shipmasters to manage their vessels and their crews, . . . whether arising from deficiency of knowledge of practical navigation or seamanship or of moral character, particularly want of sobriety."[20]

Not only was the letter unfortunately phrased, but it also sought its information from the British consuls, who, because of their position, were apt to come in contact only with the worst elements in the merchant service. The reports of the consuls make dismal reading, and one is led to wonder how it is possible, if the picture is at all true, that British ships could make their way across the seas.[21] British masters and seamen were pictured as incompetent, ill-educated for their positions, frequently drunk, with the result that ships of other nations were often used in preference to British ships. However, it was also reported that generally the masters of first-class merchant vessels were fully competent. With due allowance for the distortion and exaggeration that resulted from the phrasing of the request, there was much truth in the reports. W. S. Lindsay, a shipowner, stated in writing of the investigations that there was "too much reason for believing that the character of British ships and the conduct of British crews were then greatly inferior to those of other nations".[22]

The replies of the consuls, together with the conclusions Murray had drawn from this mass of material, were laid before the Foreign Secretary, Lord Aberdeen. Murray felt that, in contrast to foreign merchant fleets, British shipping was declining. He observed that there was insufficient control over British masters and seamen; that no attention was given to the education of men for the British merchant service; that merchants and owners had no means of ascertaining the character and capability of the masters they employed; and that, as a result, owners depended upon insurance for the safety of their property. Murray felt that the merchants and owners could not be entirely blamed for this situation, for "if a merchant can protect without difficulty his individual interests, he will [not] take much thought and trouble about the public interest and general good".[23]

Murray suggested that the time had come to change the existing method of regulating the merchant navy, as there was no co-ordination whatsoever between the nine departments which at that time administered the merchant shipping laws, and not one of them alone nor all of them together could act in a way which was best for the welfare of the entire merchant navy and the country as a whole. This end could be best achieved, Murray stated, by establishing "a Board or Department of Commercial Marine". He suggested the Board of Trade as the logical office in which to establish such a department, since it appeared to be "the office to which the mercantile community naturally look in regard to everything relating to trade, whether on shore or at sea".[24]

The Foreign Office duly transmitted this proposal to the Board of Trade, where a record in the minute book states "consideration postponed".[25] There the matter rested; six years were to elapse before Murray's proposals were put into effect.

With ample evidence before them calling for parliamentary action in establishing compulsory examinations, the government fell back upon the alternative proposed by Thomson in 1837, that of voluntary examinations. In April 1844 a deputation from Liverpool, Glasgow, and other shipping centres met the Board of Trade and presented proposals to establish local boards to examine the qualifications of masters and mates.[26] Since these boards were to have no powers of compulsion, the plan was one which had the approval of shipowners as well as those officers who were fearful that compulsory examinations would cost them their jobs. The Secretary of the Admiralty sought opinions on the practicability of the plan from the chief magistrates and others in the principal seaport towns. The responses were evidently favourable, for on 19 August 1845, by an Order in Council, the Board of Trade instituted a system of voluntary examinations, to go into effect on 1 November.[27] The Board, however, did not actually control the execution of the order. Responsibility for conducting the examinations was delegated to Trinity House in London, and to branch boards consisting of the Sub-Commissioners of Pilotage at Plymouth, Milford, and Great Yarmouth; Trinity House at Hull, Newcastle, and Leith; the board for licensing pilots at Glasgow and Liverpool; and the Ballast Board at Dublin. The Order in Council laid down the subjects and conditions of the examinations, but otherwise the local boards were left to conduct the tests in any manner they desired, with Trinity House in London setting the highest standards.[28] But the move was unpopular not only with the owners, who resented any interference with their powers of hiring, but also with many officers who maintained that an examination would not prove seamanship. Nor did candidates flock to the examining boards as eagerly as the government had hoped, for there was no practical advantage to be gained by the possession of a certificate of competence. By the end of 1846 barely 200 men had passed the examinations.[29] In order to apply more pressure to masters, the Admiralty issued an order that after 23 March 1847 no ship would be chartered by the Admiralty unless the masters and mates held the necessary certificates. Shortly thereafter the regulation was extended to other ships chartered by the government.[30] Although the lack of qualified officers meant that the government frequently had to ignore these regulations, they had a visible effect upon the numbers presenting themselves for examination. By 1850, over 3,000 had passed the test, including all officers having higher positions in ships holding government contracts.[31]

Although some progress had thus been made toward achieving one end, little or none, aside from the fact that it was the Board of Trade that instituted the voluntary examinations, had been made toward centralized administration. An Act of 1845 for the protection of seamen had imposed upon the Board the duty of checking crimping by granting licences to persons who signed on crews for merchant ships, but the Board did not exercise actual executive power, since the administration of the Act was turned over to the Admiralty. A more interesting development occurred in 1846 when an Act for the survey of steamers granted the Board of Trade the right to appoint surveyors for passenger ships and to inquire into accidents, thereby giving the Board jurisdiction over a limited amount of shipping.[32] In the Steam Navigation Department of the Board of Trade is to be seen a small beginning of the Marine Department.

In 1847, further investigations were made into the condition of British seamen. The Board of Trade requested the Foreign Office to undertake an investigation similar to that of 1843 to gain information on the operation of pension funds for seamen for the information of a Royal Commission that was soon to be appointed. Accordingly the Foreign Secretary, Lord Palmerston, directed the consuls to report on the condition of shipping in foreign ports with particular attention to Murray's suggestions for a department of commercial marine. The replies served only to confirm the previous findings, for they showed that little improvement had taken place in the intervening four years.[33]

The consular reports of 1847 along with those of 1843, accompanied by a memorandum drawn up by Murray, were presented to Parliament in 1848. The condition of the merchant navy, Murray concluded, was a disgrace to the nation. If the Navigation Acts were to be repealed and British shipping were to be exposed to the full force of world competition, the situation could not be allowed to exist. Regardless of how much British shipowners might deprecate government interference, Murray pointed out that it could not be denied that many ships were sent to sea "navigated in a manner that injures British interests, and reflects discredit on the national intelligence".[34] Murray asked whether it was reasonable that the lives of thousands of seamen should be imperilled and large amounts of property endangered because owners had the right to place incompetent persons in charge of their vessels. He reiterated his belief that the time had come for government action:

> "The condition of the sailor, and the necessity of improving our system of navigation and management now observable in our merchant vessels, so as to ensure their not losing ground, as compared with foreigners, would alone appear to require the exclusive attention of a competent department; for it is clear that individuals, however much their personal interests may be concerned, cannot, or will not, make inquiries, or take the necessary steps."[35]

The government apparently hoped that the publication of these papers would force the shipowners into action. On 15 February 1848 Henry Labouchere, the President of the Board of Trade, stated in Parliament that he hoped the papers would convince owners it was greatly to their advantage for the government to act quickly to put an end to the conditions described in the consular reports.[36] However, legislation of this sort had to be postponed until after the repeal of the Navigation Acts. The opposition of the shipowners to the repeal of these measures, which they considered essential to continued maritime supremacy, was strong and obdurate; it would not have helped matters to antagonize them further by first imposing new and highly unpopular restrictions upon the conduct of their trade. However, both in the testimony before the Select Committees on the Navigation Acts and in the debates on the measure in Parliament, is to be found additional evidence for the need for legislation to establish standards of competence for the merchant service.[37] The repeal of the Navigation Acts in 1849 made even more essential the enactment of this newer type of legislation. Sheltered behind this protective legislation, the owners had not always kept up with the latest developments in the industry. Not only were they often technologically out of date, but they were equally backward in providing for the welfare of their seamen. The industry with its many organizations of shipowners could have taken steps to police itself. It had not done so, and as a result, it has been stated that the industry was "an ill-conditioned vessel into which to pour the new wine of *laissez-faire*".[38]

Thus it was that a government pledged to free trade moved to enact as soon as possible legislation that would put into effect the reforms suggested by Murray in 1843, which Buckingham had unsuccessfully placed before Parliament in 1837. On 12 July 1849, two weeks after the passage of the statute repealing the Navigation Acts, the President of the Board of Trade, Henry Labouchere, presented to the House two Bills embodying the government's proposals, primarily so that the measures could be thoroughly understood and discussed during the recess by the public and the interests involved.[39] The government proposed to deal with three subjects—light dues, pilotage, and the qualifications of masters and mates. One of the chief features of the proposal was its emphasis upon centralization of administrative authority as compared with the many decentralized boards which then controlled merchant shipping. Labouchere proposed to substitute a central government board for the local boards which controlled light dues. He proposed to give the responsibility for the examination of masters and mates to the Board of Trade and to create a Department of Mercantile Marine.[40] The system of voluntary examinations, which had varied in strictness and uniformity, was to be replaced by a compulsory examination under the direction of the new marine department. Public officers were also to be substituted for the licensed agents who procured crews. Public shipping offices were to be established in the principal ports of the kingdom, and all shipping agreements were to be signed in the presence of the shipping officer.

In 1850 the battle began in earnest. On 11 February Labouchere introduced the Bill in Parliament dealing with the qualifications of masters and mates. The shipping interest, which had an opportunity to study the proposals between sessions, was unwilling to surrender its freedom without a struggle. The shipowners, even better organized after their fight for the Navigation Acts, showed a certain recklessness in their opposition. A radical wing centred primarily in London desired absolute freedom from control as a reward for their acceptance of free trade.[41] On the other hand, the Liverpool Chamber of Commerce, in a memorial submitted to the Board of Trade, although expressing hostility to centralization, none the less showed a desire to compromise to arrive at workable legislation. The Liverpool group held the matter of centralized administration to be of cardinal importance and expressed a desire to allow the large ports to elect local boards to supervise the examinations and to appoint shipping officers. In a letter replying to the Liverpool owners, Labouchere insisted that if any uniformity of system were to be maintained, the ports could not elect their own examiners. Experience proved that local institutions were more apt to show partiality and to fall into disrepute than a government department controlled by Parliament and public opinion. Although stating his belief in the wisdom of a policy of governmental non-interference with business, Labouchere wrote:

> "To say that it is to be left to chance whether a grossly ignorant and incompetent master or mate shall be allowed to take charge of a ship, crew, and cargo, and that the sailor shall be abandoned to all the frauds to which the crimpage system subjects him without protection, after a fatal experience has demonstrated the mischief of these practices, appears to me to be utterly inconsistent with the duty of Parliament and of the Government."[42]

The Times, which repeatedly throughout the century raised its voice loudly and fearlessly in the cause of marine reform, could see nothing wrong with establishing a supervisory power independent of the shipowners, nor could it understand how the interests of the shipowners were to be damaged by compelling them to hire competent officers. The condition of British seamen was a national issue, and *The Times* pleaded that the Bill should not "be left to the mercy of the casual, or interested, or purely mischievous obstruction".[43]

Thoughts of this sort were lost on the shipping interest. In mid-April 1850 a general meeting of shipowners was held in London for the purpose of taking steps to induce the government to postpone action on the Bill, and to institute a full inquiry into the need for legislation. A shipowner, speaking in distinct opposition to the temper of the meeting by advocating the immediate passage of the Bill, was shouted down. These remarks roused to a great fury George Frederick Young of the General Shipowners Society, whom *The Times* had termed "the Pangloss of the Shipping Interest". He attacked the government course recklessly, criticizing the reports of the consuls as a great libel against the merchant service and sneering at the great concern felt for the British seamen. Young felt the Bill proposed to extend the present British policy of treating sailors as children, for it "told the sailor not to depend on himself or his exertions, but to consider himself a mere child who would, in all things, be protected from the rapacious hands of the shipowners".[44]

The owners' opposition to the Bill, which they termed "a paltry, puerile, trashy

piece of legislation", forced the government on 20 April to withdraw the measure and
to substitute for it a revised Bill.[45] The essential principle of the Bill, to establish a system
of compulsory examinations and to put an end to crimping by the establishment of
public offices, was unchanged, as was the provision to establish a Marine Department
of the Board of Trade. However, opposition of the owners had forced the government
to make a major concession on the matter of the local boards rather than risk no legislation at all. The Board under the new plan was to nominate four of the proposed
twelve members of the local boards, to have a right to fix the plan of examination, and
to have a concurrent power to appoint examiners.[46] Although the government perhaps
felt that the presence on the local board of the mayor and stipendary magistrate of the
town would counteract the six members to be elected by the shipowners, this was not
in fact true, for these officials in a port town were all too likely to be members of the
shipping interest.[47] This concession was in fact a major defeat for the government on
an important provision of the Bill. The change meant that the local boards were from
the outset nothing more than local shipowners' associations under a different name, and
the new Marine Department was thus handicapped from the outset. Despite this
alteration designed to placate the owners, the Bill faced more opposition after it
advanced to its second reading on 20 June. Although Labouchere agreed that the
measure stood in need of further alteration, he requested that the changes be made in
committee, for to withdraw the Bill at that late date would be equivalent to defeat for
legislation which he considered to be long overdue. Although there were more complaints, definite efforts at obstruction, and continued pleas for further investigation of
the need for legislation, the Bill passed successfully through Parliament and went into
effect on 1 January 1851.[48]

The Act was a lengthy one of 124 clauses. It established a central agency in the Board
of Trade to "undertake the general superintendence of matters relating to the British
Mercantile Marine".[49] The powers of the Admiralty with regard to merchant seamen
were transferred to the Board. Local marine boards were established at all the principal
ports. The examination of masters and mates was made compulsory, but no one was to
be unfairly penalized by this provision. Those who had obtained certificates under the
old system of voluntary examinations could exchange them for the new Board of
Trade certificates. Those already in the service who were unwilling to take the examinations could obtain certificates showing previous service. Shipping agreements
in the foreign trade were to be signed by seamen before a shipping master who was to
be appointed by the local marine board. The Board of Trade was empowered to
appoint a secretary for the new Department as well as two persons with nautical experience to assist in the administration of the Act.[50]

The immediate effects of the Act once it had been put into operation were curious.
One of the chief complaints of the owners had been that their rights were being
ignored in the sudden tender concern for the condition of seamen. But no sooner had

the Act come into operation than Parliament was flooded with petitions from seamen, who, *The Times* stated, had contracted "an equally ignorant antipathy" to the new system.[51] The agitation was stirred up largely by lodging-house keepers who found their activities circumscribed by the new statute. The sailors of the north-east ports struck and refused to work the provisions relating to the supply and signing of seamen. On 24 January 1851 seamen attacked the new shipping office at North Shields, and the situation became so serious that the mayor was obliged to request the Admiralty to send a war steamer to protect shipping. The protest movement spread to other ports. On 24 February London seamen met in order to consider means of securing redress of the grievances imposed upon them by the new Act.[52] The government refused to be swayed by the agitation. Labouchere stated that the measure, which had been framed for the benefit of the seamen, would operate in their best interests.[53] However, by May, the fears of the seamen were abating, and complaints about the operation of the Act were coming from such places as Sheffield and Manchester, neither of them maritime towns.[54]

Thus, over the protests of the shipping interest and of the intended beneficiaries of the Act, a new era in the regulation of merchant shipping came into being. The need for a central office to superintend the mercantile marine had long been demonstrated, and action could no longer have been postponed. It was thus that a government committed to free trade, and with an aversion to regulating the details of business enterprise, imposed upon one of Britain's leading industries an Act which regulated some of the minutest details in the operation of the shipowner's business. From the evidence that had accumulated since the days of Buckingham's proposal to enact this very sort of legislation, it is difficult to reach any conclusion other than that the shipowners by their own lack of concern brought regulation upon themselves.

NOTES

1. *Hansard*, 3rd ser., XXXVIII, 1222.

2. Further details of Buckingham's work and the background of the movement for marine reform can be found in Jane H. Wilde, "British Legislation Concerning Shipping and Safety at Sea, 1803–1894" (Unpublished Ph.D. Thesis, University of Wisconsin, 1955).

3. *Parl. Papers*, 1836, XVII, 3–8.   4. *ibid.*, 8–11.   5. *Hansard*, XXXVII, 164–91; XXXVIII, 1222–5.

6. *ibid.*, 1222.   7. *ibid.*, 1225.

8. *Parl. Papers*, 1836, XVII, 703–4; 1843, IX, QQ. 934–41, 424, 1110–14, 2397, 5793–6, 5812–3.

9. *Nautical Magazine*, VI (1837), 688–9; VII (1838), 163. *Parl. Papers*, 1843, IX, QQ. 1920–2, 604–5.

10. *The Times*, 14 Mar. 1842.   11. *Hansard*, LXV, 764–6. *Nautical Magazine*, XI (1842), 347–9.

12. *Hansard*, LXV, 766–7. *Nautical Magazine*, XI (1842), 281–3; XII (1843), 206, 259–60, 274, 390–1; XIII (1844), 95–8. One correspondent felt that Fitzroy's measure did not go far enough, stating that until an Act was passed for the general supervision of the merchant service, it would remain in a degraded state. *Nautical Magazine*, XII (1843), 227–9.

13. *Hansard*, LXVI, 1277.   14. *Parl. Papers*, 1843, IX, QQ. 1103, 1110–14, 890, 3084–5.

15. *ibid.*, QQ. 5533–5, 5542–5, 5555–8, 5593.   16. *Economist*, 9 Nov. 1844.

17. *Parl. Papers*, 1843, IX, 4, 11.

Notes

18. *Nautical Magazine*, v (1836), 213; vii (1838), 153-4, 160; xi (1842), 818-19, 281; xiii (1844), 98. *Economist*, 20 Apr. 1844. *Parl. Papers*, 1843, ix, QQ. 1, 210-11, 5532.
19. *Westminster Review*, xlii (1844), 60.   20. *Parl. Papers*, 1847-8, lix, 1-4.
21. *ibid.*, 5-138.
22. W. S. Lindsay, *A History of Merchant Shipping and Ancient Commerce* (1874-6), iii, 48.
23. *Parl. Papers*, 1847-8, lix, 1.   24. *ibid.*, 2.
25. Sir Hubert Llewellyn Smith, *The Board of Trade* (1928), 103-4.
26. *The Times*, 20 Apr. 1844.
27. *Nautical Magazine*, xv (1846), 70-2. Smith, *The Board of Trade*, 104.
28. *Parl. Papers*, 1847, lx, 2-5. The *Nautical Magazine*, noting that officers showed a preference for Trinity House, recommended that the examinations be taken in London, thereby avoiding "the disagreeable consequences too sure to arise from local prejudice or influence": xv (1846), 664.
29. *Parl. Papers*, 1847, lx, 9-11. *Nautical Magazine*, xv (1846), 662-3.   30. *ibid.*, 1847, xvi, 364.
31. *Parl. Papers*, 1850, liii. *Nautical Magazine*, xvi (1847), 364.
32. 8 & 9 Vict., c. 116; 9 & 10 Vict., c. 100.   33. *Parl. Papers*, 1847-8, lix, 145-434.
34. *ibid.*, 141.   35. *ibid.*, 142.   36. *Hansard*, xcvi, 671-2.
37. *Parl. Papers*, 1847, x, QQ. 3182-3, 3391-414, 3426-33. *ibid.*, 1847, x, QQ. 4233, 4248-50, 5316-7. *ibid.*, 1847, x, QQ. 7808-10, 7815. *Hansard*, xcviii, 1019-20; xcix, 31.
38. R. H. Thornton, *British Shipping* (1939), 82. Cf. Lindsay, *History of Merchant Shipping*, iii, 27-8; Sir John H. Clapham, *An Economic History of Modern Britain*, i (1930), 438-41.
39. *Hansard*, cvii, 212-48.   40. *ibid.*, 227-9.   41. *The Times*, 4 Mar. 1850.
42. *ibid.*   43. *ibid.*, 11 Mar. and 9 Apr. 1850.   44. *ibid.*, 18 Apr. 1850.
45. *Commons Journals*, cv, 243.   46. *Hansard*, cxii, 110-13.
47. J. Havelock Wilson, *My Stormy Voyage Through Life* (1925), 76. Also comments of Thomas Gray, the Marine Secretary, in *Nautical Magazine*, xi (1871), 227.
48. *Hansard*, cviii, 108-22, 1066-79, 1372-5, 1423-6, 1445-52; cxiii, 12-14, 80-6, 211-21, 476.
49. 13 & 14 Vict., c. 93.
50. Thomas Henry Farrer (later Lord Farrer), whom Labouchere employed to draft the Bill, was appointed as the new Marine Secretary, thus beginning a long and distinguished career at the Board. In 1865, when he was appointed Permanent Secretary to the Board, Farrer was succeeded by the Assistant Secretary, Thomas Gray. These two men, who between them held the position of Marine Secretary for over forty years, exerted a powerful influence over the development of the Department and of merchant shipping legislation.
51. *The Times*, 30 Jan. 1851. *Parl. Papers*, 1851, liii.
52. *The Times*, 24, 25, 27, and 30 Jan. and 25 Feb. 1851.   53. *Hansard*, cxiv, 1167.
54. *ibid.*, cxvi, 508.

3 British oceanic mail contracts in the age of steam, 1838–1914

FREDA HARCOURT

In the two decades after the Napoleonic wars Britain's naval supremacy was undisputed, but her position in mercantile shipping was far less assured.[1] Development of the new marine steam technology presented an opportunity not only to correct the balance but to take the lead. As soon as the viability of ocean steam navigation had been demonstrated, public pressure demanded government action to encourage capitalists to invest in such high-risk ventures.[2] Communication was as important for government as it was for individuals. The huge empire Britain had acquired by 1815 could be more efficiently administered and more effectively defended with rapid and regular communication by sea; and at a time when world trade and British industrial output were both expanding significantly the new technology could equally benefit trade, industry and financial transactions. In the 1830s government adopted the policy of developing ocean steam navigation by way of mail contracts. Government support was essential because the primitive state of the art of early steam navigation made operating costs high. Subsidies at this juncture therefore enabled British shipyards and shipping companies to establish a lead which was not surpassed for a century.

Sea mail had been carried by naval vessels and by masters of sailing ships. In the 1820s the Post Office began to use specially built steam vessels in home waters. There they competed with enterprising private owners who offered to carry cargo and deck passengers (for which government ships were not suitable) and mail as well. Even on short runs with well developed traffic, competition reduced profits because early steamships were so expensive to work. Private owners resented government vessels. Their operating costs were easily met, and it was alleged that they were a drain on the national purse and less convenient for the public.[3] Extravagance in government departments had become a lively political issue and in 1834 the Post Office yielded to pressure by awarding the first mail contract to a private company, the General Steam Navigation Company, for a service to Rotterdam and Hamburg.[4] In the next year, in response to demand from British and Indian mercantile interests, a government subsidy enabled the East India company to begin a mail service by steam between Bombay and Suez, a move as much political (to counteract French influence) as commercial in intention because it enabled the newly developed overland route across Egypt to speed up communication with India. Naval steamers then carried mail through the Mediterranean to England.[5]

Shortly afterwards the pace quickened. In 1837, following a series of parliamentary reports, control of the mail contracts passed to the Admiralty, though other departments were also involved.[6] Several contracts for domestic routes, and one to the Peninsular Steam Navigation Company for Spain and Portugal soon followed.[7] But it was the three long-distance contracts that were the most momentous for British maritime history. By 1840 contracts were in place for the North Atlantic (Samuel Cunard),[8] the West Indies and South America (Royal Mail Steam Packet Company),[9] the Mediterranean, to connect with India and China (Peninsular & Oriental Steam Navigation Company),[10] and, five years later, the western Pacific (the Pacific Steam Navigation Company).[11] This basic network ensured continuous and regular communication to Britain from the western Pacific across the isthmus of Panama, from China and India across Egypt and the Mediterranean, and frequent services across the Atlantic. In the 1850s contracts provided services to south and west Africa and to Australia as well. Other States followed where Britain led, but this bold initiative to fund new specialist companies, most of them incorporated by royal charter, guaranteed their pre-eminence on, and for many years control of, these major sea lanes.

A review of the mail contract system falls into two phases. In the first period, heavy initial investment was required which would not show a return for a considerable time. A fleet of ships for regular and punctual services, and coal and repair depots in distant ports, had to be established. So great were the risks involved that investment would not have been undertaken by private capital alone. It was inherent in the whole enterprise that monopolies would be created and that large and powerful companies would be the beneficiaries. The second phase was marked by the revolution in technology wrought by the perfection of the compound engine in the 1860s.[12] This made long voyages economically viable without subsidy and inaugurated an era of fierce competition on the high seas, with new British entrants and with foreign companies, some of which were subsidised by their own governments. Though the monopolies characteristic of the early years were ended, the same contractors continued to receive subsidies which enabled them to preserve their dominant position for several years.

I

If ocean-going steam vessels were a novel form of transport in the 1830s, so also were the problems associated with the award of mail contracts. The Admiralty

had little idea of how to cost a commercial undertaking and advertised for tenders to 'ascertain how many persons were inclined to speculate in steam'.[13]
Shipowners naturally aimed to get as much money out of government as they
could; the Admiralty was bent on cutting expenditure. Yet, since there were few
owners in possession of vessels of the required size, horse-power and build or
with the capital available to build them, the Admiralty was to a large extent in the
owners' hands.[14] The Admiralty instinct seems to have been to look to 'good
names' and to decide on 'considerations of commercial and general policy' rather
than strictly nautical grounds.[15] This may account for the award of the North
Atlantic contract, not to the two companies which had already begun to work the
route in anticipation of their tenders being accepted, but to Samuel Cunard, the
Canadian shipowner and contractor, who journeyed to Britain for the purpose
and cleverly used his influential friends to gain the ear of the Admiralty. No
doubt Cunard's first-hand experience of American shipping, matched by his
ambitious plans to challenge it, were to his advantage. So also was the much
lower subsidy he accepted.[16]

The West Indies and Gulf of Mexico contract was assigned by the Treasury
after confidential discussions with a group of prominent City bankers and merchants, many of them connected with the politically powerful West India Committee. Like Cunard, the Royal Mail group did not set up a company or order
vessels to be built until after the contracts were certain.[17] Only for the third, the
Mediterranean route, was there something like competition between aspiring
applicants, because the distance was shorter, and here the Admiralty could make
better estimates of cost. The small company whose 'better class of vessels' had
won the Peninsular contract in 1837 had therefore to make strenuous efforts to
get the Mediterranean route at an acceptable price. The managers formed the
much larger P&O company by merging three smaller ones, a move which gave it
access to larger vessels; and their Peninsular contract enabled them to make
shrewder estimates of cost than other competitors. Yet the Admiralty inclined towards a group of 'names' from the Bank of England and from the largest mercantile houses trading with the East even though they had not actually formed
their proposed company and had no ships afloat. It was only P&O's persistence,
practical experience, informed bargaining, and intention to incorporate the City
group (which was partially achieved) that finally secured it the Mediterranean
contract.[18] The extension to India and China in 1845 was arranged after much
private negotiation between P&O, the East India company, the India Board and
the Admiralty.[19]

Admiralty estimates were based on running costs and wear and tear but took
no account of the first cost of ships, the interest on capital or of depreciation,
omissions quickly pointed out by the commercial operators. The norms for support became 5–6 per cent for each of insurance and depreciation, 10 per cent for
repairs and maintenance, and a 6–8 per cent return on capital, roughly 25 per

cent on capital overall.[20] These sums were translated into a notional cost per mile for each route; this varied from £1 for the Suez–Calcutta line, 10s 6½d on the north Atlantic and 12s 2d to the West Indies, to 5s 3¾d for the west Pacific; these figures were reduced with time.[21]

Surprisingly, the Admiralty made no allowance for earnings from freight or passengers, though shipowners pointed out that profit on any line depended on such receipts. As they were not 'mercantile men' themselves, Admiralty officials professed that they were ignorant of such matters.[22] Thus the subsidies to private companies were specific to the carriage of mail and to Admiralty purposes. All postage revenue on fixed-subsidy contracts went to the Post Office. On almost every route the amount of subsidy far exceeded the income from postage.[23] Contractors' earnings from these other sources were limited only by the nature of the trade on a particular route and by the build of early steamships, in which most of the available space was occupied by machinery and coal. Freight had therefore to be of the low-volume, high-value variety. In this respect P&O was well placed. Large shipments of specie to and from the East at first commanded the rate of 15 per cent, soon reduced to 12·5 per cent, then fell to a more sensible 2 per cent (1 per cent below the rate in naval vessels).[24] Opium from Bombay to China made this unsubsidised line one of P&O's best earners. Freight carried by steam attracted lower insurance and interest charges, so shippers readily switched from sail to P&O. Silk from China and indigo from India, carried on subsidised lines, were also highly valued.[25] The number of passengers wanting to travel by steam seemed inexhaustible — P&O's passengers at first came almost entirely from government and the army, with a sprinkling of merchants; but a brisk tourist trade in the Mediterranean grew up once steamships were available.

On the North Atlantic emigrants formed the major source of earnings for Cunard, but cargo was also carried on that busy trade route.[26] The Royal Mail company, by contrast, was at a relative disadvantage. The West Indies had a declining economy and South American States lacked the infrastructure to support a substantial traffic in goods or passengers. Only after 1860 was this handicap remedied.[27] The Pacific Steam company was a somewhat unusual case. Since 1836, when the possibilities of steam communication with the west coast of South America were first looked into, consular pressure on the local authorities in Chile and Peru gained for the future contractor exclusive privileges in coastal waters for ten years. The Pacific company began operating in 1840 but suffered losses until a subsidy was negotiated in 1845. The amount granted allowed nothing for interest, insurance or the establishment and maintenance of coal depots and workshops. Presumably exclusive rights to the trade were thought to be equivalent to those allowances. Through co-operation with the Royal Mail company a continuous line of communication was established from the Pacific to Britain. Both lines benefited from the discovery of gold in California in 1848.[28]

Subsidies imposed restraints on contractors. Ships were required to work to a fixed timetable between designated ports, with penalties for lateness or failure to provide a vessel; vessels had to be of a specified tonnage and power and had to be approved by the Admiralty; so did their complement of officers and crews; a small number of government passengers had to be carried at reduced cost, and the luggage of official passengers had to be carried free, as well as a quantity of naval and government stores; an Admiralty officer, who had considerable authority on board, had to be carried on each mail ship to take charge of the mails, he and his servant having free passage.[29] All these conditions led shipowners to regard themselves as 'fettered' by restrictions of which unsubsidised vessels were free.[30] But there were many compensations. Mail ships always had priority over other ships in port; their port dues were lower wherever this could be negotiated or required of local authorities; the prestige of being a 'Royal Mail steamer' was highly prized; and of course the subsidy itself placed them in a class of their own. In the first phase the duration of long-distance contracts varied between seven and twelve years. For shorter routes contracts sometimes continued from one year to another. All contractors appreciated the importance of being the first on any line. Their perspicacity stood the test of time: it was rare indeed for a company to lose a contract once in possession.[31] For their part, officials found it easier to deal with companies they knew whose competence had been reasonably demonstrated rather than to start afresh with untried companies.

Shipowners habitually complained that their expenses as mail carriers were far higher than those incurred in ordinary shipping, but they were compensated by the subsidies. All ships owned by a contractor were subsidised, and it was advantageous to link unsubsidised but profitable branch lines to the mail lines. P&O's opium line has already been mentioned. Another was the branch to the Levant and Black Sea ports, which linked with the main line between England and Alexandria at Malta. Regular arrivals and departures at designated ports and at fixed times enabled shippers and passengers to make their arrangements in advance, saving time and money for themselves and ensuring earnings for the steamers.

There was more substance to the assertion that the type and size of vessel built under Admiralty supervision for a contract was, in the early years at least, far more costly than ordinary trade could bear. Indeed, the most compelling argument in favour of continuing to subsidise the original contractors hinged on the investment in ships: the large capital required to start a new major route would be wasted if the ships were to be employed for no longer than the term of a single contract. If the example of P&O is taken as typical of other large contractors in the first phase, the amount of capital invested in ships was very large. Between 1840 and 1867 the first cost of P&O's ships amounted to about £5 million.[32] The combined subsidies received for that period amounted to £7·4 million. Looked at in this light, there would have been an even greater loss of capital to the State than to the company if P&O's contracts had been terminated

Table 1. *P&O mail money as percentage of operating cost and receipts
for each of five years* (£000)

Years	Subsidy	Operating cost	%	Receipts	%
1840–45	379	1,286	29	1,581	23
1845–50	1,089	2,763	39	2,918	37
1850–55	1,126	3,939	28	4,163	27
1855–60	1,574	8,043	19	7,701	20
1860–65	2,079	9,260	22	9,029	23
1865–70	2,382	10,110	23	8,979	26
1870–75	2,831	8,605	32	7,774	36
1875–80	2,655	6,629	40	7,366	36
1880–85	2,322	7,285	31	8,746	26
1885–90	2,097	8,032	26	9,764	21
1890–95	1,768	8,633	20	9,770	18
1895–00	1,754	10,396	16	12,699	13
1900–05	1,625	10,754	15	13,035	12
1905–10	1,571	11,491	13	13,213	11
1910–14	1,184	10,360	11	12,137	9
1840–1914	26,436	117,586	22	128,875	20

Sources. P.P., Mail Contracts; N.M.M., P&O/6/52, Accounts,
P&O/3/31, Receipts and Expenditure.

or, worse, if it had had to be liquidated. Alternatively, taken as a percentage of
gross receipts from freight and passage, subsidies were generous: 37 per cent
in 1845–50, when P&O began operations east of Suez, and it remained at or
above 20 per cent until 1890, only falling into single figures from 1910. Against
operating costs, the proportions were very similar.[33]

Whatever the cost, the success of the contract system in achieving national
aims was generally acknowledged. If the Lord Bishop of Calcutta's belief that
steam communication opened 'the floodgates of measureless blessings to mankind' was somewhat exaggerated,[34] the more sober conclusion of a parliamentary inquiry in 1853 was that the system was fully justified:

> the ocean has been traversed with a precision and regularity hitherto deemed imposs-
> ible, — commerce and civilization have been extended, — the colonies have been
> brought more closely into connection with the Home Government, — and steam ships
> have been constructed of a size and power that, without Government aid, could hardly
> at least for many years, have been produced.[35]

Such praise, however, was tempered by a contrary tide of opinion. With free trade now the dominant political ethos, subsidies for oceanic steam shipping came under increasing scrutiny. Besides being costly, they were seen as a hindrance to the true operation of the market by their fostering of monopoly.

By this time, too, improvements in technology, most notably the substitution of iron for wood and the adoption of screw propulsion, encouraged competition on the medium-range routes and made contests for contracts a real possibility. In the 1840s the old-established Austrian Lloyd company, whose steamers had hitherto been employed mainly in Turkish waters, opened a line from Trieste to Alexandria which encroached on P&O's domain. Seizing on the first hint of competition to force down P&O's Mediterranean subsidy, the Admiralty terminated that contract and called for tenders; only after a long wrangle did the company admit defeat and agree to a lower figure. The outside contender for the contract — a new British company — had neither the ships nor the capital to undertake the contract but the Admiralty had learned to deal roughly with a contractor who was obviously doing well out of government support.[36]

On the Atlantic more substantial competition appeared in 1847 after Congress in the United States adopted the mail contract system. This threat brought immediate reaction from Cunard. In his anxiety 'to stop these new lines, even if I got scarcely anything for it', he persuaded the Admiralty to extend his contract (not yet expired) by twelve years and to raise the subsidy so that he could run weekly steamers to New York and 'prevent these rival lines of packets running against us'.[37] Undeterred, the American Collins line competed successfully with Cunard until 1850, when both companies saw that an agreement on rates and earnings was the more sensible course. This co-operation ended because in a reversal of policy the American government decided to stop subsidies, whereupon Collins collapsed.[38] But in the 1850s a number of new companies appeared on the Atlantic: the Allan line, funded by the Canadian government, the Messageries Impériales, with a French mail contract for Brazil, the unfunded Inman Line and two German companies, North German Lloyd and Hamburg-American, all three supported by the burgeoning emigrant trade from Europe. Cunard hastened to secure his position by negotiating in private for another twelve-year extension and a larger subsidy. These changing circumstances evoked even stronger hostility to the contract system, not least because of its increasing cost.[39]

In the prevailing climate of opinion Cunard's arrangements turned out to have unpleasant political consequences, and a parliamentary inquiry in 1860 revealed other objectionable features as well. Departmental confusion abounded; so little communication took place between the different offices that contradictory decisions were taken (as had happened with Cunard) and none seemed able to exercise overall control. Reform of the whole system was plainly overdue, and a new one was put in its place in 1861. Administration of the contracts was now returned to the Post Office but ultimate sanction rested with the Treasury. Contracts were for the first time brought into the parliamentary arena in that all future contracts had to lie on the table of the House of Commons, together with the Treasury minute, so that they could be challenged before they came into operation. Other recommendations, however, were hedged with ambiguities. There was to be open competition, so often advocated, but it could be modified at the discretion of the executive. Existing contracts were not to be renewed, except when efficiency warranted it, though economy might not. Objections to long contracts were supported by the Post Office, which believed that short ones would make shipowners take advantage of every modern improvement in the interests of speed and reliability; but the committee did not recommend short contracts because they would not have been fair to capitalists who had already made substantial investments in the contract's operation. One recommendation was unequivocal: where there were several lines and much traffic, as on the North Atlantic, subsidies should be done away with. Mail should be carried for the sea postage or according to weight on the poundage system.[40]

Under the new Post Office regime a number of minor changes were made in the contracts themselves. The obligation to carry government passengers remained, but now at full cost. Survey of vessels passed to the Board of Trade; Admiralty officers were no longer obligatory on all routes; masters could take charge of the mails, and mail ships began to carry the humbler Post Office sorters to deal with them. Size and horse-power gave way to average speeds and, later, to a fixed number of days between terminal ports. The old requirement for vessels to be able to carry guns was dropped. Mail ships had rarely used them, and then only against pirates.[41] In calculating the amount of subsidy the Post Office tried to introduce more businesslike methods which took account of cargo and passengers carried, but it frequently happened that factors other than purely postal considerations hampered these efforts.

II

By the 1860s, then, with oceanic steam shipping economically as well as technologically viable, government thinking on State assistance had seemingly changed. As the new era for steam navigation began, it was accompanied by a demand for a more self-evidently political justification for the maintenance of mail subsidies. The breakthrough in technology signified by the perfection of the compound engine was the most dramatic feature in a decade of rapid change. British shipbuilders and engineers had established a lead which enabled the cost of building ships to fall at the same time as operating costs declined. The American civil war finally removed the threat of competition from the USA and was instrumental also in stimulating and speeding up the internationalisation of world trade. New channels of communication became available with the completion of transcontinental railways in the USA and Canada and the opening of the Suez Canal. The effect of all these changes was a flood of new steam shipping, both British and foreign, and a sharp fall in freight rates. Competition was at last a reality. The expansion of world trade provided opportunities for newly industrialised States to break into old lines of shipping and to create new ones. To reduce the effects of competition the larger shipowners, prominent among them the big contractors, sought refuge in Conferences. These could work effectively only if they operated across national boundaries, but the ideology of nationalism which began to dominate the State system demanded greater visibility of national symbols. Shipping, able to display national flags on the high seas and in distant ports, was regarded as a particularly potent representation of national power. The consequence was that the contract system spread all over the world, and in addition other forms of government support were devised as States tried to assert their maritime presence on oceans already dominated by Britain.

The earliest example of this aggressive new maritime nationalism was the huge subsidy given by Napoleon III in 1860 to the Messageries Impériales so that it could challenge P&O's monopoly in the China silk trade.[42] Competition underwritten by a foreign government was a new phenomenon in the East. P&O, in the grip of a serious financial crisis in the mid-1860s which made the renewal of its contracts of the greatest importance, was able to turn the French threat to good account by launching a campaign to counteract Parliament's intention of opening all contracts to competition. This was denounced as 'Free Trade gone mad', while P&O's role as the flagship of Britain's imperial strength in the East was extolled.[43] The outcome was a new contract in 1867 which flouted nearly every recommendation of the 1860 committee. The company's various contracts were consolidated in a single document (thus strengthening its hold on all the Eastern routes), a larger subsidy than before was voted, and the duration of the contract was twelve years, longer than any term previously enjoyed by P&O.

Cunard's renewal at about the same time also showed that a powerful company could thwart government intentions. On the North Atlantic the competition included several other British shipowners as well as the two German companies. In 1866 the Post Office proposed to abandon the old contract system as the 1860 committee had recommended, and to replace it with a service paid for according to the weight of mail carried. Four companies — Cunard, Inman, North German Lloyd and Hamburg-American — were asked to participate. When Cunard refused the whole scheme was upset. The Post Office had no option but to revert to a contract — now euphemistically called a subvention — though at a much lower figure; and when the Inman Line, which had previously offered to carry mail for the sea postage only, colluded with Cunard by putting in an identical offer for the service, the Post Office had to accept that competition on the Atlantic could take place only on Cunard's terms. Once this was understood, Cunard and Inman agreed to take part in the poundage scheme as well. The continuation of the contract meant that Cunard's ships had still to be available for national service if required. In the 1870s the poundage system was extended to include the White Star Line, which now joined Cunard and Inman in a separate category of Atlantic carriers: because their ships were faster, their rates for the weight of mail were substantially higher than those for two new-comers to the mail service — the Guion and Anchor Lines. The German lines were paid according to the lower Postal Union rates.[44]

In 1883 the Post Office again resolved to do away with all contract services on the North Atlantic, and to adopt the American practice of taking up, by the month, the most efficient vessels sailing from Liverpool. The resistance of Cunard and White Star again prevented the Post Office from having its way en-tirely, because the companies insisted on contracts for carriage by weight. Now, however, these were to be for no longer than one year at a time. Inman and North German Lloyd carried on under the previous arrangements.[45] The con-tract system had thus been greatly reduced. But Cunard's loss of the older fixed-payment contracts meant that it ceased to have large injections of government money at regular intervals, and this factor undoubtedly contributed to the com-pany's deteriorating position in the 1890s, when it began to fall badly behind the Hamburg-American company in size and speed of ships, and therefore of com-petitive carrying capacity.

A number of British and foreign companies competed vigorously with Royal Mail, the other major contractor on the Atlantic. In order to retain its position, this company had to accept a considerably lower subsidy for the West Indies ser-vice in the 1870s, and the South American service changed to the poundage system.[46] Royal Mail's financial and management problems reached crisis point at the turn of the century, and its demise was only averted when it came under new management in 1903. By then, however, the company's trade had been eroded by a newcomer to the area, the Elder Dempster company. This Liverpool company, engaged in West African shipping and related enterprises which it shared with the German Woermann company, saw an opportunity to break into the Caribbean by seizing on government's newly awakened interest in the prob-lems of poverty in that area — part of Joseph Chamberlain's aim to develop Bri-tain's imperial estates. In 1900 Elder Dempster started the Imperial Direct Line to Jamaica with a contract for the encouragement of fruit exports. This line, with better and faster ships, was well placed to bid for the West Indies contract when it was put out to tender in 1903. Final approval of the new contract depended on the agreement of the several island governments. Royal Mail waged a deter-mined campaign in Britain and the West Indies to prevent this usurper from taking its place. In the end neither company got the contract. It was allowed to lapse, to the detriment of the smaller islands, which were deprived of a regular mail service. Royal Mail itself underwent a transformation, partly because of its dynamic new management but also because, 'unfettered' by the mail contract, its activities were diversified and the company became the focus of a revitalised shipping empire.[47]

German subsidies for new lines to Africa, Asia and Australia roused cries of unfair competition from the late 1880s onwards. Their function was for the most part more political than economic, and British contractors were happy enough to work with them in various conference agreements. Japanese shipping, however, presented a challenge of quite a different order in the decades before 1914 and represents the most extreme form of government intervention. Coming late to international trade, Japan saw (as Britain had done fifty years earlier) a strong mercantile marine as the key element in a strategy to create and develop an industrial base.

Constrained by the 'unequal treaties' before 1899, Japan was unable to raise barriers to foreign shipping. The government had therefore to adopt various other protective devices to support national shipping and shipbuilding. In many respects this support was based on European models, as, for example, the formation in 1885 of a large new subsidised company, the Nippon Yusen Kaisha (NYK), but there were significant differences, one being that the government and imperial house were its largest shareholders, with an active role in the company's affairs. This Japanese company first made possible the development of local markets in Korea, northern China and Vladivostok. Then, continuing its role as a 'national policy company', NYK began new long-distance lines to India, Australia and Europe. The integration of shipping with related industries enabled Japan to pursue an industrial strategy with singular determination. By 1896 NYK had broken into the Indian cotton trade and the European Homeward Conference, both dominated by P&O, thanks to resolute backing from the Japanese government.[48]

One of the recognised functions of subsidised companies was to bring imperial possessions closer to the metropolis. The British contractors achieved this objective, but their domination of colonial trade bred resentment as local economies began to develop, especially as colonial governments were expected to contribute to the subsidies negotiated in London. The Indian government constantly grumbled about payments it had to make not only for its own postal services but for mails to Ceylon and China as well.[49] When steam services in Indian coastal waters were contracted out in 1862, the small British India company was preferred to P&O; and Alfred Holt's Blue Funnel line had many champions in the East as a stalwart opponent of P&O. Officials in the Indian army and civil service, who formed the bulk of P&O's passengers, constantly railed at it for its high passage rates. This antagonism came to a head in 1902, when the Indian government ordered a boycott of P&O ships which was not lifted until the company agreed to allow a 5 per cent commission on the passage money to the government.[50]

Similarly, the Cape Colony refused to accept the contract concluded in London with the Union Steam company in 1873. Colonial agitation against it brought to light scandalous maladministration in the contract departments and caused the downfall of a Cabinet Minister and a postmaster-general.[51] Instead, a new entrant, the Castle company, was engaged to carry mail for the sea postage, an arrangement which provided the Cape with a cheaper, speedier and more frequent mail service.[52] Australian colonies also followed their own wishes in the 1870s, some adopting the Pacific, others the Suez route with the newly formed Orient Line, set up to compete with P&O.[53] The New Zealand government arranged its own mail services in the 1880s to ensure greater reliability.[54] These initiatives were reactions to economic dependence on the mother country, but, as so often happened, competing companies sooner or later found it expedient to combine. On its formation in 1900 the Australian Commonwealth adopted other forms of colonial assertion. Tariffs were imposed (as had already happened in Canada), and legislation was enacted to prevent coloured labour from being employed in Australian ports. This struck at the employment of low-paid Lascar crews by P&O and Orient.[55] Talk of setting up a government shipping company came to nothing because of the cost involved. In the latter part of the century even the impoverished West Indian islands were required to contribute to their postal service, and this caused great resentment.[56]

Despite these efforts to assert their independence colonial governments looked to Britain for protection not only from the mail contractors but from foreign competition as well. At the Conference of Colonial Premiers, held in London in 1897, the government was asked to insert a clause preventing contractors from levying excessive freight charges and from giving any preference to foreigners.[57] Sir Thomas Sutherland, spokesman for shipowners, opposed these conditions, demanding to know how the mail contract could be 'identified with patriotic trade, and yet leave [a company] the freedom to carry on its business against foreign competition';[58] but restrictive clauses appeared in the next round of major contracts.[59]

Among the most important functions of the mail contracts, and the principal demand made by the State of all subsidised companies, was that their ships should be available to the government in any national emergency. Subsidised companies had therefore to remain carriers of a specialised kind. A contract implied the loss of freedom to engage in other than shipping or shipping-connected activities. It is impossible to determine how much companies lost by this restriction, but it is abundantly clear that they all gained substantially in purely monetary terms whenever they took part in emergencies and wars. The only European war in the nineteenth century which depended on sea transport first demonstrated the great advantage of steam. No fewer than thirty-seven vessels were hired from the principal British contractors to carry French and British troops and supplies to the Crimea.[60] Imperial expansion in the nineteenth century was accompanied by 'little wars' with rich rewards for merchant ships carrying troops, *matériel* and stores to distant theatres. The importance of the overland crossing for rapid troop movements was not immediately grasped by the Cabinet when the Mutiny began in India: P&O's first offer to convey troops was refused. But once in operation, the utility of the shorter route was seized upon. Steam itself was a valuable asset in war.[61] For the Abyssinian Expedition in 1867–68 the Admiralty hired P&O ships to convey coal to the East by steam — unprecedented and costly but quick. It was said that the expedition could not have begun without P&O's assistance and the Admiralty asserted that this service alone justified the contract system.[62] P&O's windfall earnings in this episode helped it to weather a serious financial crisis. The South African War, longer and larger in scale than any other imperial conflict, was worth £1·2 million to P&O between 1899 and 1903,[63] aside from troop movements, which had begun before the war and continued for some time after it. Since Britain was so dependent upon the Indian Army, and the navy's transports were inadequate, hired ships, usually P&O's (though BI also supplied troop transports after 1906), regularly exchanged regiments between Britain and India.[64]

In other ways, too, contractors were expected to contribute to the State's defence. The idea that ships served as 'nurseries to our sailors', if it ever had validity, had certainly lost it after mid-century, when recruitment for shipping fell as more opportunities of employment offered on land. This concern led in 1859 to a scheme to encourage officers of mail ships to join the Royal Naval Reserve — which P&O at least tried hard to enforce.[65] In the late 1880s the agitation about Britain's inadequate naval strength prompted the establishment of the Armed Cruiser Subvention. This involved a select number of fast modern vessels, suitable for conversion to armed cruisers, for which an annual retainer was paid to the companies concerned. Cunard, White Star, P&O and Orient were among the participating companies. For them the payments were 'pure profit'; they need do nothing except consult the Admiralty on how to strengthen the chosen ships, and submit plans for large new liners for approval.[66] The companies also had the obligation to see that a proportion of their officers were RNR men, and a penalty was imposed if they failed to do so. A separate document ruled that only British ships should be employed in any new mail contract.[67] This precaution was directed at foreign ownership on the Atlantic but it did not prevent German carriage of mail by weight.

After 1900 naval experts questioned the need for the armed cruiser scheme, because no British company was building ships to match the size and power that German yards were turning out. Nor was this the only concern. In 1902 an entirely new threat confronted British shipping. This was the seemingly unlimited wealth of the American Morgan combine, which enabled it to buy up several important companies, including White Star. Furthermore, Congress decided once more to subsidise American steamships. Clearly the challenge from across the

Atlantic had to be met by extraordinary measures, because this was perceived as no 'ordinary' competition but 'an attack on a vital industry' by a foreign government.[68] A new protective policy for Cunard was adopted, consisting of a large annual subsidy and a long-term government loan so that two very large ships could be built, under Admiralty supervision, to outpace any foreign liner on the Atlantic.[69] It was this turn of events which made the Armed Cruiser Subvention redundant, and it was abandoned.

III

The fact that Britain's predominance in shipping and shipbuilding by 1914 was still overwhelming despite the efforts of all her competitors showed the importance of her early start in ocean steam navigation, and this in turn owed much to the contract system. The aims of providing regular world-wide mail services, of binding the different parts of the empire more closely to the centre, and of fulfilling 'Admiralty purposes' by providing transports were all achieved.

Constraints on contractors limited them to specialist functions. The work they did and the subsidies they received tended to lead to conservative business policies, and this conservatism enabled them to hold on to their contracts. Officials were perceived as men with 'a love of those they knew, a disbelief in those they did not'[70] — men unlikely to view unconventional business strategies with favour. In a real sense, the longer a contract was held the more comfortable the relationship between government and company. Royal Mail's launch of a whole range of new business initiatives as soon as it had become disengaged from its contract in 1905 indicates the sort of opportunity others might have seized in similar circumstances. Just as instructive, however, is how hard that company fought to keep the contract. The *status quo* was an easier option.

However respectable and responsible a contractor's conduct might be, there were inevitable conflicts of interest between the State and the private company. Contractors themselves were confused about their role: were they private or public enterprises? As private companies their best interest was to seek profitable trades wherever they were to be found; as national businesses they had to accommodate themselves to State interests. The two were not always compatible from the point of view of business strategy (though in monetary terms State service was profitable). P&O, often called upon for State service, regarded itself almost as 'an external Department of the Government'.[71] But this exalted status did not prevent serious distortion of the company's commercial interests, as for instance during the long battle with the Post Office to be allowed to send mails through the Suez Canal. The resistance in Britain to the 'patriotic policy' which advocated no preference in freights for foreign nationals reinforces this point.

There was tension too between government and companies over the cost of the major mail contracts at each renewal, a complicated bargaining process that could take up to two years. The time and effort put into it was a measure of the importance of the subsidies. For companies, renewals were always a 'turning point' in their affairs[72] when, as far as possible, they would try to reconcile their own interests with those of the State, and when business decisions were likely to depend more upon the amount and conditions of the next subsidy than upon the opportunities available. At each renewal a large building programme would be embarked on; indeed, subsidies could be regarded as building bounties, though there is no hint that they were thought of in that way. The reduction in subsidy of the Cunard and Royal Mail companies may well have been the major factor in causing their loss of competitiveness by the 1890s.

Another kind of tension occurred when contracts and their renewal were debated in Parliament. This involved lobbying, appeals to 'public' opinion and much batting of free-trade slogans and well used protectionist sentiments to and fro. Parliament's control of contracts was not always effective, and the Cabinet had sometimes to intervene to resolve disputes when it was politically expedient to do so.

The Post Office's zeal for economy often clashed with wider policy aims, as for instance when Cunard threatened to stop building 'expensive and powerful steamships only suited to the special requirements' of the mail service if its subsidy was stopped in 1866. The Post Office finally succeeded in ending Cunard's subsidy in 1883, a rational move if the mail service alone was taken into account but contrary to the 'Admiralty purposes' of the mail contracts. A much cheaper alternative to the North Atlantic subsidy was found for a time in the Armed Cruiser Subvention. This was patently inadequate. The Admiralty demanded large, fast vessels at least equal to those of any foreign power; the massive rescue operation for Cunard in 1902 showed that economy and national needs were not compatible in the context of international competition and perceived threats to Britain's maritime dominance.

The cost of mail services when bound up with defence objectives raises the question whether contracting with private companies was the most economical way of achieving them. In 1840 contemporaries thought it was, because it shifted some of the cost on to private capitalists. At that time stimulation of trade was also a prime objective, and it was assumed that the contract system would eventually wither away when contractors became self-sufficient through the commercial side of their business. This did not happen. Foreign competition on the Atlantic as early as 1847 was seized upon as a warning that vigilance could not be relaxed. In the 1850s several practical demonstrations of the usefulness and economy of private steamships in war and emergencies underlined the advantage of fleets of suitable and readily available vessels at the State's command.

When competition became general after 1865 and the conference system was devised to regulate trade, companies vied with each other in the services they could offer to shippers and the travelling public. Larger and faster steamers were in any case necessary, because of the economies of scale. In this phase of international shipping the unquantifiable element of prestige became a particularly important factor. National flagship companies could not afford to be inferior to their rivals, nor would governments have wished them to. This was brought out in innumerable parliamentary exchanges and press commentaries.

Mail contracts, though quickly established as essential for the initial launch and organisation of oceanic shipping, attracted adverse criticism throughout the period. Alfred Holt, the Liverpool shipowner, denounced them as a waste of public money and because they enabled contractors to compete unfairly with ordinary British companies. He accused Britain of setting a bad example to foreigners, who were then blamed for using mail contracts to achieve their own national aims. His 'revolutionary' alternative involved building small, fast, cheap vessels which would carry mail and nothing else, a scheme which would have done away with the large and luxurious mail ships of the day that were so costly. Though the Post Office seemed taken by the low outlay of Holt's proposal (not realising that it would be a reversion of the Post Office steam packets of the 1820s), the insignificance of his special vessels when compared with heavily subsidised foreign liners (he had little expectation that foreign governments would follow this example) was a stumbling block, quite apart from the loud protests of P&O, whose subsidy would have been directly affected.[73]

Holt's idea, if adopted, might well have provided the faster, cheaper mail service that the Post Office constantly aspired to. But mail contracts served many purposes. In an era in which sea power was so integral a part of international trade and diplomacy, contracts acted as a multi-functional mechanism for carrying out those purposes. At the start these included the expansion of trade, the capture of the major sea routes and the encouragement of British shipbuilders. All were achieved by the great contracting companies whose business strategies had enabled them to carry out these national polices. Without subsidies none of these would have been achieved so quickly and so completely. Who would have denied that 'the organisation of a complete postal system [was] . . . for the advantage of mankind at large; and if the price has been high, the object has been worthy'? The mail contracts therefore served both as a support and as a spur to the new technology of oceanic steam navigation. In time all the contractors became less innovative and were challenged or overtaken by newcomers, whether British or foreign. The fact that P&O was the last of the big contractors to retain its large subsidy and its pre-eminent position is not mere coincidence. This company's status was safeguarded because its Eastern lines were central to imperial interests, and its prestige an invaluable national asset. As long as P&O could build ships fit to carry the King-Emperor to India it was properly fulfilling its role as 'a business of national importance'.

Notes

1 H. J. Dyos and D. H. Aldcroft, *British Transport: an Economic Survey from the Seventeenth Century to the Twentieth* (Leicester, 1971), pp. 231–9; F. Neal, 'Liverpool Shipping 1815–1835', Liverpool M.A. thesis, 1962, pp. 61, 71, 125–6.
2 H. L. Hoskins, *British Routes to India* (1928), pp. 87 ff.; *Select Committee [S.C.] on Postal Communication with Ireland, Report, Parliamentary Papers [P.P.]*, 1831–32, XVII (716).
3 P. Bagwell. 'The Post Office steam packets, 1821–36, and the development of shipping on the Irish Sea', *Maritime History*, I (1971); H. Robinson, *Carrying British Mails Overseas* (1964), chs. 1–11, pp. 118–23.
4 S. Palmer. '"The most indefatigable activity": the General Steam Navigation Company, 1824–50', *Journal of Transport History*, third series, 3 (1982).
5 *S.C. on Steam Communication between Suez and Bombay, P. P.*, 1850, LIII (693), Correspondence, 1834–37; *S.C. on Contract Packet Service, P.P.*, 1849, XII (571), qq. 1574 ff.
6 *Sixth Report from Commissioners . . . [on] Management of the Post Office Department, P.P.*, 1836, XXVII [51], p. 145.
7 *Contracts entered into between the Government and the Peninsular and Oriental Steam Packet Company, P.P.*, 1847, XXXVI (117), pp. 1–6.
8 . . . *Contract . . . respecting the Conveyance of Mails to . . . America, P.P.*, 1839, XLVI (566); *Packet Service*, 1849, XII (571), qq. 2048–101; F. E. Hyde, *Cunard and the North Atlantic* (1975), pp. 5–8.
9 R. G. Greenhill, 'British Shipping and Latin America, 1840–1930: the Royal Mail Steam Packet Company', Exeter Ph.D. thesis, 1971, ch. 1; *Royal Mail Steam Packets, P.P.*, 1852, XLIX (318), 1850 contract.
10 *Contracts, P&O*, 1847, XXXVI (117), pp. 6–22.
11 *Packet Service*, 1849, XII (571), 2702–57.
12 F. E. Hyde, *Blue Funnel: a History of Alfred Holt and Company of Liverpool, 1865–1914* (1957), pp. 14 ff.
13 *Packet Service*, 1849, XII (571), qq. 936, 962.
14 *Ibid.*, qq. 1521–7.
15 *Steam Communication*, 1850, LIII (693), pp. 95–6.
16 Hyde, *Cunard*, pp. 5–7.
17 *Packet Service*, 1849, XII (571), qq. 2427 ff.
18 *Ibid.*, qq. 1540–9, 1811 ff.
19 *Ibid.*, qq. 1241 ff., 1652–9, 1875 ff.
20 *Ibid.*, qq. 1241–62, 1354–410, 1629; *Steam Communication*, 1850, LIII (693), Paper (B).
21 *Packet Service*, 1849, XII (571), qq. 1390–410, 1639 ff.; *House of Lords [H.L.]*, 1847, 5 (225), *S.C. on Post Office Revenue*, Appendix 8, for a breakdown by the Admiralty of the cost of P&O's proposed Eastern service in 1844; *Steam Communication*, 1850, LIII (693), Paper (C); for example, in 1888: P&O, India and China, 6s 8¾d, Royal Mail, 5s 4½d, *Parliamentary debates*, 3rd ser., CCCXX, c. 1364.

22 *Packet Service*, 1849, XII (571), qq. 1321–3, 1346–52, 1394–425, 1739–61.
23 *Report of the Committee on Contract Packets, P.P.*, 1852–53, XCV (195), pp. 4–5 and Appendix (C). In 1852 subsidies amounted to £822,390 out of a total Civil Service Estimate of £4·2 million. Revenue from postage was £443,782.
24 National Maritime Museum [N.M.M.], P&O/15/1, 8 December 1840; *S.C. on Steam Communication with India, Second Report, H.L.*, 1851, 10–II (187–II), q. 3816.
25 *S.C. on Steam Communication with India, Second Report, P.P.*, 1851, XXI (605), pp. vii–viii, qq. 4153 ff., 5697 ff.; N.M.M., P&O/73/1, Egypt — Passengers and Freight Overland, 1852–7:

Year	Passengers	Cargo (tons)	Cargo (£ million)	Specie (£ million)
1852	2,257	957	1·1	3·4
1857	8,293	3,694	5	26

26 Hyde, *Cunard*, ch. 2. IV.
27 R. G. Greenhill, 'Latin America's export trades and British shipping, 1850–1914', in D. Alexander and R. Ommer (eds), *Volumes not Values: Canadian Sailing Ships and World Trade* (St John's, Newfoundland, 1979).
28 *Packet Service*, 1849, XII (571), qq. 2702–57. A rival bid (q. 2757) might also have affected the outcome of the negotiation.
29 *Contracts, P&O*, 1847, XXXVI (117), 1–22; *Contract . . . America, P.P.*, 1839, XLVI (566); *West India Contract Mail Service, P.P.*, 1851, LI (406).
30 For example, P&O/6/2, *Tenth Annual Report*, 1850, p. 8.
31 Royal Mail was probably the only company to lose its contract before 1914; see below, p. 10.
32 N.M.M., P&O/3/25–33, 5/612, Ships' Cost.
33 N.M.M., P&O/6/52. Annual Accounts. See table. Royal Mail's subsidy, 1840–60, constituted 40 per cent of receipts, and ships' cost, 1840–1900, amounted to £7 million, see Greenhill, 'British shipping', pp. 15, 223; the cumulative subsidy to 1900 was £10 million (my calculation).
34 N.M.M., P&O/30/1, *Abstract of Proceedings of S.C. . . . on Contract for Proprietors*, November 1849, III.
35 *Contract Packets*, 1852–53, XCV (195), *Report*, para. 2.
36 *Packet Service*, 1849, XII (571), qq. 1473–527, 1734–6, 2371–85; N.M.M. P&O/30/1, *Abstract*, III; *H.L., Steam Communication*, 1851, 10–II (187–II), qq. 5323–93, 5775.
37 *Packet Service*, 1849, XII (507), qq. 2066–76.
38 Hyde, *Cunard*, pp. 37–44.
39 *Postmaster General's Reports*, annual. The cost had reached £948,000 by 1859.
40 *S.C. on Packet and Telegraph Contracts, P.P.*, 1860, XIV (328), *First Report*, pp. v–xiii.

41 By P&O against opium pirates on the China Sea in the 1850s.

42 *S.C. on East India Communications*, P.P., 1866, IX (428), Appendix 9, *Convention*; N.M.M., P&O/30/3, *Comparisons and Contrasts*, 24 July 1867.

43 *Parl. Deb.*, 3rd ser., CLXXXIX, cc. 658–704; N.M.M. P&O/6/3, *Corr. Between the Directors . . . and the Postmaster-General*, 15 February 1867, *Memorial . . . on . . . Postal Service . . .*, 27 June 1867, with *Opinions of the Press*.

44 *Contracts . . . and Correspondence*, P.P., 1867–68, XLI (42-42-III); *S.C. on Mail Contracts*, P.P., 1868–69, VI (106).

45 *Post Office, American Mail Service*, P.P., 1878, XLVI (92); *Post Office (Conveyance of Mails to New York)*, P.P., 1884–85, XLV (99); *Post Office Mail Contract (America)*, P.P., 1887, XLIX (165).

46 *West India Mails*, P.P., 1863, XXXI [3217]; Greenhill, 'British shipping', p. 42.

47 R. G. Greenhill, 'The State under pressure: the West India mail contract, 1905', *Business History*, IX (1969); P. N. Davies, *The Trade Makers: Elder Dempster in West Africa, 1852–1972* (1973), pp. 86 ff.; E. Green and M. Moss, *A Business of National Importance: the Royal Mail Shipping Group, 1902–1937* (1982), chs. 1–3.

48 W. D. Wray, *Mitsubishi and the NYK, 1870–1914: Business Strategy in the Japanese Shipping Industry* (Cambridge, Mass., 1984), 92–7, 126–66, 223–45, 285–300.

49 *East India*, 1866, IX (428), *Report*, paras. 20–1, qq. 466 ff.; Public Record Office [P.R.O.], T1/6768A. file No. 20107/3, T1/6401A, 1890 for criticism of P&O in India, 1855–60.

50 N.M.M. P&O/30/85, P&O to Post Office, 17 June 1904; P&O/12/3, Correspondence, 7 May–12 July 1904.

51 F. Harcourt, 'Gladstone, monarchism and the "new" imperialism', *Journal of Imperial and Commonwealth History*, XIV (1985); pp. 36–7.

52 Robinson, *Mails*, 176–83; A. Porter, *Victorian Shipping, Business and Imperial Policy: Donald Currie, the Castle Line and Southern Africa* (1986), ch. 2.

53 J. A. Maber, *From North Star to Southern Cross* (Prescot, 1967), ch. 25; Robinson, *Mails*, pp. 239, 241.

54 *Ibid.*, 212–16.

55 A. T. Yarwood, *Attitudes to Non-European Immigration* (Melbourne, 1964), chs. 2, 7.

56 Greenhill, 'British shipping', pp. 43–6.

57 P.R.O., BT 11/2, c. 4099, 1902, Minute on Re-solution . . . on Mail Subsidies; *Report of the Eastern Mail Service Committee*, P.P., 1904, XXIII (Cd. 2082), para. 19.

58 N.M.M. P&O/30/3, P&O to General Post Office, 3 August, 1906, pp. 2–3.

59 *Cunard Steamship Company Limited*, P.P., 1903, XXXVI (Cd. 1703), Treasury Minute and Agreement; *Post Office (East India, China and Australia Mails)*, P.P., 1907, XLVII (311), Contract, paras. 31–3.

60 *Return of Transport Steam Vessels supplied by Companies Holding Contracts . . .*, P.P., 1854–5, XXXIV (24).

61 N.M.M., P&O/1/104, Minutes, August–October 1857.

62 *S.C. on the Abyssinian War*, P.P., 1868–69, VI (380), qq. 1240–69 and Appendix 7; *S.C. on the Abyssinian Expedition*, P.P., 1870, V (401), qq. 3869–86.

63 N.M.M., P&O/3/31, Receipts, 1875–1914.

64 N.M.M., P&O/4/13–16, Departmental Reports, Trooping.

65 The French invasion scare was responsible for this initiative. N.M.M., P&O/1/105, Minutes, November–December 1859, January–February, 1860.

66 *Correspondence on Subvention of Merchant Steamers for State Purposes*, P.P., 1887, LII (649), and P&O/51/3, Agreement, 14 May 1888.

67 *Post Office Mail Contract (America)*, P.P., 1887, XLIX (165), Treasury Minute, 23 May 1887.

68 *S.C. on Steamship Subsidies*, P.P., 1902, IX (385), *Report*, para. 42.

69 *Cunard Agreement (Money) Act*, P.P., 1904, I [Bill 293]. The loan was for £2·6 million at 2½ per cent for twenty years. *Cunard*, 1903, XXXVI [Cd. 1703], raised the fixed sum for carriage of mails by weight to £68,000 minimum and when the two new ships were in service this was to be £150,000 p.a. See also Hyde, *Cunard*, pp. 137–58.

70 Picton Library, Liverpool, Julian Holt Collection, 920, HOL/2/12, Memorandum by Alfred Holt, 15 December 1897. I am greatly indebted to Mr Julian Holt, who holds the copyright to these papers, and who kindly allowed me to see them.

71 N.M.M., P&O/30/1, P&O to General Post Office, 31 March 1886.

72 N.M.M., P&O/12/2, Confidential Letter Book, 13 September 1895.

73 Picton Library, Holt Collection, 920 HOL 2/13, Correspondence and Notes, July 1896.

4 Distance tamed: steam navigation to Australia and New Zealand from its beginning to the outbreak of the Great War

FRANK BROEZE

Situated almost precisely at the opposite side of the globe, Australia and New Zealand (henceforth collectively referred to as ANZ) were amongst the last of the main trading areas of the modern world economy to be connected to its North Atlantic core by steam shipping. The purpose of this article is to analyse the broad development of steam navigation on that long-distance route (or, perhaps more accurately, that bundle of routes) between the creation of the very first regular services, in 1852, to the coming of the Great War in 1914, when the sailing ship had been pushed back into a small number of the least remunerative intercontinental bulk trades, such as those in wheat and timber. The introduction and diffusion of steam navigation on the oceanic freight and passenger markets of the world, in which the import and export trades of ANZ occupied such a prominent position, was a complex process, in which many more factors than an 'automatic' substitution of sail through a gradual shift in the relative production costs of steam and sail were involved.[1] Of course, technological change and the resulting improvements in the cost, quality and organisation of steam shipping services were of great importance, but an approach wholly or predominantly based on a simple supply and demand model would fail to distinguish between the many and varied segments of the oceanic freight market on the one hand and those of the world's shipping industry on the other; and, moreover, would overlook political and entrepreneurial factors.

It is virtually textbook orthodoxy to state that the diffusion of the steamship led to the binary division in world shipping between tramps and liners which was (with the exception of the rising oil tanker business) largely maintained until the 1950s.[2] Historically, the steamship operated at the upper end of the market, gradually expanding its custom from mail, bullion, passengers, high value freight and perishables to ever cheaper and bulkier goods as well as migrants. Conversely, at any one time and on any one trade route, there were segments of the market which could, and others which could not, be handled by steam, and between the two extremes of sail and steam a grey area of competition often existed. In other words, there was a certain hierarchy of market segments in which transport costs (if one takes the supply side) or freight/passage rates (from the customers' viewpoint) increased with the quality of the service offered. In order to assess the progress made by steam, it is indispensable to differentiate accordingly within the freight market.

It is, however, not sufficient to distinguish between the various trading goods and classes of passengers demanding (or being induced to demand) oceanic transport. Geography in its many manifestations tended to create divisions within what, at first sight, could have been regarded as a uniform and homogeneous freight market. The location of ANZ's major ports, both within the region and in relation to the broader areas of the Indian Ocean, East Asian, and Pacific Ocean trade routes, as well as the size of their respective hinterlands helped to determine whether steam could be utilised at all, and how steam shipping services could be introduced and developed to some but not to others. While the particular site of some ports could be a factor of importance as well (for example, the unsuitability of the unimproved port of Fremantle for steamers), the intense rivalry between ports and colonies probably did more than anything else to determine the layout and quality of ANZ's mail and, in consequence, steam communications with Britain until well into the 1880s.

Moreover, political intervention, mainly through the awarding of mail subsidies and migrant contracts, enabled steam shipping to be established at times and on routes where this otherwise might not have been possible at all, or where the quality of the service offered would have been of a much lower quality. The very political nature of the process of awarding mail contracts and the subsidies which went with them introduced a whole array of external influences into the shipping scene which could seriously interfere with the ordinary market forces at work. Conversely individual entrepreneurs or companies could astutely use government policies for their own purposes. After all, the quest for government subsidies or favours is just another of the many diverse tactics shipping companies could (and did) employ in order to advance network expansion, market penetration, profitability, security, or status. In short, during a considerable time, a synergic relationship existed between government and private enterprise. Hence, in the final analysis, the development of steam navigation between Britain and ANZ was, like any other comparable instance of technological diffusion in transport, the product of the interaction not just of demand and supply, but also of entrepreneurial activity and innovation, as well as technological and political influence.

Mail subsidies and the monopoly of the P&O

The first steamer to reach Australia was the small *Sophia Jane*, which arrived in

1831 at Sydney. Making the voyage largely under sail, this vessel was intended for the New South Wales coastal trade. For some considerable time such delivery voyages were to remain the only direct 'steam link' between Britain and the colonies; they made no impact on the way in which sailing ships monopolised that imperial trade route. Nevertheless, the growth of regular steam services on the Australian coasts made the colonists thoroughly aware of the advantages to be gained from the introduction of steam navigation on the route with their mother country, source of virtually all immigrants and market-place for the bulk of their export produce. When in 1838 the prospectus of an India Steamship Company was publicised through the colonial press, intense interest was expressed in the enterprise.[3] The company aimed at opening a steam service between Britain and Calcutta via the Cape of Good Hope, where a branch line would start for the Australian colonies. The projected company was one of several contenders for the imperial mail contract soon to be awarded on the prime trunk line of the Empire, Britain–India.

The India Steamship Company did not get off the ground, but despite its failure it was important for several reasons. First, it was the first instance for Australians to be affected by the momentous change in British policy concerning the carrying of mail over long sea routes. Since 1837, on routes where private companies were established or were willing to become engaged, the Post Office awarded mail contracts to such companies who, in return for a considerable subsidy, were obliged to carry the mail in regular services, and meet specified conditions (in terms of size and speed of vessel, frequency, etc.).[4] Paid by the Post Office, but administered by a specially created division within the Admiralty, this system of mail subsidies became an instant success when the troubled Peninsular Steam Navigation Company on its route to Portugal and Spain demonstrated that it could decisively improve both the quality of the actual mail service and the financial results of the company.[5] While the Post Office saved money, the subsidies meant that navigation could now be established on long sea routes where otherwise it would not have been commercially viable. The consequence was, almost immediately, a symbiosis of imperial policy and commercial/shipping interest, as government prepared to write out tenders for new mail steamer routes and businessmen could organise shipping companies in the knowledge that on the major routes of the Empire there would be mail subsidies to support private shipping enterprise.[6] From now on it was no longer a question of whether but of when and via what route ANZ was to be linked up by steam.

Secondly, the proposal by the India Steamship Company demonstrated that steam communication between Britain and ANZ did in the first instance not have to be established over the full distance of a direct link, but could be effected through a regional link with a trunk line running to another part of the Empire. Thus, it could be expected that Australia might be reached earlier than otherwise would have been the case. As the contract for the service to India, however, was awarded for the overland route via Egypt, the chances for such an indirect connection waned and the matter dropped out of public interest. Moreover, the contract went to the Peninsular SN Co., enlarged and now styled Peninsular & Oriental Steam Navigation Co. (P&O), for whom the route to India was a natural extension of their Iberian service. Incorporating some of the most prominent Indian commercial interests, it was presently able to use the conclusion of the Opium War (1842) for the opening of a further mail service from India via Singapore to Hong Kong, and to elevate itself into a position of imperial/strategic as well as commercial prominence. Unavoidably enjoying a monopoly on its routes, the company could wield considerable power; steam would not reach Australia before it was ready to perform the service itself.

In 1846, when the deep economic crisis which had followed the 1838–41 Australian boom had subsided, agitation began in London as well as the colonies for the establishment of mail communications by steam. An outward mail service maintained with sailing ships between London and Sydney had existed since 1844, but it was a source of general disappointment and derision.[7] The leading merchants in the trade, steam enthusiasts and naval officers combined forces in public meetings, which became battlegrounds for the protagonists of the different routes to Australia. With Melbourne and the other ANZ port towns still far smaller than Sydney, it was the interests of the latter which gained the day. A crucial factor in its desire for the quickest possible service was the newly established P&O trunk service to China. A plan was adopted for a feeder line through Torres Strait between Sydney and Singapore to connect with the existing P&O network. As the P&O itself felt that despite a subsidy the Australian service would not be profitable and thus showed no interest in the project,[8] a new company was formed.

The origins, organisation, and demise of the India & Australia Royal Mail Packet Company provide a telling insight into the dynamics of early steam shipping.[9] Backed actively by the greater part of the leading merchants involved in the Australian trade, the composition of its Board of Directors reflected how the new company arose directly out of the needs, resources, and interests of that trade. The necessary capital was rapidly raised, a secretary appointed, and a mail contract obtained. All hinged, however, on the willingness of the P&O to co-operate with the newly formed India & Australia. Not surprisingly, the Directors of the P&O showed themselves unwilling to abandon their own chances for future expansion in the area and refused to give any assistance. As no government department was willing to force the issue, the India & Australia had no option but to liquidate itself.[10]

The inability of the leaders of the Australian trade to break through the stonewall of the P&O fell in the twilight of the Navigation Acts. Long shielded against the incursions of *laissez-faire* ideology because of its supposed vital role in maintaining imperial security, Britain's merchant fleet from 1850 had to compete on equal terms with the vessels of all other nations. At the same time, and not entirely dissociated from the urge for fundamental change in shipping policy, the monopolistic practices and other abuses of some mail steam shipping companies had alerted parliamentary opinion to the fact that the system of awarding mail contracts to individual companies, even if this was done after the issuing of tenders, could be both economically and ideologically harmful.[11] The resulting enquiry of the 'Select Committee on Steam Communication with India . . . and Steam Communication between England, India, China, Australia, New Zealand or any of them' (1851) led, despite strong resistance on the part of the P&O to the decision by government that in future mail contracts should be divided, whenever possible, over two contestants.[12] As the next eight years were to show, the resilience of the P&O with its overland route and established Asian network on the one hand, and the very severe technological and commercial problems involved in steam navigation over long ocean routes with little traffic on the other, were to nullify any such political attempt to create effective competition.

In 1852 the British government awarded contracts to two companies for rival steam services to Australia. New Zealand was as yet too insignificant, and too far away from Sydney, to warrant inclusion; it had to await the opening of transpacific steamer routes before it could begin to think of throwing off its trans-Tasman dependence on Australia. One half of the service was to be executed by the P&O through a two-monthly line starting at Singapore, with calls at Albany (Western Australia), Adelaide, Melbourne, and Sydney. The British government had insisted on the southern route so as to include as many colonies as possible, but in consequence both Sydney, at the end of the line, and the P&O were less than satisfied. The company had, in fact, accepted to undertake the Australian service only as an integral part of a comprehensive Asian contract which netted it an annual subsidy of no less than £199,000. Despite boom conditions during the gold rushes the service ran at a loss, and the outbreak of the Crimean War provided a welcome excuse to abandon it, although the highly lucrative China run was maintained. By that time the contractant for the alternative mail route, directly from Britain around the Cape of Good Hope, had already given up its operations.

The Australian Royal Mail Steam Navigation Company, in fact, performed only eight round voyages between May 1852 and June 1854, although its contract, involving an annual subsidy of £26,000, was based on a bi-monthly schedule.[13] Numerous technical and other problems had beset the company when the chance to have all vessels taken up by the Admiralty for the Crimea gave it the opportunity to withdraw. During the war Australia was thus without any mail services by steamer; a mail contract was given to the flamboyant owner of clippers, James Baines (whose vessels were not much slower than the previous service by steam), while a number of non-subsidised steamers made their way down south. Only the exceptional *Great Britain* could establish itself, and for over twenty years was to maintain a solitary track around the world along the routes of the sailing ships, carrying both freight and passengers.[14] All others found that the trade involved distances as yet too long and with too little remunerative freight. Amongst the many projects was also a plan to cross the Pacific Ocean from the isthmus of Panama via New Zealand to Sydney — the first of many such ventures which could provide Sydney with an alternative to being after Melbourne on the Indian Ocean route, as well as locate New Zealand on Britain's network of direct intercontinental steam communications (across Panama direct steam links with both Britain and New York existed).

Also after mail subsidies were awarded again, at the conclusion of the Crimean War (1856), the new contractant was not able to perform the required monthly service. The European & Australian Royal Mail Company was unable to maintain an overland service via Egypt, which, for part of the way, competed directly with the P&O. A hefty subvention of £185,000 per year was insufficient to overcome managerial and technical problems.[15] Virtually by default the Australian mail contract returned to the P&O. Initially from Suez via Mauritius, but from October 1859 through a branch line from Galle (on the southern tip of Sri Lanka) the P&O resumed its sailings to Sydney; this time the calls under way were at Albany (where a locally owned steamer carried the South Australian mail to Adelaide) and Melbourne.

Utilising the strength of its resources, experience and established network of Asian services to the full, the P&O had, during the preceding decade, defeated both government ideology and at least half a dozen rivals. By being the first east of Suez, it had been able to gain a complete monopoly over all Indian, Chinese, and Australian mail services. It was annoyed but not troubled when after several scandals (in which it was not itself involved) the administration of the mail contracts in 1861 was returned from the Admiralty to the Post Office, and the Treasury insisted that tenders be advertised widely. No other company tendered in 1864 for the Australian contract (awarded at £120,000 for a monthly service), and when three years later the Post Office went so far as to invite the French Messageries Impériales to tender for the Indian and Chinese contracts, the P&O was able to stir up 'such an outburst of protective chauvinism in and out of parliament that competition with Britain's premier shipping company was made to look like high treason'.[16]

The monopoly of the P&O, of course, did not mean that steam was now dominant in the Australasian or even Australian trades. Its steamers carried only mail, bullion, first-class and cabin-class passengers, and some very small volumes of high-value freight — in short, the top of the freight market. At the ports of call of the company little competition existed from sailing ships, although some passengers preferred them. But sailing vessels (and a very few, largely incidental, steamers) still carried virtually all imports and exports, second-class and third-class passengers, and all immigrants. Moreover, in those colonial ports not immediately served by the P&O (such as Wellington and Auckland; Hobart, Brisbane, and Fremantle) competition remained between the alternatives of shipping directly from and to Britain by sail or using feeder services in order to hook into the P&O network.

From monopoly to maturity

Four major changes revolutionised the ANZ shipping trade and brought it to maturity during the twenty years or so after the opening of the Suez Canal and the introduction of the compound engine caused a dramatic influx of steam tonnage into the Indian Ocean and Asian seas: namely the founding of new mail lines in opposition to the P&O, the transition from sail to steam in the middle and lower reaches of the freight market, the introduction of foreign steamship companies, and the formation of shipping conferences in order to regulate competition between the participants in the trade.[17] As ANZ had, relatively, much less to gain from the new interoceanic link with Britain and Europe than, for example, India, many developments which were accelerated in the Indian trade as a result of the dramatic shortening of the distance between India and the shipping core of the world were slightly later in coming to Australasia. On the other hand, the opening of the transcontinental railroad across the USA — completed in the same year as the Suez Canal — suddenly made the transpacific route to Australasia a viable alternative to the Suez route.[18] In consequence, for some time it was a dynamic force of considerable significance rather than the 'minor partner' which it later became.

Transit time by P&O steamer between Britain and Australia via Egypt and the Suez Canal was considerably shorter than by sailing ship, but with monopoly had come complacency. Most vocal amongst the complainants were the merchants of those colonial port cities which were left out altogether from its route or of those under some relative disadvantage. Adelaide, Brisbane, and all Tasmanian and New Zealand ports stood offside, while Sydney increasingly resented being at the end of the line thereby receiving its mail days after Melbourne. Agitation in Sydney grew for the establishment of a transpacific service to give New South Wales communication with Britain in equal time as Melbourne enjoyed. Several attempts to link up with Panama had failed even more miserably than the Cape rivals of the P&O had done,[19] but the linking of San Francisco by rail to New York or Southampton promised a much better chance, if only because the great potential of the USA could now be tapped.

A coalition was formed between New South Wales and New Zealand, which country, being connected to the P&O network by no more than a local feeder service across the Tasman, had remained worst off of all ANZ colonies. This coalition became imperative as the result of the terms of the New Australian mail contract of 1873.[20] Finally, a call at Adelaide had been included, but the government of Victoria had been able to insist that the main line terminate at Melbourne, so that now Sydney was reduced to feeder status with a small coastal steamer carrying its mail and passengers. Such dependence could not be tolerated. In June 1875 the governments of New South Wales and New Zealand combined awarded a ten-year contract to the American Pacific Mail Steamship Company for a four-weekly service from Sydney via Auckland to San Francisco. The American company did not sell its services cheaply: the annual subsidy to be paid by the two colonial governments was no less than £100,000, or about £7,600 per individual voyage.[21] With a travelling time to Britain of about forty-one days Sydney's overland route across the American land bridge just matched the speed of the P&O's westward route from Melbourne. Also the ships employed, including the 2,700 ton *Zealandia* and *Australia*, which could carry 170 first-class, 30 second-class, and 100 third-class passengers, were quite comparable. Equality had, at last, been achieved but at what a price! Moreover, the transpacific route would, until the opening of the Panama Canal, never be able to be a significant carrier of trade goods or migrants, and any advantages gained through its adoption could not, in consequence, be more than temporary and partial.

As indicated earlier, the opening of the Suez Canal had had no immediate effect on the Australasian trade, as distances to Australian and New Zealand ports were only marginally cut. But in combination with the diffusion of the far more efficient compound and subsequently also triple-expansion marine engine it was only a matter of time before both the P&O and the sailing ships in their various segments of the ANZ freight market were challenged. There were great opportunities to be grasped as all Australasian colonies continued their rapid economic expansion, but the sheer length of the voyage and commercial obstacles to be faced necessitated a considerable combination of entrepreneurial and financial resources if these opportunities were to be transformed into a commercially viable steam shipping company.

This combination was achieved in 1877 when (after some experimental sailings) the Orient Line came into being as the result of two of London's most prominent shipping brokers in the Australian trade, Anderson Anderson & Co. and F. Green & Co., joining forces with the Pacific Steam Navigation Company.[22] Anderson's and Green's were also owners of sailing ships, but it was their pivotal position and function as brokers, mediating between and intimately knowing both the demand and supply sides of the Australian trade, which gave them the necessary knowledge and connections to risk the introduction of a regular steam service — in addition to and not instead of, it should be stressed, the sailing ship traffic, which they continued to handle.[23] I shall return later to this remarkable aspect of the Australian trade, but what matters here is that the new line from the beginning was not limited to the top end of the market served by the P&O. With their immense experience in the freight and migrant trades (F. Green & Co., moreover, had recently amalgamated with the very first and long-time leading broker in the trade, Devitt & Moore),[24] the two firms aimed their venture across the whole spectrum of the market, excluding only the cheapest bulk goods. Their ships, accordingly, were to be designed on totally different lines from the mail steamers of the P&O although they also included accommodation for first-class passengers. Initially, however, no new steamers had been ordered for the trade; for a step of such strategic significance the risks involved were still too large. Instead, and it is inviting to speculate that otherwise the venture would not have originated as it did as early as 1877, an agreement was entered into with the Pacific SN Co., which in consequence of overspeculative ordering during the boom of the early 1870s was now saddled with a large surplus fleet. Aimed at the Magellan Strait trade to the west coast of Latin America, not incomparable to Australian conditions, these ships and with them the new service immediately proved to be successful.

In early 1878 Anderson's and Green's took up their option to buy the Pacific SN Co.'s steamers and formed the Orient Steam Navigation Company for the purpose; the Pacific SN Co. itself did not wish to remain behind, and a joint service, under the management of the London firms, was set up. From January 1879 its frequency was increased to four-weekly and additional sailings were made whenever the managers were able to acquire surplus custom. At the same time, the crucial decision was taken by Orient SN Co. to invest in a new, custom-built and fully competitive pair of steamers. While Pacific SN Co. for the time being continued to move its west coast steamers into the trade, in 1879 and 1881 its partner launched the standard-setting *Orient* and *Austral*. Having already shown that a profitable steam service could be maintained without a subsidy, the Orient SN Co. with the introduction of these most modern vessels (with its 5,386 tons the *Orient* had a coaling capacity of 3,000 tons as well as accommodation for 120 first-class, 130 second-class and 300 third-class passengers and considerable freight space) was ready to take on the P&O. For the first time this company was faced with competition from a rival using superior technology and aiming at the almost complete range of passenger and cargo trades. In 1879 already the P&O had reacted by doubling the frequency of its service to Melbourne, and two years later it adopted direct sailings from London instead of the branch service from Colombo. It could, however, not prevent the Orient Line from capitalising on the linking of Melbourne and Sydney by rail (1883) and the profound resentment of New South Wales. In 1883 that colony signed a mail contract in which the P&O and Orient Line shared a now weekly service, whereby the mail was carried by train from Melbourne to Sydney.[25]

The success of the Orient Line was a commercial milestone in itself, but at the same time it gave the impetus to a decade of revolutionary change. It challenged the P&O in the luxury market, but simultaneously demonstrated that sail could now be replaced in the mass-migrant and most commodity trades. Coinciding with the rapid rise of the frozen meat and dairy exports from ANZ, which provided attractive back-loading opportunities, it precipitated a new wave of investment in steamers and a transition to steam on all routes incorporating the major ANZ ports. In doing so, it turned Sydney away from the transpacific route, which was incapable of carrying freight in any significant amounts, and provided a new challenge as well as new opportunities to New Zealand.

The first colony to move was Queensland. Disappointed in the effects of an earlier feeder service to Singapore, it concluded in 1881 a mail and emigrant contract with the powerful British India Steam Navigation Company (BI) for a direct London to Brisbane service. Controlling the Indian coastal trade and in receipt of mail subsidies for lines into the Persian Gulf, to East Africa, the Dutch East Indies, and South East Asia, that company could see the Queensland line as a natural extension of its growing network of Indian Ocean services.[26] BI's Queensland service was such a success, in both the existing traffic it served and the potential markets it helped to develop (especially in mass-migration and railway material) that London managers Gellatly's and their successors, Gray Dawes & Co., adopted the practice of chartering additional tonnage for the outward voyage. While sailing ships formerly had had to overcome the imbalance of Australian import and export volumes by seeking return freights to Europe in the Indian and Pacific Oceans, these ships were predominantly dovetailed into the carriage of refrigerated cargo from New Zealand. Thus, successively the Ducal, Shire, and after the coalition of 1904 the Federal–Houlder–Shire Lines entered the Queensland service of BI, as did the New Zealand Shipping Company.

In New Zealand since 1879 there had been experiments in establishing direct steam communication from Britain. The colonial government showed a particular interest in the matter, as only in this way could immigration (which the transpacific route did little to promote) be boosted in the face of increasing steam shipping to its Australian rivals. In 1882 it offered an annual subsidy of £30,000 to encourage the establishment of a regular service, and it was this prize that first induced the two largest brokers and owners of sailing ships in the trade in Britain to amalgamate. The new concern, Shaw Savill & Albion Company (SS&A), then teamed up with the locally owned New Zealand Shipping Company to accept the government contract for a fortnightly steam service.[27] The outward route was to run via the Cape of Good Hope and Hobart, thus also giving Tasmania its first direct steam link with Britain; homeward the voyage went around Cape Horn, catering for the New Zealand export trades, which the Pacific Mail could not carry. The actual introduction of steamers took another few years, but significantly SS&A in the meantime entered into an agreement with the White Star Line, which was reducing its sailing ship trade to Australia but had a surplus of steam tonnage for its North Atlantic operations. With these modern vessels SS&A received a material infusion of the same kind that had some six years earlier been of such importance to the Orient Line. White Star in the process acquired a major shareholding in Shaw Savill which proved to be a source of strength during the second half of the 1880s when the New Zealand economy went into a severe crisis. In 1889 the annual mail subsidy was withdrawn. New Zealand Shipping Co. could not be rescued under local control and in 1890 came into the hands of London interests led by Edwyn S. Dawes, senior partner in Gray Dawes & Co., the London managers of BI, which already was chartering New Zealand Shipping Co. tonnage for its outward Queensland service. With this sale the only colonial participant in the Indian Ocean route to ANZ had disappeared; the limited financial resources of Australasian business and the high costs of colonial labour would make a return in future well-nigh impossible. Only across the Pacific, where the only competition came from high-cost American enterprise, the New Zealand-based Union Steam Ship Company and (since 1893) the Australian-owned Canadian–Australasian Line could maintain a presence.[28] The latter connected at Vancouver with the Canadian Pacific Railway, but despite the popularity of its 'All-red' service the Pacific remained negligible as a migrant and freight route to the Antipodes.

While the main reason for this lack of development was, of course, the very nature of the land-bridge connection across North America with its two transhipment points, the gradual transition from sail to steam on the Suez and Cape routes also helped to reduce its attractiveness. Besides the mail companies now others switched over to steam and thus were able not only to satisfy demand but were also likely to stimulate it through the continuous expansion and improvement of services. The major impetus was given in 1882 by Geo. Thompson Jr & Co. when they introduced the triple-expansion-engined *Aberdeen*. With this vessel they specifically aimed at the lower end of the market, which they had been serving for a long time with their large fleet of sailing ships. Apart from forty-five first-class passengers the *Aberdeen* could carry up to 650 migrants.[29]

The 'annihilation' of the sailing ship, in Professor Graham's words,[30] began with the introduction of the *Aberdeen*. But the transition to steam was by no means immediately achieved. The *Aberdeen*, after all, was only 3,684 tons and Thompson's introduced their next steamers at such a slow rate that it was not until 1894 that their Aberdeen Line was able to offer a monthly service. Moreover, they hardly reduced their large fleet of sailing ships and managed sail and steam not so much as rival but as complementary parts of their business. The same was very much the case with the Shaw Savill & Albion and New Zealand Shipping Companies across the Tasman, and London shipping brokers like Trinder Anderson & Co., Houlder Brothers, J. Gavin Birt & Co., or Allport & Hughes; and after the amalgamation of F. Green & Co. and Devitt & Moore the latter retained control over the sailing ship operations (owning and broking) of the new concern. In 1880, shipbrokers Houlder Bros, who also owned a sizeable fleet of sailers themselves, became the London loading agent for the steamers of Wm Lund & Co. as well as the leading Hamburg firm Robert M. Sloman, but it was not until 1888 that they put their own first freight steamers into service.[31] As all these examples from the Orient Line to Houlder's also show, the transition to steam in the ANZ trades arose largely out of the pivotal functional and organisational role played by the established shipping brokers; the introduction of steamers on their individual berths was in each case determined by a combination of their perception of the possibilities of the market and their ability either to raise finance for the purchase of steamships or to act for owners who themselves were not willing or able to enter the freight acquisition business. But, as will be seen, this dominance of the brokers also caused a remarkable lengthening of the commercial life of the sailing ship and gave a unique character to the conferences in the ANZ trades.

In consequence of the innovating role of the brokers and their follow investors during the mid-1880s, enough steam tonnage was introduced to draw virtually all ANZ immigrants away from sailing ships and to cater for the needs of the rapidly expanding exports of meat and dairy produce. By contrast, the general trade to ANZ as well as the homeward wool trades remained important preserves for the sailing ship. While in 1884–5 53 per cent of all Sydney wool exports were carried by steamer, this figure had only increased to 56 per cent in 1894–5; while the volume carried had risen from some 200,000 to about 700,000 bales.[32] The main reason for this resilience of the sailing ship in the liner shipping sector lay in the nature of the Australian trade and, in particular, in the imbalance between the outward and homeward volumes of trade. Generally speaking, imports (including migrants) far outran exports; by contrast, during the wool season (say from November to March) the balance was usually reversed. In consequence, it made excellent sense to keep the extra cargo capacity of the sailing ships moving in a seasonal rhythm aimed at carrying the surplus of freight on offer during the wool season which the steamers could not handle. In consequence, some shipowners/brokers, like Thompson's/Aberdeen Line, Devitt & Moore/Orient Line, Trinder Anderson & Co. or Houlder Bros, operated mixed fleets in order to cope with the additional demand for freight space during the wool season, but others did not. Outside the wool season the latter shipowners were not able to find direct return employment for their steamers and, in consequence, had to seek business elsewhere. Their situation was, in fact, very similar to that which had faced most British intercontinental shipping to Australasia throughout the whole of its economic development since white settlement.[33]

In some cases, such as that of the Tyser Line or the New Zealand Shipping Company (through contracts with New Zealand freezer works), it was the return employment, already fixed beforehand, which brought the ships outward to Australia in charter to shipbrokers or British India SN Co.'s Queensland service. In other cases, such as Gellatly Hankey & Sewell's Mogul Line, outward voyages to Australia outside the wool season were combined with homeward employment from China.[34] From the viewpoint of this article perhaps most important was a significant integration of the ANZ freight markets; smaller but comparable connections existed between Fremantle, Hobart, and Fiji through the steamer service (begun in 1884) of Trinder Anderson & Co., who continued also to run sailing ships for the wool trade.[35]

Despite the partial survival of sail, but that (outside the pure bulk trades) in relatively close connection with owners and brokers of steamships, the Australasian trade by the late 1880s had come to full maturity. That decade was, indeed, a most propitious period for the investment of massive funds into steam shipping. The spectacular rise of the refrigerated meat and dairy exports (which caused a massive demand for homeward steam services) was easily matched by booming immigration, consumption, and investment, especially in railways and construction. From 1882 to 1889 no less than 303,313 immigrants arrived in Australia from Britain, and to those may be added several tens of thousands who embarked in the Mediterranean or travelled from Germany and France on the new services the Norddeutscher Lloyd and the Messageries Maritimes provided. During the late 1880s growth accelerated even further in Australia (while New Zealand languished) and the P&O, after introducing its four *Golden Jubilee* mail steamers in 1887–8, finally moved to counter the Orient Line on all fronts by the beginning of a freight line around the Cape of Good Hope. In this the company was matched by a second German line, the Hamburg-based Deutsch-Australische Dampfschiffs-Gesellschaft.

Conferences and concentration

It was in these years of rapid change and expansion, too, that the conference system was introduced into the Australian trade. In December 1876, hard on the heels of the formation of the first conferences in the Indian trade, eight leading London shipping brokers, some of whom also possessed fleets of sailing ships, founded the Associated Australian Owners and Brokers (AAOB, more popularly known as 'Davis' after the shopkeeper above whose premises the members met).[36] On the basis of a flexible system, largely but not exclusively determined by the historical performance of the firms over the previous three years in terms of the number of ships they had loaded, the AAOB agreed on a division of market shares amongst its members, fixed commission charges, and raised freight rates in the outward trade. Within a few years the deferred rebate (5 per cent) was introduced to cement the loyalty of customers and soon the brokers had gained the necessary 'power to regulate the rates of freights at their will'; 'both shipowners and shippers [were] completely under their control'.[37] Separate but similar agreements existed in the trades to Tasmania and Western Australia.

Because of the great imbalance in the volumes of Australian imports and exports, however, it was impossible to achieve any such order in the homeward trades to Britain: part of the year there was far too much tonnage and during the wool season there often was an acute shortage which could only be filled by outsiders. With the gradual transition to steam of the participating brokers and owners in 1884 the deferred rebate was also applied to outward steamers. Indicative of the dynamics of the freight market during a period of rapid expansion of shipping space, in 1890 the steam rebate had to be raised to 10 per cent while sail remained at its former level. By now, however, the explosive growth of ANZ's refrigerated exports had created a specialised sector within the homeward trades, which was virtually incontestable by tramps and thus should have lent itself to the formation of agreements between participating companies. It was the direct consequence of such monopolistic control which in 1886 led the Nelson group of meat interests to set up its own shipping line (the Tyser Line),[38] just as Vestey's in 1909 began the Blue Star Line. But as Nelson's success in New Zealand and the continued ability of colonial governments and large exporters in Australia to play off the various members of AAOB against each other demonstrated, with too little suitable tonnage on the market outsiders found entry easy to achieve so that as yet no stable and comprehensive conference could be formed.

In the early 1890s the Australian trade received a severe setback, when a severe cyclical crisis was followed by widespread drought. The conference collapsed for some time. Several of the non-subsidised companies failed or withdrew. The P&O abandoned its migrant/freight service and in 1894 the Orient Line passed its dividend. From 1895 recovery gradually set in, as it had done a few years earlier in New Zealand. In both cases it was marked by pronounced improvements in the quality of steamers and services.[39] The benchmark in New Zealand was set in 1893 with White Star's introduction of the *Gothic* (7,755 tons, 14 knots) with unprecedented comfort for her 104 first-class and 114 third-class passengers. Its *Delphic* of 1897 could already carry some 1,000 migrants in temporary accommodation. After the turn of the century the New Zealand trade really took off, and ships were introduced such as Shaw Savill's 12,345 tons *Athenic* (1902, 100 first-class, 100 second-class and 200 third-class passengers; surpassing the size of the largest vessel on the Australian run), and New Zealand Shipping Co.'s *Ruahine* of 1909, with similar capacity. As White Star (Shaw Savill's major shareholder) concentrated its efforts on the North Atlantic and Australia (which trade it re-entered in 1899), Shaw Savill greatly expanded its own fleet. For it as well as New Zealand Shipping steerage migration became the main outward trade, and between 1910 and 1914 both companies expanded their fleets rapidly, mostly with vessels of a temporary capacity of up to 1,000 migrants. Their outward route still included Hobart, but as the Tasmanian economy remained unable to absorb any significant number of new arrivals, it hardly benefited from this direct connection with Britain.

In Australia shipping began to recover in 1895. Major steps in this trade were the foundation of the Federal Line in 1895 (significantly resulting from the transition to own steam shipping of the three amalgamated sailing ship brokers, Allport & Hughes, John Potter & Co., and J. Gavin Birt & Co., all members of AAOB); Wm Lund & Co.'s establishment of their own Blue Anchor Line (1896); and the introduction by the Norddeutscher Lloyd of the *Oldenburg* and *Feldherren* classes and its use of its intermediate Atlantic steamers during the southern summer season, the first ships of over 10,000 tons to sail to Australia. The P&O and Orient Line undertook fleet renewal programmes after the mail contract of 1897 (which reduced the passage between Tilbury and Melbourne to thirty-one days six hours); Houlder Bros expanded greatly; and in 1899 the White Star Line re-entered the Australian trade with modern steam tonnage featuring the exciting concept of one-class through-deck accommodation. By 1904 the Federal Line had built up 'a fleet of eleven cargo-passenger vessels of the most modern type', totalling some 68,000 tons.[40] In the same year it formed with Houlder Bros and Turnbull Martin & Co. the Federal–Houlder–Shire Line, which consortium provided a monthly around-the-world service between Britain, Australia, and New Zealand. This meant a rationalisation of services through enlargement of scale, which White Star the following year matched through its takeover of the Aberdeen Line.

With the recovery 'Davis' had also regained its former strength. It also associated with a comparable organisation in Germany which included both German steamship companies and the leading sailing ship broker, August Blumenthal of Hamburg.[11] Antwerp was included in their range of ports and in 1895 the deferred rebate for both sail and steam was standardised at the high rate of 10 per cent.[12] Shortly later also a New York–Australia conference was established (as well as minor ones from Singapore and China), so that virtually the whole of the import trade of Australia was under the control of a small number of shipping conferences with largely overlapping membership; in New Zealand the same observation applied. It is important to stress the continued participation of sail in these conference trades (thus, largely outside the range of the bulk trades). In 1906 the total number of cargo steamers sailing from Britain to Australia (excluding Tasmania and New Zealand) was 120, against fifty-four general cargo sailers; from New York the figures were thirty-one steam and twelve sail.[13] Taking into account that also fifty-two mail steamers should be included and that the average capacity of the steamer (say 6,500 tons) was considerably larger than that of the sailing ship (say 3,500 tons), still some 15 per cent of all general cargo was carried by sail. For the participating companies the conference system brought the obvious advantages of order, profitability, and confidence resulting from a strong hold over their customers. With the gradual decline of the imbalance between import and export volumes and, at the same time, the existence of the specialised refrigerated sector of the market, it is understandable that several attempts were made to emancipate the latter from its organisationally diffuse state with scattered secret rebates and competitive contracts to a comprehensive conference.[44] The P&O Chairman, Sir Thomas Sutherland, a great believer in law and order, was a prime mover behind such schemes; it was, however, not until 1913 that he was successful in creating the Australasian Refrigerated Tonnage Committee.[45]

In several instances the conference system as it was applied in ANZ was subjected to scrutiny by public authority.[46] Although Sutherland claimed that the most wide-ranging of these, the Royal Commission on Shipping Rings (1906–9), would not have been heard of but for some problems in the South African trade,[47] it is obvious that opinion in ANZ ran strongly against it. In both countries in 1906 consideration was given to the establishment of government-owned shipping lines to break the hold of the foreign lines and establish services to Britain at more advantageous conditions.[48] Yet, at the same time as many shippers complained about the level of the freight rates, there was also recognition that the conferences, whose position in the trade was founded on their application of the onerous deferred rebate mentioned earlier, had brought major benefits to the trade. Amongst the most important of these were reckoned to be the equal treatment of all shippers, small and large; the equalisation of freight rates throughout the year instead of the sharp fluctuations which had resulted from the seasonal availability of wool freight; the regularity of sailings, whether the ships were full or not; the confidence with which shippers could plan ahead and the considerable improvements in the quality of shipping services as companies could equally confidently plan ahead and re-invest funds into steamers of a size and quality ahead of actual demand.[49] Especially since the establishment, in 1902, of the Australasian Merchants' Association, through which the combined shippers could provide some counterweight against the joint power of the shipping companies at least at the British end of the line a more positive attitude existed towards the conference. Here the material advantages 'Davis' and its associates brought were deemed more important than the sense of powerlessness resulting from the unflinching application of the deferred rebate, which so incensed Antipodean opinion.[50] It is also clear that the conferences served foreign exporters to Australia at such rates of freight that the oceanic distance was no tariff barrier but, instead, necessitated the imposition of highly protective measures to assist colonial manufacturing.

Expansion of capacity and modernisation of the fleet indeed never stopped. Alfred Holt & Co.'s Ocean Steam Ship Co., which had previously only been involved in the Singapore–Fremantle run, in 1910 also entered the eastern

Australian trade, and by 1914 the total tonnage employed by the major companies was well over twice the amount of ten years earlier. P&O and Orient Lines had to follow the German lead and introduce vessels of over 10,000 tons; for the latter company this had been achieved under extremely difficult circumstances after its partner, Pacific SN Co., had been absorbed by the Royal Mail group, which subsequently attempted to capture a share of the Australian mail contract and with it the upper end of the market.[51] The largest ship in the trade, White Star's *Ceramic*, measured no less than 18,481 tons. In the migrant trade several new operators gained entry through contracts with the Victorian government (besides Tyser, the Indra, and Milburn Lines; with the Star Line they in 1914 formed the Commonwealth & Dominion Line). ANZ was served by better ships (even if they were significantly slower than those on the North Atlantic though faster than those of the Royal Mail to the River Plate) and services than ever before, and that in a period in which migration (boosted by assistance schemes of both New Zealand and all six Australian states) leapt ahead in tandem with the rapid economic growth of both dominions.

With the overall growth of steam shipping, however, came also a marked concentration of control and ownership, which considerably strengthened the hold of the new, much bigger, groups over the trade. Very much in line with developments in other sectors of the world's shipping industry and, indeed, the world economy as a whole,[52] from about 1900 a process of growth, rationalisation, and concentration through co-operation and merger, corporate power-play and unashamed empire building gained momentum, which was in fact not to culminate until after the Great War, but of which the foundations had been firmly laid before it broke out in 1914. The P&O, after absorbing the initial challenge of the Orient Line, under Sutherland's leadership acted as the 'leader of the pack'; it had a special understanding with the foreign mail companies and probably 'protected' the Orient Line in its battle with the Royal Mail; moreover, by taking over Lund's Blue Anchor Line (1910) and subsequently introducing the successful B-class of migrant and freight steamers, it became a formidable all-round company. In one of the greatest shipping events of the time it merged in 1914 with British India SN Co.[53] Perhaps better understood as the takeover of P&O by BI's Chairman, the powerful Lord Inchcape, this merger has often been depicted as the coming together of the 'trunk line P&O' with the 'feeder BI', but this is a very misleading simplification, especially in the ANZ trades. Although BI possessed a considerable power base in the Australian coastal trade, it still ran its direct London–Queensland line (although this had lost some importance since the P&O and Orient mail steamers terminated their service at Brisbane) and from the early 1890s had been closely associated with the New Zealand Shipping Co. and Turnbull Martin's Shire Line (which since 1904 operated within the Federal–Houlder–Shire consortium). A further rationalisation in 1912 had resulted in NZS Co. taking over both the Federal Line and the Australian interests of Houlder.

Thus, in 1914 Inchcape had established a trading hegemony, which during the next five years he rounded off by the outright purchases by the P&O of NZS Co. (1916); the Union Steam Ship Co. (with the Canadian–Australasian Line, 1917); and one half of Anderson Anderson & Co., managers and owners of the Orient Line (1919). Besides this giant group (totalling some 2 million tons)[54] stood the ANZ 'wing' of the International Mercantile Marine Company, the 'Morgan Trust', which included the White Star Line, Shaw Savill & Albion and through them also since 1905 the Aberdeen Line.[55] Leaving out of consideration the much smaller migrant lines (four of which in 1914 joined in the Commonwealth & Dominion Line, which two years later was in turn absorbed by the revitalised Cunard Line, White Star's traditional rival on the North Atlantic), there were only Holt's Ocean Steam (Blue Funnel), the Messageries Maritimes, and the two German lines to complete a formidable combination of power. The ANZ trade was well served by a technologically efficient and responsive ocean transport system. In comparison to the largest Atlantic passenger liners, the Australasian steamers were perhaps no more than second-class, but without a further deepening of the Suez Canal and virtually all ports in Australia and New Zealand, no great improvements in size or speed could be made. The Dominions Royal Commission in 1914 praised its general standards, except for the low speed stipulated for its mail steamers: just over 15 knots while 18 knots was the absolute minimum desirable.[56] But the exposure of the dominions to the power of a very small number of large to very large shipping concerns could not but raise grave questions as to the price these were able to exact as a result of their monopolistic position.

Many factors on both supply and demand sides acted together in the origins and full development of steam navigation in the Britain–ANZ trade: some were structural, such as technological innovation and diffusion; entrepreneurial drive, competition, and risk taking; corporate reorganisation and combination; the growth of passenger traffic and ANZ's imports and exports, especially those requiring refrigerated transport; and the political intervention of both imperial and colonial governments through mail subsidies. Others, such as the shift of surplus steamers from other trade routes (Pacific SN Co., White Star), were largely incidental. Central in this process of steamship diffusion, however, stood the shipbrokers. As their functions were often taken over by the steamship companies they founded, they have often been overlooked; the conclusion of this article can only be that a full reassessment of their historical role is long overdue. Similarly, despite some hesitant beginnings,[57] as yet no systematic and comprehensive attempt has been made to integrate the development of the ocean transport network of Australia and New Zealand into the general economic history of the countries; it is hoped that the cursory overview offered in this article may stimulate such endeavours.

Notes

1 Such a pure substitution model is offered in C. K. Harley, 'The shift from sailing ships to steamships, 1850–1890: a study in technological change and diffusion', in D. N. McCloskey (ed.), *Essays on a Mature Economy: Britain after 1840* (1971).

2 See, for example, S. G. Sturmey, *British Shipping and World Competition* (1962), ch. 10; A. D. Couper, *The Geography of Sea Transport* (1972), ch. 6; or C. E. Fayle, *A Short History of the World's Shipping Industry* (1935), ch. 10.

3 *Sydney Herald*, 19 November 1838.

4 P. Bagwell, 'The Post Office Packets, 1821–36, and the development of shipping on the Irish Sea', *Maritime History*, I (1971), pp. 4–28; H. Robinson, *Carrying British Mails Overseas* (1964), ch. 12.

5 Three 'house histories' of the P&O have appeared to date: B. Cable, *A Hundred Year History of the P&O* (1937); D. Divine, *Those Splendid Ships* (1960); and D. and S. Howarth, *The P&O Story* (1987). A briefer but informative overview is given in J. M. Maber, *North Star to Southern Cross* (Prescot, 1967), ch. 1. Maber's book, subtitled *The story of the Australasian seaways*, contains 'potted' histories of all steam shipping companies which at one time or another carried passengers to Australia and/or New Zealand and, despite being aimed at the general reader market, is an important source. Two more critical studies deal with the P&O during its early years: D. Thorner, *Investment in Empire. British Railways and Steamshipping Enterprise in India, 1825–1849* (Philadelphia, 1950), ch. 5; and F. Harcourt, 'The P&O Company: flagships of imperialism', in S. Palmer and G. Williams (eds), *Charted and Uncharted Waters* (1982), pp. 6–28.

6 R. H. Thornton, *British Shipping*, 2nd ed. (Cambridge, 1959); Robinson, *Carrying British Mails*; P. N. Davies. 'The development of the liner trades', in K. Matthews and G. Panting (eds), *Ships and Shipbuilding in the North Atlantic Region* (St John's, Newfoundland, 1978), pp. 175–99; and F. Broeze, 'The international diffusion of steam navigation: the myth of the retardation of Netherlands steam navigation to the East Indies', *Economisch- en Sociaal-Historisch Jaarboek*, XLV (1982), pp. 77–95.

7 Robinson, *Carrying British Mails*, pp. 187–9; J. Bach, *A Maritime History of Australia* (West Melbourne, 1976), p. 108.

8 National Maritime Museum (Greenwich), P&O Archives, Minute Book, Court of Directors, II, 450–5, report by committee . . . on the subject of steam navigation with Australia, 7 July 1848.

9 The short-lived career of the India & Australia can be traced in Public Record Office (Kew), Board of Trade 1/464/668 and 41/319/1831, and Colonial Office 201/420, fos. 423–49; also General Post Office (London), 29/51.

10 Maber, *North Star to Southern Cross*, erroneously

ascribes the demise of the company to bankruptcy (p. xii).

11 See, for example, the *Reports of the Select Committees* (House of Commons) *on the Halifax and Boston Mails* (1846), and *on the Contract Packet Service* (1849).

12 *First Report, Select Committee on Steam Communication with India* . . ., Chairman, Lord Jocelyn (1851).

13 Maber, *North Star to Southern Cross*, ch. 2.

14 *Ibid.*, ch. 3; G. Blainey, *The Tyranny of Distance* (Melbourne, 1966), pp. 208–9 overlooks the introduction of the mail contract liner services and singles out the *Great Britain* as the only one of the early steamers to be successful.

15 Maber, *North Star to Southern Cross*, ch. 11.

16 Harcourt, 'The P&O Company', p. 12.

17 For studies discussing the growth of steam shipping east of Suez see F. E. Hyde, *Blue Funnel 1865–1914* (Liverpool, 1957), *Shipping Enterprise and Management. Harrisons of Liverpool 1830–1939* (Liverpool, 1967), and *Far Eastern Trade 1860–1914* (1970); M. Fletcher, 'The Suez Canal and world shipping, 1869–1914', *Journal of Economic History*, XVIII (1958), pp. 556–79; D. A. Farnie, *East and West of Suez* (Oxford, 1969), ch. 4; and Broeze, 'International diffusion of steam navigation', pp. 87–92.

18 It is worth stressing that in the vision of its main political promoter, the American Secretary of State William Henry Seward, the transcontinental railroad was as much a device to link the USA from coast to coast as the first stage of the total steam link between New York and America's industrial centre in the north-eastern states and her commercial markets across the Pacific, and even the middle section of the shortest route from England to China, India, and Australia. Seward's broad views on 'American commercial Empire' were based on what he perceived to be the main constituents and dynamics of Britain's economic development and policies, which specifically included the granting of mail subsidies for steamer services between the east coast and Brazil and Argentina, and from San Francisco to East Asia. The ten-year contract for the latter route was awarded to the Pacific Mail Steamship Company in 1865. See E. N. Paolino, *The Foundations of the American Empire. William Henry Seward and U.S. Foreign Policy* (Ithaca, 1973), chs 2, 5, and 6, esp. p. 36; and J. C. B. Hutchins, *The American Maritime Industries and Public Policy 1789–1914* (Cambridge Mass, 1941), pp. 529–31.

19 Maber, *North Star to Southern Cross*, chs 9 and 16.

20 K. Sinclair, 'Australasian inter-government negotiations 1865–80: ocean mails and tariffs', *Australian Journal of Politics and History*, VI (1970), pp. 151–76; Maber, *North Star to Southern Cross*, p. 71.

21 Maber, *North Star to Southern Cross*, p. 71. Pacific Mail had just lost its lucrative San Francisco to China

contract with the American government, and in consequence was more than eager to enter the Australian trade.

22 C. E. Morris, *Origins, Orient and Oriana* (Brighton, 1980), chs 2 and 7, *passim*; Maber, *North Star to Southern Cross*, ch. 25.

23 On the centrality of the brokers in the Australian trade see the testimony of P&O's Chairman, Sir Thomas Sutherland, in *Royal Commission on Shipping Rings* (1909), IV, q. 20666. No systematic history of the sailing ship sector of the Australasian trades has as yet been made, but one should see R. V. Jackson, 'The decline of the wool clippers', *The Great Circle*, II (1980), pp. 87–98. Much anecdotal information is contained in B. Lubbock, *The Colonial Clippers* (Glasgow, latest reprint 1975).

24 National Maritime Museum (Greenwich), Devitt & Moore Papers, item 56, 'Devitt and Moore from 1836 onwards'; Maber, *North Star to Southern Cross*, ch. 17; A. G. Course, *Painted Ports: The Story of Messrs Devitt & Moore* (1961); and C. Jones, *Sea Trading and Sea Training* (1936). Sir Thomas Lane Devitt for many years was chairman of the Orient Line.

25 Sinclair, 'Australasian inter-governmental negotiations'; Maber, *North Star to Southern Cross*, pp. 102–3. The Orient Line with the new mail contract switched its ships on the outward run from the Cape to the Suez route, on which, as a result of the opposition of the P&O at Aden, it for some time had to establish a coaling station at Diego Garcia.

26 G. Blake, *B.I. Centenary 1856–1956*, ch. 6; Blainey, *Tyranny of Distance*, pp. 219–20; and Bach, *Maritime History*, pp. 146 and 195. Through the specific geographic configuration of Queensland BI well-nigh inevitably became deeply involved in the coastal trade of the colony and, in consequence, set out to become a dominant participant. The main controversies over this extension of the power of BI are discussed in S. Jones, *Two Centuries of Overseas Trading: the Origins and Growth of the Inchcape Group* (1986), ch. 5, 'Maritime enterprise in Australia . . . 1887–1939'. See also N. L. McKellar's massive *From Derby round to Burketown: The A.U.S.N. Story* (St Lucia, 1977), chs 4–6.

27 S. D. Waters, *Shaw Savill Line: One Hundred Years of Trading* (Christchurch, 1961), chs 5–6, *From Clipper Ship to Motor Liner: The Story of the N. Z. S. Co., 1873–1939* (Wellington, 1939); Maber, *North Star to Southern Cross*, chs 26–7; and W. J. Oldham, *The Ismay Line, The White Star Line, and the Ismay Family Story* (Liverpool, 1961), pp. 71–2.

28 S. D. Waters, *History of the Union S.S.Co. of New Zealand, 1875–1940* (Wellington, 1940); Maber, *North Star to Southern Cross*, chs 39–40 and 46.

29 Maber, *North Star to Southern Cross*, ch. 33; K. T. Rowland, *Steam at Sea: A History of Steam Navigation* (Newton Abbot, 1970), pp. 152–3; and Blainey, *Tyranny of Distance*, pp. 266–7. Somewhat surprisingly, the *Aberdeen* does not figure in J. Guthrie, *A History of Marine Engineering* (1971). A comparison of the vital statistics of the *Aberdeen* with those of the *Orient* most clearly shows the contrasting marketing policies of the Aberdeen and Orient Lines.

30 G. S. Graham, 'The ascendancy of the sailing ship 1850–85', *Economic History Review*, 2nd series, IX (1956–7), p. 87.

31 E. F. Stevens, *One Hundred Years of Houlders* (1950), chs 4–6; E. Hieke, *Rob. M. Sloman Jr.* (Hamburg, 1968), pp. 145–60.

32 Jackson, 'The decline of the wool clippers', p. 88.

33 F. Broeze, 'British intercontinental shipping and Australia, 1813–1850', *Journal of Transport History*, new series, IV (1978), pp. 189–207.

34 G. Blake, *Gellatly's 1862–1962* (1962), ch. 6; and S. Marriner and F. E. Hyde, *The Senior: John Samuel Swire 1825–98. Management in Far Eastern Shipping Trades* (Liverpool, 1967), pp. 146–50. It was the reactions of the China Conference against the seasonal incursions of the Mogul Line which brought the latter to test the legality of conference agreements; in final instance, the House of Lords in 1891 dismissed its case.

35 Bach, *Maritime History*, pp. 164–74, contains a most informative and perceptive account of the operations of Trinder Anderson & Co. to Western Australia. With their sailing ships until after the turn of the century they provided direct sailings to London from several loading places, often no more than tidal flats, in the north-west of the colony/state.

36 Quite some attention has been devoted to 'Davis' in the literature: B. M. Deakin (with T. Seward), *Shipping Conferences: A Study of their Origins, Development and Economic Practices* (Cambridge, 1973), ch. 2, pt. 4; Bach, *Maritime History*, ch. 8; and K. A. Moore, *The Early History of Freight Conferences* (1981). Apart from a limited amount of material emanating from company archives (such as that used by Bach), by far the major source of all information is the *Royal Commission on Shipping Rings, I–IV, Reports, Evidence and Appendices* (1909). Many witnesses gave valuable testimony, but none more so for our subject than Sir Thomas Sutherland, Chairman of the P&O (IV, qq. 20489–669), Sir Edward Montague Nelson, Australasian frozen meat magnate and director of the Tyser Line (IV, qq. 13535–733), H. A. Sanderson, General Manager of the White Star Line (IV, qq. 18342–773), and Edward Behenna Tredwen, senior partner in the prominent merchant house of Gilbert J. McCaul & Co. and Chairman of the Australasian Merchants' Association (III, qq. 2620–3092 and IV, qq. 14527–765). In the Tasmanian trade in 1886 F. Green & Co., Staley Radford & Co., Shaw Savill & Albion and the New Zealand Shipping Co. as loading brokers equally divided the departures to Hobart amongst themselves in order to maintain a two-weekly service, J. F. Archer, *A History of Staley, Redford & Co. Ltd. 1875–1975* (Chichester, 1975), p. 108.

37 Saul Samuel to H. Parkes (Premier of New South Wales), 2 December 1881, quoted in Bach, *Maritime History*, p. 162.

38 *Royal Commission on Shipping Rings*, IV, q. 13605* (Nelson).

39 See the various company histories referred to earlier as well as Maber, *North Star to Southern Cross*. For the Australian service of the Norddeutscher Lloyd see O. Seiler, *Hapag-Lloyd: 100 years of Liner Shipping Far East/Australia* (Hamburg, 1985). The operations of the second German company in the trade, DADG, were critically analysed by its former managing director, O. Harms, in *Deutsch-Australische Dampfschiffs-Gesellschaft, Hamburg* (Hamburg, 1933).

40 Maber, *North Star to Southern Cross*, p. 255.

41 Bach, *Maritime History*, p. 175; Harms, *DADG* ch. 8 ('Vereinbarungen'); and Hieke, *Sloman*, pp. 159–60.

42 *Royal Commission on Shipping Rings*, III, q. 2722 (Tredwen).

43 *Ibid.*, q. 2622, no. 16 (Tredwen). In the same year departures from Hamburg to Australia included forty-eight steamers (137,068 nrt) and, still, as many as nineteen sailers, measuring 34,432 nrt (Harms, *DADG*, app. 1).

44 Bach, *Maritime History*, pp. 177–83, contains an insightful account of the struggle for control over the Victorian refrigerated trade in 1894. Much evidence on the working of the refrigerated market was given to the Royal Commission on Shipping Rings by Nelson (see note 36).

45 Bach, *Maritime History*, p. 184.

46 *Royal Commission on Shipping Rings*, I, Report no. 12.

47 *Ibid.*, IV, q. 20495.

48 Commonwealth of Australia, *Report from the Royal Commission on Ocean Shipping Service* (Melbourne, 1906), 1–37. Australia, in particular, was a strong force behind the setting up in 1918 of the Imperial Shipping Committee; significantly, its representative was H. B. G. Larkin, the manager of the government-owned Commonwealth Shipping Line (who, interestingly, had made his career with BI before he moved to state enterprise).

49 Besides the admirably clear and well developed evidence of Tredwen (see note 36) one should also see that of Frederick William Grimwade (III, qq. 124–1435) and J. McLaren (IV, qq. 13960–14526), the latter a largely hostile witness.

50 Perhaps best expressed by H. W. Berry, merchant and shipping agent of Melbourne: '. . . where they should be our servants, they are our masters'. (Commonwealth of Australia, *Royal Commission on Ocean Shipping Service*, q. 6084).

51 Morris, *Origins, Orient & Oriana*, pp. 69–71; E. Green and M. Moss, *A Business of National Importance: The Royal Mail Shipping Group 1902–1937* (1982), pp. 24 and 30 does not mention this rare failure of Royal Mail at that time to reach its corporate objective.

52 Sturmey, *British Shipping*, ch. 14; D. H. Aldcroft, 'The depression in British shipping, 1901–11', in *Studies in British Transport History* (Newton Abbot, 1974, orig. publ. 1965), pp. 112–13. The exact dynamics of this process of concentration remain to be researched. See also Hutchins, *American Maritime Industries*, ch. 15; and V. Vale, *The American Peril: Challenge to Britain on the North Atlantic 1901–04* (1984), ch. 1.

53 Cable, *One Hundred Years P&O*, pp. 202–7; H. Bolitho, *James Lyle Mackay, First Earl of Inchcape* (1936), pp. 119–20; Blake, *B.I. Centenary*, pp. 172–4; and Jones, *Inchcape Group*, p. 56.

54 Bolitho, *Inchcape*, p.119.

55 In this case it seems clear that amalgamation was the result of depression, as the Aberdeen Line lost its independence after it had left the Australian Conference in the aftermath of the post-Boer War collapse of the freight market (Commonwealth of Australia, *Royal Commission on Ocean Shipping Service*, q. 217).

56 *Royal Commission on the Natural Resources, Trade and Legislation of Certain Portions of His Majesty's Dominions, Second Interim Report* (1914), pp. 25–7 and 60–1. Very detailed evidence on the financial aspects of the size and speed of ships on the Australian run was given by Professor Sir J. H. Biles, *Ibid., Minutes of Evidence taken in London in January 1914* (1914), pp. 14–25.

57 Blainey, *Tyranny of Distance*; and R. V. Jackson, *Australian Economic Development in the Nineteenth Century* (Canberra, 1977) contain the beginnings of such an analysis; significantly, despite some specific passages in the text, the index of G. R. Hawke, *The Making of New Zealand. An Economic History* (Cambridge, 1985) has no entry for 'shipping'.

5 McGregor Gow and the Glen Line: the rise and fall of a British shipping firm in the Far East trade, 1870–1911

MALCOLM COOPER

I

The success of the British shipping industry until the outbreak of the First World War depended to a considerable extent upon a group of liner companies formed in the middle decades of the nineteenth century. While some of the early formations, such as P&O and Royal Mail, were built around generous state subsidisation, the majority began as small, family-based organisations carrying a limited range of cargo on a single route. The slow improvement in the profitability of the steamship broadened the base of the industry, bringing a new generation of tramp owners into the bulk-carrying trades, but the established liner companies remained the leaders of the British mercantile marine. When other nations began to contest the sea lanes towards the end of the century, it was these companies which first bore the weight of competition.

The historiography of the British shipping industry has tended to portray the initial response to the foreign challenge as successful. Until 1914 at least, British firms were seen as having held off their rivals reasonably well. Even Aldcroft, that stern critic of the Victorian entrepreneur, was unable to find serious fault with the performance of shipowners, and other historians have tended to follow his lead.[1] Detailed studies of such successful firms as Alfred Holt's Blue Funnel Line and Harrison's Charente Steamship Company have reinforced this general impression, painting a picture of dynamic adaptation to the changing requirements of the trade.[2] It was only in the aftermath of the First World War that Britain's domination of the sea lanes was thought to have been seriously undermined.

There was, however, another side to the development of the shipping industry. As Craig once remarked, entrepreneurial success stories are often the exception rather than the rule.[3] A surprisingly large number of pioneer steam shipping companies did not survive as independent entities until the First World War. Faced with increasing competition, rising costs and prolonged trade depression, British shipping entrepreneurs frequently found themselves unable to continue profitable operation. By 1914, names like Anchor, Dominion and White Star in the North Atlantic; and Shire, Glen and China Mutual in the Far East were only maintained under the aegis of other firms. The British liner trade as a whole was in the midst of a massive structural transformation which would leave most of its vessels under the ownership of a handful of groups — P&O, Ellerman, Furness Withy, Cunard and Royal Mail.[4]

It is too easy to see this process of agglomeration as a dynamic response to competition. As Wray, has already argued with reference to the 1914 merger of P&O and British India, it was actually reflective of stagnation and of a defensive mentality produced by foreign success.[5] Many of the pioneers of British liner shipping only accepted merger or buy-out as an alternative to extinction. In the case of at least one of the resulting combines, Lord Kylsant's Royal Mail, the final product was little more than the collective manifestation of individual weakness.

Within this context, the present study will examine the history of one of the more distinguished casualties of the pre-war period, McGregor Gow & Co., commonly known as the Glen Line. It would be rash to present this company as a perfect microcosm of any part of the shipping industry. None the less, its record does present many features common to a wide sector of the British liner trade. Founded to exploit the potential of steam propulsion in one narrow avenue of sea transport, the Glen Line achieved early success, but then failed to adapt to increasing competition and changing freight requirements. Unimaginative management completed the process of deterioration, leaving the company in such a position that independent survival was no longer possible. Thus, it joined a casualty list of entrepreneurship, the very length of which was indicative of widespread ill health in the sector.

II

In common with many mid-nineteenth-century liner firms, the Glen Line emerged from a shipbroking business.[6] A. C. Gow & Co. had operated in Glasgow for two decades before purchasing its first sailing vessel in 1867. This vessel was placed in the South American trade, but its three sail successors were designed for service in the East Indies. The impetus towards consolidation around the latter trade was provided by the opening of the Suez Canal and simultaneous advances in the design of the compound steam engine. The first steamship, *Glengyle*, was despatched to the East late in 1870, and by the end of the decade eleven steamers were maintaining a regular service organised around the seasonal import of China tea.[7]

When the service was inaugurated, the senior partners in the firm were the deceased founder's brother, Leonard Gow, and James McGregor, a Highland Scot who had worked his way up through service in the company office. Of the two, McGregor was very much the innovator. Whilst Gow's interest remained largely financial, McGregor moved to London in 1873 to assume management of McGregor Gow & Co., the organisation created to run the steamer service to the East. The good results achieved in the early years of operation were the product of McGregor's knowledge of the trade and tight control of decision-making. The surviving correspondence between John Swire, founder of the Far East freight conference, and the Holt brothers, owners of the rival Blue Funnel Line, clearly demonstrates that McGregor was seen to be one of the shrewdest judges of operational requirements in the 1870s and early 1880s.[8]

The company's early prosperity was based on a simple formula: building up a modern fleet with a reputation for speed and reliability established through the carriage of China tea to Britain. The 1860s had witnessed a dramatic increase in the importance of the tea trade following the opening of the Yangtze to foreign navigation. During that decade the trade remained largely in the hands of sailing vessels, but the opening of the Suez Canal allowed compound engined steamships to offer a faster, more efficient service.[9] The annual race to earn the highest freights by getting the first teas of the season to British markets remained as much the centre of the China trade as it had in the days of the tea clippers. Swire, who knew the trade as well as anyone, was in no doubt as to the value of speed: 'As long as tea is tea', he told Alfred Holt, 'a first arrival with nothing behind it this side of Gibraltar is worth at least 50*s* [per ton] extra freight, and given a fast reliable steamer, buyers will combine to let her have a start.'[10] By building vessels designed for speed, the Glen Line was able to establish itself as the leader and be assured of the prestige necessary to win other freights in a trade which rapidly became glutted with excess tonnage.

In this context, it is interesting to compare Glen Line vessels with those of its rivals. *Glenfruin*, which entered service in 1880, was typical of the ships built for McGregor Gow & Co. during its heyday. Iron-built, it measured 2,985 g.r.t. and was capable of 13 knots. The Blue Funnel steamer *Cyclops* entered service in the same year as one of a class of ten ships forming the backbone of the Liverpool-based service of Alfred Holt & Co., Glen's largest non-subsidised rival; it was almost a third smaller at 2,064 g.r.t. and could make only 10 knots. Swire, whose firm represented Blue Funnel in the East, was convinced that Holt's ships were too small and too slow, and held up the Glen steamers as examples of the ideal design.[11]

The Glen Line won the tea race for three successive years in the mid-1870s, and its vessels frequently returned high profits. *Glenroy*, introduced to the trade in 1872 at a cost of £36,800, earned a total profit of £21,000 on its first three voyages. It had more than covered construction costs by the end of its eleventh voyage in January 1878, earning a further profit just in excess of £40,000 before realising £14,000 on sale in 1890. Overall, it returned an annual average of 13·6 per cent on initial investment. *Glenfruin*, whose career with the firm stretched from 1880 to 1897, did not prove as profitable, largely because the trading conditions for which it was built did not last into the second half if its lifetime. None the less, it did return an annual average of 8·5 per cent on cost.[12]

Table 1 gives some indication of fleet growth during the first decade of operations. Surviving records do not permit a detailed analysis of business performance, but Glen's voyage results do compare favourably with those of its larger rival Holt. In 1881, for example, Holt's Blue Funnel Line realised £238,900 on fifty voyages — an average voyage profit of £4,700 — while the Glen Line realised £134,399 on twenty-four voyages — an average profit of £5,600.[13] Apart from Holt, Glen was also in competition with the two regular mail carriers, Britain's P&O and France's Messageries Maritimes, as well as several smaller British firms (most notably Jenkins's Shire Line and Skinner's Castle Line), but by the end of the 1870s the company had established a reputation second to none. Commenting in October 1880 on the possible consequences of the break-up of his infant shipping conference, John Swire saw the Glens as 'the best working plant in the trade', and 'the greatest favourites with shippers', to be the best placed of the non-subsidised lines to face cut-throat competition. Almost a year later a P&O agent in China reported that the Glens, as 'the most desirable conveyance', were obtaining more than their share of homeward cargo.[14]

The Glen Line's established position at the top of its trade helps to explain why McGregor was an ardent supporter of the shipping conference. The operations

Table 1. *Fleet growth and voyage profits, 1871–81*

Year	No. of ships	Gross tonnage	No. of voyages	Voyage profits	Profits per ton	Av. voyage profits
				£	£	£
1871	2	3,764	2	8,224	2.18	4,112
1872	3	5,882	4	27,994	4.76	6,999
1873	6	12,410	3	15,082	1.22	5,027
1874	7	14,864	10	28,972	1.95	2,897
1875	7	14,864	13	38,490	2.59	2,961
1876	7	14,864	13	37,710	2.54	2,901
1877	10	22,654	16	65,377	2.89	4,086
1878	11	25,567	16	60,790	2.38	3,799
1879	11	25,567	20	54,038	2.11	2,702
1880	12	28,552	22	108,568	3.80	4,935
1881	12	29,923	24	134,399	4.49	5,600

Source. Glen MSS, OA113, Steamer Earnings, 1871–98.

of this institution, first established by Swire in 1879, are too complicated to describe here.[15] The overall purpose, however, was straightforward: to prevent ruinous competition by agreeing on freight rates and binding customers to them through a deferred rebate of part of the original charge. Much of the literature on conferences, written either from the point of view of their clients, or with the dangers of monopoly in mind, has portrayed them as aggressive attempts at forcing prices up and controlling the market. In fact, their objectives were more defensive in nature. In the Far East trade, as elsewhere, conferences were formed to protect established trading positions against the arrival of new tonnage and consequent rate-cutting to unprofitable levels. Conferences usually only fought interlopers who did not have the resources to maintain the struggle. In other cases, particularly when subsidised European and Japanese lines attempted to break into British-dominated trades late in the century, the conferences frequently allowed the newcomers into their ranks after only brief resistance. McGregor, running a small line depending on high returns from high-quality service, was more vulnerable to rate-cutting than most of his competitors. It was, therefore, not surprising that he was converted far earlier, and far more whole-heartedly, to Swire's scheme than the latter's own clients, the Holt brothers, who operated smaller, slower, less expensive vessels on a larger scale.[16]

In its first two years of operation, the conference added approximately £0·5 million to the profits of its members. Glen's share in this increment was reflected in the high voyage profits for 1880 and 1881.[17] Other aspects of the firm's performance within the conference, however, hinted at the long-term weakness of its trading position. In the 1880s Glen persistently carried more than its allotted share of conference cargo on the homeward voyage, compensating other participants through the existing pooling arrangement. On the outward leg the situation was reversed. To take just one example, Glen carried only 15 per cent of the cotton goods shipped by conference steamers to China and Japan in January–August 1885, while Blue Funnel carried 64 per cent.[18] Glen's prosperity was disproportionately based on the tea-dominated homeward trade. When that trade began to stagnate in the mid-1880s, McGregor Gow & Co. was more vulnerable than many of its competitors.

III

The decline of the Glen Line began in the mid-1880s. Until the beginning of that decade fleet expansion had continued at a steady pace. In 1880 Glen was operating twelve ships to Blue Funnel's nineteen. By 1890 the relative balance had altered decisively to the latter's advantage: Glen was still operating twelve vessels while Blue Funnel ran twenty-nine. Table 2 demonstrates that Glen was also falling behind in the size of individual units — as was also the case with one

Table 2. *Fleet growth in the Far East trade, 1870–1900*

Year	Glen Line			Shire Line			Blue Funnel Line		
	A	B	C	A	B	C	A	B	C
1870	(1)	1,614	(1,614)	(0)			(6)	12,596	(2,099)
1875	(7)	14,864	(2,123)	(2)	3,316	(1,658)	(16)	32,937	(2,059)
1880	(12)	28,552	(2,379)	(4)	7,212	(1,803)	(19)	39,295	(2,068)
1885	(13)	34,541	(2,657)	(7)	15,910	(2,273)	(22)	46,245	(2,102)
1890	(12)	34,817	(2,901)	(9)	24,660	(2,740)	(29)	65,661	(2,264)
1895	(12)	37,072	(3,089)	(5)	14,548	(2,910)	(30)	90,028	(3,001)
1900	(9)	33,240	(3,693)	(7)	23,997	(3,428)	(34)	154,004	(4,530)

Note. A: number of vessels in service at end of year; B: total tonnage of A; C: average tonnage of A.

Source. E. P. Harnack, 'Glen Line to the Orient', *Sea Breezes*, XXIX (112), (1955), pp. 284–5; W. A. Laxon, *The Shire Line* (1972), pp. 34–7; D. Haws, *Merchant Fleets, 6: Blue Funnel Line* (1984), pp. 41–64.

of its smaller rivals, Jenkins's Shire Line. As the century neared its close, the Far East trade was increasingly dominated by several large firms, leaving the smaller lines in a more and more precarious market position.

Profitability also passed its peak in the mid-1880s. Average voyage profits stayed well above £3,000 until 1886, but in most years thereafter they barely exceeded half that figure. The data in table 3, based on an incomplete set of voyage returns, illustrate the extent of the decline: in that it under-represents older, less profitable vessels, the decline might actually have been steeper. New vessel acquisition followed a similar pattern. Having introduced sixteen vessels between 1870 and 1885, the company introduced only seven between 1885 and 1900. It also failed to keep abreast of increases in the size of individual units. At the turn of the century, the largest vessels in the Glen fleet were the *Glenorchy* and the *Glenturret* of 1896, each of just under 4,700 g.r.t. In contrast, Holt's *Idomeneus* class, of which nine were built in 1899–1900, measured between 6,700 and 7,050 g.r.t.

Explanations for the Glen Line's decline can be sought in two areas. In the first instance, the pattern of trade on which early prosperity was based began to change in the 1880s. In the second, management failed to respond adequately to these changes, leaving Glen to compete with outmoded equipment and business ideas.

Glen had risen to prominence by exploiting the China to Britain tea trade. Its vessels earned very high freights in the tea season, but even in the 1870s such earnings were being used to subsidise out-of-season operations. Jardine

Table 3. *Estimated average voyage profits, 1882–97*

Year	Estimated total voyages[a]	Voyages recorded[b]	Estimated average voyage profits (£)[c]
1882	26	22	3,673
1883	28	18	3,296
1884	26	14	3,837
1885	26	16	3,234
1886	28	14	5,136
1987	30	19	1,085
1888	30	20	2,375
1889	28	20	3,875
1890	24	11	1,348
1891	26	15	1,795
1892	24	21	1,388
1893	22	18	2,096
1894	24	16	1,990
1895	24	17	2,279
1896	26	16	969
1897	24	17	1,617

[a]Calculated on basis of two voyages per vessel per year.
[b]Voyages for which results available.
[c]Average profits of voyages in b.
Source. Glen MSS, OA113, Steamer Earnings, 1871–98.

Matheson & Co., Glen's agents in the Far East, often had difficulty in finding remunerative unseasonal homeward freights. One early expedient was to employ steamers in short-haul trades in the East to keep them on station for the opening of the next tea season. Another was to send boats which missed the British peak season for teas to New York with similar cargoes. Neither course was particularly successful. By 1873–74 Glen steamers were frequent callers at Japanese ports, but the low freights to be earned in the local rice and coal trades could not support the tea carriers' high fuel bills and manning costs. In the second half of the decade more and more vessels carried tea to New York, but such voyages rarely earned enough to compensate for the consequent disruption of the British outward service or the poor cargoes produced by an under-developed USA to Britain service.[19]

Similar problems existed in the British outward trade. Despite the advantages of an established London berth, the company had difficulty in finding dependable sources of full cargoes. In its early years of business, the outward trade to the East was dominated by Midlands textile goods.[20] By 1878, Blue Funnel was despatching one ship a week from Liverpool with freights at 20s to 25s a ton. Glen could not match these rates at the discount of 10s necessary to compensate shippers for the cost of transporting goods to London. In August of that year the firm wrote to Jardine Matheson of the 'great folly on our part of sending out boats under such unfavourable circumstances'. A few weeks later, having just despatched *Glenearn* with only 500 tons of cargo after nearly three weeks on the berth, it was considering reducing the service to a maximum of one vessel a month and the possibility of laying up vessels until market conditions improved.[21]

Holt was able to maintain a frequent service in depressed market conditions with small and cheap-to-operate craft. The larger and faster Glen liners could not be made to pay under such circumstances. They required long stays on the berth to fill up when cargo was in short supply. They could not depend upon superior speed to earn the higher rates necessary to cover their operating costs because cheap carriage was a greater inducement to most outward shippers than was rapidity of transport.[22]

The Glen management was not oblivious to this problem. In 1878 it purchased a smaller, slower steamer off the stocks (subsequently renamed *Gleniffer*), commenting to its China agents: 'We fear fast boats are not sufficiently appreciated, as we find slow going vessels with small consumption get the same rates of freight as our fast going vessels, and are of course very much more profitable.'[23] This realisation, however, made no long-term impact on company policy. James McGregor remained convinced of the future of speed and by 1882 had disposed of both *Gleniffer* and the only other vessel of similar capabilities, the pioneer *Glengyle*.

None of these problems was potentially fatal as long as the tea trade provided dependable compensation. Unfortunately, China tea was driven from the British market after the early 1880s by its stronger flavoured Indian equivalent. Imports of China tea, which had stood at 137 million lbs in 1873, fell to 16 million lbs by 1913. Other changes in international trade further altered the requirements of the Far East shipping service. British yarn was driven from its near monopoly of the Chinese market by Indian and Japanese competition. British exports to the East were increasingly dominated by machinery, other metal goods and chemicals, while tea imports from the region were replaced by rice, sugar, silks, tobacco and bean oil.[24]

These alterations in trade were the first cause of the downturn in Glen's fortunes. They did not by themselves produce collapse. The rival Blue Funnel Line responded to the same set of circumstances with a massive expansion programme which left it the unquestioned leader in Britain's carrying trade with the East. A comparison of respective responses to the challenge reveals entrepreneurial failure as the real cause of Glen's decline.

Throughout the 1880s and early 1890s, the ageing Holt brothers resisted pressure to expand and modernise their fleet but continued to run a slow but reliable service. By maintaining regular sailings and reducing rates as low as the market seemed to require, the Holts retained a large portion of the regular freight market. Conservatism had its short-term costs, but the gradual accumulation of resources through a refusal to pay occasional windfall dividends ultimately helped underwrite a brighter future. When a new generation of Holt managers introduced a policy of rapid expansion around the construction of larger vessels designed for bulk transport, it was able to achieve dynamic growth. In eight years at the end of the century, Blue Funnel brought twenty-three new ships (totalling 141,767 g.r.t.) into service, and added another thirteen modern vessels of 76,100 g.r.t. through the purchase of the rival China Mutual Steam Navigation Co. At the same time it extended its services in the transpacific, Japanese and Australian trades, placing itself in a strong position to face increasing foreign competition in the decade leading up to the First World War.[25]

A different brand of conservatism allowed a second generation of Glen Line managers few such opportunities. Two expansion projects were allowed to founder in the 1870s. In 1873 the firm attempted to interest Matheson & Co., the London affiliates of its Far East agents, in taking a financial stake in new building. The deal fell through as a result of McGregor's refusal to surrender any measure of personal control in exchange for an infusion of capital. He particularly resisted the idea of reconstituting the line as a joint stock company.[26] In 1876 fresh tonnage was introduced in the form of vessels of the State Line, a Glasgow-based firm normally engaged on the North Atlantic run and managed by Glen's Scottish parent, A. C. Gow & Co. No attempt was made to broaden the service to take account of the different capabilities of these vessels, which were withdrawn after failing to pay in the tea trade. Any hope of fresh help from this source ended in 1883 with Gow's refusal to accept a lower management fee from the financially troubled State Line.[27] Thereafter, Glen gave up the search for outside help and settled down to run its ailing tea-dominated service entirely from its own resources.

The key to Glen's managerial performance was the character of its founder. James McGregor's energy and acumen were the prime engines of success in the early years, but in the last decade of his life McGregor became much less effective. Large sums of money were taken out of the business to maintain a high standard of living for the founder's family.[28] More importantly, the elder McGregor proved unwilling to undertake financial arrangements which might revitalise the business. Most of the original sixty-fourth shareholders were bought out as money became available, leaving the individual vessels almost entirely in the hands of the McGregor and Gow families. Profits were disposed of in handsome dividends and little attention paid to building up reserves. Finally, McGregor refused to transform the business into a limited liability joint stock company, denying it the opportunity to raise fresh capital on the grounds that 'a limited company meant limited honesty and that a proper shipowner should own 64/64ths in his ship'.[29]

Related to this failure to embrace financial expansion was a failure to explore fresh areas of business. Studies of some of the more successful British shipping lines reveal a fairly uniform pattern of response to the difficult trading conditions around the turn of the century. Faced with increasing competition and structural changes on the routes where they had first made their names, firms like Cayzer's Clan Line, Harrison's of Liverpool, and the Blue Funnel Line diversified their operations, opening new services to different parts of the world.[30] Alternatively, some concerns, such as the West African lines of Alfred Jones and the emerging Inchcape group in the Indian Ocean, sought vertical integration within the whole process of overseas trade.[31] The Glen Line took neither course. It followed its competitors in extending the original line north to Japan, and in calling more intensively at intermediate ports in India and the Straits, but failed to spread its fortunes beyond this extended route. In particular, it denied itself systematic access to the rich possibilities of the new north Pacific service. By the time Glen went out of independent existence, its rival Blue Funnel was sharing 75 per cent of the cargo on this route with the Japanese firm Nippon Yusen Kaisha (NYK) and obtaining 27 per cent of its total voyage receipts from it.[32] Beyond the development of its own small brokerage in China, there is no evidence at all of Glen adopting the alternative business strategy and investing in the trading economies of its shipping customers. The firm remained a one-route shipping line to the end.

IV

On the elder McGregor's death in 1896, control of the company passed to his three sons — Allan, Bertram and Douglas. Far from being saved by the arrival of a new generation, the Glen Line slipped further into decline. While the financial practices of their father had left Glen's new managers with fewer options than those allowed their Holt contemporaries by the more stable performance of their predecessors, their response showed little energy. The new managers showed signs of having their business instincts dulled by a leisured upbringing, exercising only intermittent guidance over the London office and withdrawing company personnel to maintain their private yachts. By the end of 1904, with the shipping industry mired in a decade-long depression, Glen was operating only six ships on an irregular Far East service. The outward route was in particular danger after the arrival of NYK on the London berth, a move which the London-based members of the freight conference, the Glen, Ben and Shire Lines, had been too weak to resist. In Glen's case the damage was not restricted to loss of freight; it also involved the departure of key personnel to work in NYK's London office.[33]

Remaining documents for the period are not particularly informative but suggest that the management was undecided as to whether it should continue to struggle along on the periphery of the regular liner trade or turn its hand to tramping.[34] In 1906 the Glen Line experienced its first brush with take-over when the shipping millionaire J. R. Ellerman became involved in its service, contributing much needed tonnage in return for a share in profits. Only persistently low profits from a neglected business network dissuaded Ellerman from continuing the experiment and consolidating the line within his growing empire.[35]

There was a sense in which the entire British liner sector was passing through a generational crisis around the turn of the century. Many of the founders of firms created in the 1860s and 1870s around the compound-engined iron vessel died or retired at about this time, leaving family-controlled organisations to their descendants. It is not necessary to embrace notions of the gentrification of the late Victorian or Edwardian shipowner to explain the subsequent sale or disappearance of many of these firms. The world shipping market was glutted with tonnage; foreign competition was driving the British flag from some trades and taking up at least a portion of others; and the cyclical pattern of shipping earnings was showing longer and deeper troughs.[36] In short, shipping was not an attractive prospect, and the temptation for sons or executors to accept almost any price to dispose of wasting assets was strong. Ellerman, for example, swallowed up several well-established lines in this fashion in 1901, while Glen's old competitor Shire was taken over by the Royal Mail Group after a series of joint management schemes had fallen through.[37] Glen itself, having failed to hold Ellerman's interest beyond 1910 and featured as the target of a German take-over bid, followed Shire into Royal Mail control a year later.[38]

Depressed trading conditions finally convinced the McGregors that financial restructuring was imperative. In 1910, Glen Line (McGregor Gow & Co.) Ltd was formed with an authorised capital of £225,000 in £1 shares. In the event, this new company only served as a vehicle for sale in 1911 to Sir Owen Philipps's Royal Mail Group. The total purchase price was just over £204,000, and the sale went through only after the brothers had discharged all existing liabilities from their own private resources. At the time the book value of the seven-vessel fleet stood at £270,000. Although this was probably an overvaluation, the McGregors had clearly not made a profitable sale. They had, for example, received only £19,300 for the firm's good will — a small sum for an asset which included valuable conference and London berth rights.[39]

After 1911 the Glen Line's fortunes were tied to those of its parent group, and as such do not form a valid area of enquiry for this article. Before concluding, however, it is worthwhile to look back over the firm's financial structure for additional clues to failure.

Until 1910 the Glen Line's capital had remained in sixty-fourth shares in individual vessels. Surviving share accounts for seven of the eleven ships which entered service before 1880 show James McGregor holding sixty-two and Leonard Gow fifty-one of the 448 shares, a combined holding of 25 per cent. The remainder was spread among fifty-four investors (mostly from the Glasgow business community), none of whom held more than 10 per cent, and only five more than 5 per cent. Analysis of the share accounts of nine of the ten vessels to enter service between 1880 and 1896 reveals a different pattern; with McGregor and his family taking up 166 shares and Gow 118 — in all, 49 per cent of the total. In the years immediately preceding takeover, the move towards concentration in McGregor hands becomes even clearer. Douglas McGregor sold his interest a few years before reconstruction, and this, together with his brothers' financial problems, had left 133 shares in the hands of their bankers by 1910. Before this, the McGregor family had controlled 291 shares which combined with seventy-eight held by the Gow family to leave only 16 per cent of the firm's capital in the hands of outsiders.[40]

The shrinking of the Gow interest exacerbated Glen's financial difficulties. A sleeping partner from the start, Leonard Gow extended his own broking and management activities through the original Glasgow firm of A. C. Gow & Co. In 1895 he combined his small tramp fleet with another Glasgow concern to form Gow Harrison & Co., which rose to become one of the larger British tramp operators with a First World War fleet of twenty-three vessels.[41] The decisive move of the Gows into shipowning in their own right was paralleled by their withdrawal from the Glen enterprise. The divergence was accelerated by a personal rift between the second generations of the McGregor and Gow families, and by the latter's insistence on a move to limited liability to protect its remaining investments. In this context, it is worthy of note that the Glen Line's shortage of capital became acute at a time when Gow fortunes were improving — Leonard senior, for example, leaving an estate of £144,103 when he died in 1910.[42]

V

Although the McGregor family remained involved in the management of the Glen Line after 1911, the company's fate was determined by that of its parent the Royal Mail Group, a subject admirably covered by several modern studies.[43] For the purposes of this study, it is necessary only to make brief comment on the take-over in the context of its time. The tendency towards agglomeration in the pre-1914 British shipping industry was symptomatic of the weakness of many of its constituent firms. It was the inability of weak financial structures to continue

profitable operation in the face of strengthening foreign competition and prolonged freight rate depression which convinced owners to sell or seek merger.
The businesses they disposed of were frequently in a parlous state, operating outdated or overcapitalised tonnage in markets already penetrated by
outsiders.

The new British combines were not well-integrated concerns like their
German or Japanese rivals. Too often they suffered as a result of their origins,
operating declining services on poorly connected routes. The Glen Line, in
particular, proved no more successful after merger than before. Ambitious
attempts to expand and modernise on inadequate foundations failed to make it
competitive and reduced its finances to chaos. Its trials until its resale to the Blue
Funnel Line in 1935 were reflective of a malaise which affected the British liner
sector not only during the inter-war period but also well before 1914.

Notes

1 D. H. Aldcroft, 'British shipping and foreign
competition: the Anglo-German rivalry, 1880–1914',
in D. H. Aldcroft (ed.), *Studies in British Transport
History 1870–1970* (Newton Abbot, 1974), pp. 53–99.
2 F. E. Hyde, *Blue Funnel: A History of Alfred Holt
and Company of Liverpool from 1865 to 1914* (Liverpool,
1957); *Shipping Enterprise and Management 1830–
1939: Harrisons of Liverpool* (Liverpool, 1967).
3 R. S. Craig, 'Aspects of tramp shipping and
ownership', in K. Matthews and G. Panting (eds),
Ships and Shipbuilding in the North Atlantic Region
(St John's, 1978), p. 209.
4 By the outbreak of the First World War, P&O
had taken over Blue Anchor and British India;
Ellerman the City, Hall and Bucknall Lines, as well as
Westcott & Laurence; Furness Withy the Warren
Line and Houlder Brothers; Cunard the Anchor
Line; and Royal Mail the Shire, Glen, Nelson, Union
Castle, Elder Dempster, Lamport & Holt, and Pacific
Steam Navigation Lines.
5 W. D. Wray, *Mitsubishi and the N.Y.K. 1870–1914:
Business Strategy in the Japanese Shipping Industry*
(Cambridge, Mass., 1984), pp. 406–8.
6 R. Davis, 'Maritime history: progress and
problems', in S. Marriner (ed.), *Business and Businessmen: Studies in Business, Economic and Accounting History*
(Liverpool, 1978), pp. 170–4.
7 A. Aiken, *In Time of War* (Glasgow, 1980), pp.
3–9; E. P. Harnack, 'Glen Line to the Orient',
Sea Breezes, 29 (112), (1955), pp. 268–71.
8 Modern Records Centre, Ocean MSS, OA300/A
and B, Swire–Holt correspondence.
9 For the sailing ship era in the Far East trade:
D. R. MacGregor, *The China Bird: The History of
Captain Killick and One Hundred Years of Sail and Steam*
(1961).
10 Ocean MSS, OA300/A, Swire to A. Holt,
24 May 1879.

11 Ocean MSS, OA300/A and B, Swire–Holt
correspondence.
12 Modern Records Centre, Glen MSS, OA113,
Steamer Earnings, 1871–98.
13 Glen MSS, OA113, Steamer Earnings, 1871–
98; Hyde, *Blue Funnel*, p. 124.
14 Ocean MSS, OA300/B, Swire to A. Holt,
28 October 1880 and 12 September 1881.
15 For a full description: S. Marriner and F. E.
Hyde, *The Senior: John Samuel Swire 1825–98; Management in Far Eastern Shipping Trades* (Liverpool, 1967),
pp. 135–83.
16 Ocean MSS, OA300/A, Swire to P. Holt, 11 July
and 17 October 1879.
17 Marriner and Hyde, *The Senior*, p. 181; Glen
MSS, OA113, Steamer Earnings, 1871–98.
18 Marriner and Hyde, *The Senior*, pp. 164–70.
19 University Library, Cambridge, Jardine Matheson MSS, Correspondence, Unbound Letters,
GB/5994, A. C. Gow to Jardine Matheson (Shanghai),
20 March 1873; Lon/14413, McGregor Gow to
Jardine Matheson (Shanghai), 10 April 1874, Lon/
16665 and 18896, McGregor Gow to Jardine Matheson (Shanghai), 29 December 1876 and 12 July 1879.
20 F. E. Hyde, *Far Eastern Trade 1860–1914*
(1973), *passim*.
21 Jardine Matheson MSS, Unbound Letters, Lon/
18182 and 18219, McGregor Gow to Jardine
Matheson (Shanghai), 29 August and 12 September
1878.
22 Hyde, *Blue Funnel, passim*.
23 Jardine Matheson MSS, Unbound Letters, Lon/
17842, McGregor Gow to Jardine Matheson
(Shanghai), 28 April 1878.
24 S. B. Saul. *Studies in British Overseas Trade 1870–
1914* (Liverpool, 1960), pp. 44–5 and 189; F. E.
Hyde, 'British shipping companies and East and
South-East Asia, 1860–1939', in C. D. Cowan (ed.),

McGregor Gow and the Glen Line   179

The Economic Development of South East Asia: Studies in Economic History and Political Economy (1964), p. 34.

25 Hyde, *Blue Funnel*, pp. 80–159.

26 Jardine Matheson MSS, Unbound Letters, GB/ 6016 and 6095, A. C. Gow to Jardine Matheson (Shanghai), 10 April and 24 August 1873.

27 Jardine Matheson MSS, Unbound Letters, Lon/ 16125, McGregor Gow to Jardine Matheson (Shanghai), 28 April 1876; Glen MSS, OA557, The State Steamship Co. Ltd, Report of Directors, 15 May 1883.

28 Glen MSS, OA361, Notes by Cameron McGregor, 16 March 1947.

29 Glen MSS, OA289, Share Accounts on Ships; OA361, Notes by C. McGregor, 16 March 1947; for general comment on financial practice in British shipping: E. Green, 'Very private enterprise: ownership and finance in British shipping, 1825–1940', in T. Yui and K. Nakagawa, *Business History of Shipping: Strategy and Structure* (Tokyo, 1985), pp. 219–48.

30 A. Muir and M. Davies. *A Victorian Shipowner: A Portrait of Sir Charles Cayzer, Baronet of Gartmore* (1978), *passim*; Hyde, *Harrisons*, pp. 82–97, *Blue Funnel*, pp. 117–42.

31 P. N. Davies, *The Trade Makers, Elder Dempster in West Africa, 1852–1972* (1973), *passim*; S. Jones, *Two Centuries of Overseas Trading: the Origins and Growth of the Inchcape Group* (1986), *passim*.

32 Hyde, *Far Eastern Trade*, pp. 167–8; for another

example of the exploitation of the north Pacific trade: S. Jones, 'George Benjamin Dodwell: a shipping agent in the Far East, 1872–1908', *The Journal of Transport History* (3rd series), VI, 1 (1985), pp. 23–40.

33 Wray, *Mitsubishi and the N.Y.K.*, pp. 308–32; Glen MSS, OA361, notes by C. McGregor, 16 March 1947.

34 Glen MSS, OA273, Freight Movements, 1901– 19; OA361, notes by C. McGregor, 16 March 1947.

35 J. Taylor, *Ellermans: a Wealth of Shipping* (1976), pp. 55–8.

36 E. A. V. Angier, *Fifty Years' Freights 1869–1919* (1920), pp. 88 and 104.

37 Taylor, *Ellermans*, pp. 205, 225–6; W. A. Laxon, *The Shire Line* (1972), pp. 10–15.

38 *Fairplay*, 8 December 1910.

39 Glen MSS, OA4088/1, Directors' Book, 17 January 1911; Companies House, London, File 111291, Glen Line Ltd.

40 Glen MSS, OA289, Share Accounts on Ships.

41 *Lloyd's List*, 6 November 1948.

42 Glen MSS, OA361, notes by C. McGregor, 16 March 1947; Aiken, *In Time of War*, pp. 18–19.

43 E. Green and M. Moss. *A Business of National Importance: The Royal Mail Shipping Group 1902–37* (1982); P. N. Davies and A. M. Bourn, 'Lord Kylsant and the Royal Mail', *Business History*, XIV (2), (1972), pp. 103–23.

Acknowledgements

The author would like to thank the staff of the Modern Records Centre, Liverpool, and Alan Reid, Honorary Archivist for Matheson & Co. Ltd, for their kind assistance. He is also grateful to Ocean Transport and Trading PLC for making the Glen Line collection available for his use, and to Matheson & Co. Ltd for permission to quote from the archives of Jardine Matheson & Co. Ltd. An earlier version of this paper was given at a symposium on 'The Shipping World and Scotland' held on 16 May 1987 in Glasgow under the auspices of the Department of Economic History of the University of Glasgow and the Scottish Maritime History Group.

6 George Benjamin Dodwell: a shipping agent in the Far East, 1872–1908

STEPHANIE JONES

Studies of British maritime and trading enterprise in the treaty ports of China and Japan in the second half of the nineteenth century have invariably relied heavily upon the archives of Jardine Matheson and Swire's.[1] The role of shipping agents in the deployment of merchant tonnage generally, and especially in long-distance trades, has not received the attention its importance merits.[2] The recent discovery of a large collection of papers relating to the Far Eastern merchant house of Dodwell & Co. Ltd,[3] a substantial proportion of which documents the work of its founder and the head of its shipping activities is therefore of particular importance. It provides an insight into, firstly, the establishment and operation of British trading concerns through the development of shipping routes to China and Japan; and secondly, the value of the shipping agent in facilitating the opening up of this distant region to trade with the West.

Before the mid-nineteenth century, Western trade with China was limited to the ports of Macao and Canton, and only members of the exclusive *Cohong*, a small group of authorised merchants whose financial and commercial resources were strictly limited by the Chinese government,[4] were permitted to undertake transactions with foreign traders. The limited demand for Western goods in China was in considerable contrast to the large local market for opium. The attempts of the Chinese government to restrict opium imports led to conflict with Britain, which imposed the Treaty of Nanking in 1842; by this treaty Hong Kong was ceded to Great Britain and the treaty port system inaugurated. Later treaties opened China further to Western commerce. The port of Shanghai became one of the most important and prosperous of the foreign settlements, especially with the development of the foreign trade of the Yangtse, whilst Hong Kong became the centre of the entrepot trade of south China generally.

Meanwhile the rigid social structure of mid-nineteenth century Japan precluded practically all contact with foreign merchants and traders, who were confined to the port of Nagasaki only. The building of large sailing vessels capable of distant voyages was expressly banned, but Commodore Perry's arrival in 1853 opened the way to change. Only with the gradual demise of the power of the *Daimyō* (the territorial lords) and the rising prosperity of the *Chōmin* (the merchants), with the resultant collapse of the Tokugawa shogunate and the Meiji restoration in 1868, was Japan prepared to trade with Western nations and accept foreign influences on her society and economy.

It was against this background that the firm of W. R. Adamson & Co. was registered in London in 1858, with its head office in Shanghai, and branches in Hong Kong, Foochow and, after the Treaty of Tientsin in 1860, in Hankow. Adamson himself had originally been sent to Shanghai in the early 1850s by a group of Macclesfield silk merchants to procure a new source of raw silk. Realising the extent of the commercial opportunities, he soon branched out to trade on his own account. In 1863 he was recorded as the owner of an ⁸⁄₆₄ share in the new Far Eastern trader *Yangtse*, built by Alexander Hall of Aberdeen for Captain Killick of the London shipping firm of Killick Martin & Co.[5] W. R. Adamson & Co., which became Adamson Bell & Co. in 1867, built up a prosperous business in the export of silk and tea. They also acted as agents for visiting shipping and dealing in the import and export trade generally.

By 1872 the partnership was operating on a scale large enough to justify the appointment of a full-time shipping clerk at its Shanghai office. George Benjamin Dodwell, born in Derby, and then aged twenty, was engaged at a salary of £400 for the first year, with a room, fire, light and medical attendance. His conditions of service laid down that he should devote his whole time and attention to the House (Adamson knew only too well the temptations to trade on one's own account) and he was allowed a 5 per cent interest on all the profits of the shipping business of the Shanghai office, on all profits earned above 7,000 taels per annum (equivalent to £2,100 sterling), an indication of the department's income. His work as a shipping agent was interpreted in a wide sense: he was to act for the owners or charterers of vessels in securing cargoes, clearances and any other business, including insurance. Rather than acting as an agent for one specific fleet of merchant vessels, as in the case of James Kirton, who acted solely for the Henleys, primarily in the English coasting trade,[6] he managed a general shipping agency business, acting for a variety of owners and principals. He was not concerned with the buying and selling of ships, their outfits, crews and provisions, but with their profitable operation through consigning and despatching vessels entering and clearing the port of Shanghai and other ports where Adamson Bell & Co. maintained branches. Adamson Bell also allowed Dodwell to take a one-tenth interest in steamers and one-fifth in sailing ships chartered for speculative voyages on the account of the Shanghai office. These percentages of the profits were not, however, allowed on commission business (on the shipment of cargo held by the firm) which was seen as the department's main activity. The final condition of Dodwell's appointment was that he should 'not indulge in racing of horses and ponies', in contrast to the largest merchant house in China, Jardine Matheson.[7]

A detailed notebook kept by Dodwell covering the decade 1873 to 1883 provides an insight into the vessels and owners for whom he acted as agent. This has been used to compile table 1, which summarises the profits of Adamson Bell's shipping business at Shanghai and Hankow. Dodwell clearly dealt primarily with steamers, the profits of which exceeded those of sailing ships after 1875. Steamships gained an early predominance in the Far Eastern trade, which specialised in high-value, low-bulk traffic such as tea, silk and passengers rather than high-bulk, low-value cargoes such as coal or timber, which continued to be carried by less highly capitalised sailing vessels. The profits achieved by the shipping department of Adamson Bell & Co. may be divided into two categories: those earned as a result of Dodwell's own speculative ventures in the chartering of vessels, and those of ships trading on consignment for the firm. Regular high profits were earned by the 'Castle' steamers (owned by T. Skinner & Co. of London) but the extension of European telegraph and cable services to all the major countries of east and south-east Asia between 1871 and 1875 soon diminished the profits of speculative trading. Success in such trading relied upon a greater knowledge of the market than that of one's competitors. When an accurate and up-to-date listing of arrivals, departures and prices of commodities was made easily available to all, this advantage was lost.

Dodwell recalled that a great deal of risk was involved in chartering, and often heavy demurrage charges were incurred through waiting for a full cargo. He regarded it as a generally unsatisfactory system, especially as he was often forced to buy his own cargo to fill the ships, 'and that is the worst thing that could happen if you were a merchant'.[8] From 1879 the profits from charters averaged a third of the total income from shipping and contributed considerably to Dodwell's earnings. For example, the profit of nearly 6,000 taels on the chartering of sailing vessels in 1881 added over 1,000 taels or over £300 to his salary, then £1,000 p.a. and, as that same year, steamers earned over 10,000 taels, his 10 per cent share was again over £300. To this may be added his share of the overall profits, 5 per cent on his department's profits exceeding 7,000 taels, which equalled nearly 1,500 taels or approximately £450. Thus in 1881 his gross earnings exceeded £2,000, doubling his salary.

Whereas Dodwell's chartering business was based on tramp steamers, the firm also acted as agents for liners trading on consignment. The regularity of the Castle and Shire line ships in their voyages to Shanghai, for example, may be seen in the contemporary commercial press. Dodwell's work as a shipping agent also led to an expansion of the firm's income from these vessels, too — in the case of the Castle steamers, by more than fivefold. Profits from the Castle fleet agency were derived from charging 5 per cent on homeward freights: one per cent of which being held on the account of each steamer. A further 5 per cent was levied on coasting cargoes obtained, and 2½ per cent was charged on payments made by Adamson Bell on the behalf of Skinners' over and above the credit which was held on the account of each steamer. A half per cent was claimed for collecting debts and one-eighth per cent on bill brokerage. Of the 5 per cent charged by Adamson Bell on rice charters, one per cent was put to the credit of the steamer. Similar arrangements existed with the other shipping lines with whom Adamson Bell dealt, including D. J. Jenkins & Co.'s Shire Line, Geo. Thompson Jnr. & Co., Killick Martin & Co. and Alex. Stephens & Sons. The results of these arrangements in terms of profits earned by Dodwell for his employers are summarised in table 1. Strangely, such detailed information has not survived for the later period.

A wide variety of cargoes was carried on consignment and by charter through Dodwell's agency work. In the early days of trading with China the export trade was dominated by tea and silk; imports were mainly raw cotton and opium. By the mid-1870s the Chinese supplied new lines of exports, such as Chinese beans, vegetable oils and bristles. Imports included cotton piece goods, kerosene for lighting, metal wares, matches, soap and cigarettes. This diversification was explained in a customs report from Shanghai in 1876: 'British merchants in China sought some other and more profitable medium than bullion in which to remit the proceeds of their imports, and a trade of greater or less magnitude . . . in consequence . . . developed in articles which a few years before were unknown among our foreign exports, such as sugar, tobacco, hides, camel's wool and straw braid.'[9]

Yet even by the end of the nineteenth century nearly 60 per cent of China's exports consisted of tea and silk. In order to consider the importance of Adamson Bell as a merchant house, in table 2 tea has been taken as an example of an important commodity handled by Western firms in China. If we consider exports of tea from the ports of Shanghai and Foochow for a few years in the 1870s for which statistics happen to survive, Adamson Bell appear among the leading firms. In 1875 the total number of chests of tea it shipped from Foochow exceeded that of any other Western firm, more than 10 per cent of all tea exports from that port. In the following year Adamson Bell & Co.'s tea shipments were only marginally behind those of Butterfield & Swire, Fairhurst & Reeves, Jardine Matheson and Westall Galton & Co. In 1877 the firm ranked fourth in tea shipments, and in 1878 seventh. At Shanghai, it was the second and third most important shipper of green and black teas respectively in 1876. In 1877 Adamson Bell & Co.'s totals were exceeded only by the firm of Maitland & Co. In 1878 they maintained their position in green teas but fell slightly to eighth ranking in black tea shipments.[10]

Such a prominent position in the tea trade thus ensured Dodwell's note as a leading shipping agent. His firm, unlike John Samuel Swire, Jardine Matheson

George Benjamin Dodwell   27

Table 1. *Analysis of shipping agency profits (net) at the Shanghai and Hankow branches of Adamson Bell & Co., 1873–83 (taels), year ending 31 March (3·33 taels = £1 sterling)*

Year		Vessels on consignment			Charters		Total	
		Castles*	Others	Total	Steam	Sail	Taels	£
1873	Steam	2686·45	1181·67	3868·12	–	–	12490·87	3751
	Sail	–	8622·75	8622·75				
1874	Steam	2821·15	227·62	3048·77	–	–	10246·83	3077
	Sail	3005·49	4142·57	7198·06				
1875	Steam	8822·75	–	8822·75	–	394·17 loss	14779·58	4438
	Sail	472·26	5878·74	6351·00				
1876	Steam	8219·72	856·16	9075·88	–	–	14174·88	4257
	Sail	–	5099·00	5099·00				
1877	Steam	7089·84	5270·76	12360·60	–	4789·44	19160·91	5754
	Sail	–	2010·87	2010·87				
1878	Steam	9442·31	–	9442·31	–	3356·76	15832·43	4755
	Sail	–	3033·36	3033·36				
1879	Steam	1405·74	3100·97	4506·71	7800·55	1804·92	17523·93	5262
	Sail	–	3411·75	3411·75				
1880	Steam	12067·72	2171·52	14239·24	5790·60	3790·95	25625·87	7696
	Sail	–	1805·08	1805·08				
1881	Steam	9549·96	7706·23	17256·19	10844·37	5899·31	36112·53	10,845
	Sail	–	2112·66	2112·66				
1882	Steam	10099·45	8067·14	18166·59	3220·45	3778·70	27960·64	8397
	Sail	–	2794·90	2794·90				
1883	Steam	13482·78	8156·47	21639·25	10760·21	510·68 loss	33225·86	9978
	Sail	–	1337·08	1337·08				

*Ships of the Castle Line of steamers, owned by T. Skinner & Co. of London.
Source. DOD 6/3, notebook of G. B. Dodwell, frontispiece.

and the American firm, Russel, did not actually invest in local steamers,[11] but otherwise his activities included all aspects of the maritime trade of Shanghai. His notebook is packed with *aides-mémoire* pertaining to his duties. He had to consider the varying charges made at the ports of arrival and departure of the vessels he represented. He had to note the costs of loading, discharge and storage of particular cargoes. He kept a record of all the 'correspondents' or contacts at foreign ports. He arranged the insurance of cargoes and vessels. He recorded the London credits of London firms operating in China. He made regular references to the fluctuations in the exchange rates between the tael, sterling and US dollars, noting that this in itself varied between different Chinese ports.

28　　　　　　　　　　　　　　　　*The Journal of Transport History*

Table 2. *Number of chests of tea shipped by Adamson Bell & Co. from Shanghai and Foochow, 1874–78*

Shanghai

Year	Type of tea	Number of chests shipped by Adamson Bell	Total number of chests shipped from Shanghai	Number of companies shipping more chests of tea than Adamson Bell in that year	Total number of companies involved in shipping tea that year
1874	Black	–	–	–	–
	Green				
1875	Black	–	–	–	–
	Green				
1876	Black	24,045	277,949	2	35
	Green	57,161	431,903	1	24
1877	Black	19,130	227,669	1	33
	Green	76,681	416,893	1	25
1878	Black	5,614	146,465	7	28
	Green	30,911	147,765	1	25

Foochow

Year	Number of chests shipped by Adamson Bell	Total number of chests shipped from Foochow	Number of companies shipping more chests of tea than Adamson Bell in that year	Total number of companies involved in shipping tea that year
1874	71,448	740,043	1	24
1875	79,053	752,520	0	26
1876	53,658	740,818	4	25
1877	52,587	644,692	3	25
1878	40,988	698,318	6	26

Overall totals

Year	Number of chests shipped by Adamson Bell at Shanghai and Foochow	Total number of chests shipped at Shanghai and Foochow	Number of chests shipped by Adamson Bell as a percentage of total tea shipments that year
1874	71.448	740,043	9·65
1875	79.053	752,520	10·51
1876	134.864	1,450,670	9·30
1877	148.398	1,289,254	11·51
1878	77.513	992,548	7·81

Source. DOD 6/3. notebook of G. B. Dodwell, pp. 104–6.

Dodwell also noted, for the years 1876–79, the vessels for which he acted as agent and the freight rates he obtained. Table 3 is a summary of the shipping movements of the season 1 May 1876 to 30 April 1877.[12] In this period, he was personally responsible for arranging the shipment of over 15,000 tons of various cargoes. Tea dominated the export trade, followed by sugar and hides, with straw goods and cotton piece goods also of importance. The largest part of these cargoes was destined for London, but the supply of goods to the United States was already significant and increased rapidly.[13] The shipment of silk goods to Lyons, comprising raw silks, silkworms and silkworm eggs, was the result of the outbreak of a silkworm disease in Europe and the need to restock the industry. The cargoes analysed in table 3 were carried in eighty-two shiploads, sixty-two by steamer and twenty by sailing ship. Dodwell's duties included the safe storage of cargoes. Great care had to be taken in the shipment of tea, which was liable to be tainted if placed in close proximity to hides or sugar cargoes. Silk and straw braid were also fragile and easily damaged.

In many of his tasks Dodwell was aided by the firm's *compradore*. It was a peculiarly Eastern custom to employ a local assistant whose knowledge of the Chinese language, customs and practices helped Western merchant houses in the day-to-day running of their affairs. They were often disliked by other Chinese as commercial 'traitors', in the employ of foreigners, working against the interest of their fellow countrymen, but they were often also envied for their wealth. They became an essential element of Chinese commercial life, not only because of the linguistic and cultural differences between East and West, but also because of continued government restrictions on trading by foreigners, the lack of uniformity of weights and measures used in different provinces, the unsettled nature of the national currency, and the unregulated issue and circulation of

Table 3. *Tons of cargo shipped by Adamson Bell & Co. from Shanghai,*
May 1876 to April 1877: destinations and commodities

	Destination						
	London		New York		Lyons	Colonies	Coast	
Commodity	Steam	Sail	Steam	Sail		Steam		Total
Tea	7,381	930	1,593	1,811	–	–	–	11,715
Straw goods	230	–	–	316	–	–	–	546
Sugar	483	954	–	–	–	–	–	1,437
Hides	707	–	1	–	–	–	–	708
Silk	23	–	–	–	19	–	–	42
Cotton and piece goods	–	–	–	–	–	–	536	536
Goatskins	44	–	–	13	–	5	–	62
Sundries	69	–	–	–	–	3	–	72
Totals	8,937	1,884	1,594	2,140	19	8	536	15,118

Source. DOD 6/3, notebook of G. B. Dodwell, pp. 120–1.

money certificates and credit bills by native banks. The establishment of the
Hongkong & Shanghai Bank, which was incorporated in 1866, helped ease
commercial transactions,[14] but the *compradore* remained a vital go-between in the
native market. He brought together local buyers and sellers, settling their
disputes, securing his principal against loss, and giving him advice on the
condition of the market generally. In theory, employing a middleman would
tend to increase the price of goods to the Chinese consumer, but in practice
experienced *compradores* created price combinations with the *compradores* of other
firms in the same trade, or with Chinese wholesale dealers. In this way he
increased his share of the profits, and the foreign traders bore the brunt of the
increase by paying more for materials for export.[15]

This formation of rings may be seen on a larger scale in Dodwell's activities as
a shipping agent: obtaining the best rates for the vessels he represented and thus
maximising his firm's commission brought him into contact with the first major
shipping conference in the Far East trade, that of 1879. Instigated by John

Swire, who founded the partnership of Butterfield & Swire, this conference helped Blue Funnel Line ships particularly, for which Swire's acted as agent. Although the Holt fleet was known for its low fuel consumption and slow passages, it required high freight rates to stay profitable, as the lengthy voyages incurred heavy overheads in terms of depreciation and interest on capital. The Castles and Shires, represented by Adamson Bell & Co., offered high-speed passages in return for higher rates: Swire's saw them as a threat to the earnings of the Blue Funnel ships.[16] However, the conference was regarded as a great success for the steamer owners and shipping agents. Arranged between Swire's, P&O, Holt's (Blue Funnel), T. Skinner (Castle), McGregor Gow (Glen), D. J. Jenkins (Shire) and Gellatly Hankey and Sewell,[17] the conference ensured that rates were kept high by offering the shipper a deferred rebate and limiting the number of departures per season.[18] Despite a clause added in 1885 which specifically stated that 'agents of conference steamers in China . . . to be prohibited from being interested . . . in opposing steamers, or in the loading of sailing vessels', Dodwell continued to load both sail and steam, as table 1 shows. He continued to represent Skinner's Castle Line, whilst his firm was employed as agent for Killick Martin & Co.'s sailing ships.

Thus in his first decade as a Far Eastern shipping agent Dodwell helped to increase the shipping tonnage handled by Adamson Bell & Co., to improve the variety and quantity of cargoes imported and exported, and to raise profits generally in the firm's Shanghai office. Despite China's great land mass and population, however, the total value of her foreign trade by the end of the nineteenth century was only £53 million.[19] Meanwhile, in the late 1870s, branches of Adamson Bell & Co. were established at the ports of Kobe and Yokohama in Japan.

The *Japan Weekly Mail*, which reported shipping arrivals and departures at Yokohama, shows that at the time when the firm was setting up in business at the port, shipping activity was limited, at a weekly average of only a dozen or so vessels clearing outwards with cargoes. Adamson Bell appear as consignees of the Castle Line steamers *Glamis Castle*, *Londoun Castle* and *Braemar Castle*, a Danish steamer and two British sailing vessels. It dispatched nine shiploads of outward cargo during the 1878 season. The three named vessels traded between the ports of Shanghai, Kobe and Hong Kong, except for the *Glamis Castle*, which sailed to New York. General cargoes, tea and coal were carried; frequent voyages in ballast indicate a shortage of goods for shipment before the expansion of Japan's overseas trade in the following decades.[20] By 1883 activity at Japanese ports had markedly increased, and with it the business of Adamson Bell. Of shipments organised by Dodwell from the firm's Shanghai office in 1883, twenty-four were destined for the ports of Kobe and Nagasaki. In the same year Dodwell handled a total of eighty-nine shiploads, acting as consignee for vessels trading to Chinese ports, such as Foochow, Swatow, Hankow, Woosung, Amoy and Newchwang.

The carriage of tea, silk and sundry goods to London, New York and Marseilles was still important.[21] When Japan's ports were opened to foreign trade, imports were mainly textile yarns and piece goods, metal wares, ships, munitions and pharmaceutical chemicals. Exports were chiefly raw silk, tea and rice, as in the case of China: in the 1880s these commodities accounted for two-thirds of outward cargoes.[22] The twenty-four shipments from Japan arranged by Dodwell in 1883 increased to fifty-seven[23] in 1889, and seventy-four in 1892.[24]

These shipping intelligence reports demonstrate clearly that the largest share of the Japanese tea trade was in the hands of the Americans. This fact, and the large American demand for silk, convinced Dodwell of the great commercial potential of a Far East trans-Pacific service. In 1883 he himself had organised the shipment of a cargo of silk across the Pacific which had sold for more than $6 million. In 1886 the Pacific and Atlantic coasts of Canada were linked for the first time by direct rail communication, and the Canadian Pacific Railway began chartering sailing ships to import goods from China and Japan. Dodwell's 1883 consignment of silk had been carried by steamer, so he now saw a golden opportunity to introduce a regular steamship service. Meanwhile the Fairfield Shipbuilding Company on the Clyde had three ex-Cunarders available for charter. The *Parthia*, *Batavia* and *Abyssinia* had been taken over in part payment for the new and larger tonnage which the firm had built for Cunard's Atlantic trade. A large proportion of the carrying capacity of these vessels was given over to passenger accommodation, which made them unsuitable for short trade runs to the Far East but ideal for a trans-Pacific passenger and freight service. Having come to an agreement with Sir William Pearce, the chairman of Fairfield's and whom he already knew (through his contacts with the Scottish Oriental Steamship Company, another of Pearce's interests), Dodwell appealed direct to Canadian Pacific, offering a ready-made steamship line, and won a three-year contract to manage the ships, which were still owned by Fairfield's. To all intents and purposes, he controlled this new shipping service, the main purpose of which was to facilitate the interchange of east- and westbound freight and passenger traffic at Port Moody, the CPR terminus.

Thus Dodwell played an important part in the expansion of his firm's business throughout the Far East, and personally pioneered the steamer links between Canada and the ports of China and Japan. But his own shipping agency work and plans to expand his commercial networks were severely curtailed by his employers. Adamson had retired in 1886 and Bell, who had succeeded him as senior partner, proved inept and profligate. The company also suffered as a result of a major change that occurred in the Far Eastern shipping trade in the late 1880s: a large number of steamers not belonging to regular shipping lines entered the trade, by accepting low freights. Dodwell was later to describe how these freights, considerably lower than those ruling before, paid only a very small profit but enabled new competition to enter the field.[25]

For Adamson Bell, bankruptcy loomed on the horizon from March 1890. On a voyage from Vancouver on the *Parthia*, beginning a month later, Dodwell and A. J. H. Carlill, the tea department manager, plotted the take-over of their moribund parent company. Their letters from this period to 1 May 1891, the date when their objective was finally realised, have survived.[26] They provide further insight into the business which Dodwell helped develop. The demand for Indian tea had caused a decline in the Foochow-to-London tea trade, and silk shipments from Japan were less in demand after the recovery of the European silk industry. Meanwhile the export trade in tea to America and also to Russia was still thriving. Dodwell saw a chance of success for a new firm if he could take over all his company's principals and 'chops', or trade marks; keep the arrangement with Fairfield's; keep the insurance agencies, and concentrate on his commission business. Slight improvements in tea and silk prices in London enabled Adamson Bell to survive a little longer. Dodwell had to maintain confidence among the firm's twenty European employees based at Yokohama, Kobe, Hong Kong, Shanghai and the London head office for over a year.

In setting up the new firm he had to raise some £20,000 capital from other employees whilst having to warn them that they would have to accept lower salaries until the new firm had found its feet. Thomas Dermer, at the London office, refused to accept a salary of only £300 a year, considering that he was worth £800. Also in London, Frederick D'Iffanger broke down completely under the strain of waiting for the Company's impending demise and withdrew from the proposed new undertaking. Dodwell's brother, Fred, based in Hong Kong, also gave cause for concern. He was given to an enthusiasm for personal speculation and trading on his own account, to the detriment of his parent firm, and, since Hong Kong was seen as the future chief earning port in the East rather than Shanghai, he had to be brought into line. Dodwell saw the fortunes of his new company hingeing on the expansion of its shipping agency work and carefully ensured that existing agencies would transfer their business from Adamson Bell's to the proposed new firm. Sealed instructions were drawn up and addressed to all constituents and agents, containing full instructions for carrying on transactions already in progress and advertising the new company, to be opened at the receipt of a single word by cable — 'Haddock'.

Carlill described how well these preparations paid off when Adamson Bell at long last expired: 'with no more delay than the time required for cablegrams to reach the chief business centres, the new firm was widely advertised, and the whole transformation was effected with a minimum of friction and disturbance'. He went on, 'never was there a more startling birth of a new firm, springing full-fledged without a pause the moment the old firm closed its doors'. Rival firms were taken aback: when they cabled their branches to try and secure the late company's agencies they found they were too late. John Swire, for example, was not slow to apply for the CPR agency and was disconcerted to discover that it had already been passed to the then unknown new firm of Dodwell Carlill & Co.[27]

In setting up his new business Dodwell planned from the beginning that it should be a limited liability company, but this status was not achieved until 1899, partly through the loss of the supply of shipping services to the CPR. Dodwell had originally entered into a three-year contract with Sir William Van Horne of the CPR; but when the shipping line had quickly established itself and shown that the level of eastbound traffic was sufficient to ensure that it would continue to pay its way, the CPR decided to run its own fast mail line in place of the old hired Cunarders. The CPR then successfully campaigned for a £60,000 annual mail subsidy for five years (£15,000 from Canada and the remainder from Britain) and commissioned the building of the Empress Line of steamers for the then new Canadian Pacific Steamship Company. Dodwell was notified that the contract he enjoyed with the CPR would not be renewed, although as the successor to Adamson Bell he was asked to continue to manage the service at the Far Eastern end. Before the creation of his new firm Dodwell had spent four months with Sir William Van Horne and various heads of departments of the CPR and had impressed them with his knowledge of Far Eastern commerce, to the extent that in 1892 Van Horne offered him the full management of the new line if he would abandon his newly-created firm and join them as an employee. Dodwell was promised complete control of CPR shipping and the freedom to develop the service as he thought best, second only to Van Horne himself. He was offered the highest remuneration paid to anyone in the CPR, a salary of £2,000 a year with commission earnings promising to equal that, totalling £4,000 p.a. Dodwell declined the proposal. He thus turned down a splendid offer from one of the world's best known railway companies, preferring the leadership of his own new and untried firm, which he had so recently rescued and rebuilt from bankruptcy. Also, by spurning the CPR, he knew he would incur that powerful company's hostility. 'It is the worst day's work you have ever done, Dodwell', Van Horne threatened, 'I will crush you'. Shaughnessy, the CPR's vice-president, added, 'Don't you attempt to start a steamship line of your own. If you do, we will run you off the Pacific'.[28]

Fairfield's, left with the redundant Cunarders, informed Dodwell that it was willing to re-enter the Pacific trade if he could find a suitable rail connection. (Almost all the Pacific steamship lines inaugurated in the late nineteenth and early twentieth centuries were controlled by railway companies.)[29] Dodwell thereupon cabled J. M. Hannaford, the traffic manager of the Northern Pacific Railroad, who jumped at the idea of forming an alternative service. Branch offices were soon established at Victoria and Tacoma. Unwilling to await the preparation of the Cunarders, Dodwell chartered the Scottish Oriental company's largest coasters to begin his new line. The Northern Pacific Steamship Company, as it came to be known, proved ten times more profitable to Dodwell's company than the Empress Line could have been, according to the memoirs of J. P. Dowling, who acted as his personal secretary and stenographer when working at the Pacific coast branches.[30] Whereas the Empresses carried only 2,580 tons deadweight and the CPR would not add extra steamers when the volume of passengers was small in the autumn and winter, the NPSS regularly chartered extra steamers when cargo was plentiful, running up to twelve vessels at any one time. This concentration on the carriage of freight rather than passengers was seen as an important element in his success.[31] The Pacific trade contributed greatly to the turnover of $20 million achieved by Dodwell Carlill in the first six months of trading from May 1891.[32]

The successful expansion of Dodwell's shipping agency work was aided considerably by the political and economic events of the last decade of the nineteenth century. Throughout this period the sizeable emigrant traffic in Japanese contract labour to Hawaii profitably filled the steerage of many of the trans-Pacific vessels chartered by Dodwell's. The Sino-Japanese war of 1894 saw the firm in an unaccustomed role of ship broking. The Japanese company Nippon Yusen Kaisha asked Dodwell to arrange the purchase of vessels for its fleet, at a commission of 5 per cent. The forty-three steamers which Dodwell purchased on their behalf brought in £80,000.[33] The Gold Rush to Alaska, with its demand for shipping space for gold prospectors and their stores, added yet further business. Dodwell's sponsored the incorporation of the Washington–Alaska Steamship Company, by the purchase of a two-thirds share in the SS *City of Seattle*. Making round trips between Puget Sound and Alaska in ten days, she grossed between $20,000 and $25,000 per voyage, paying a 400 per cent dividend on the initial investment over four years. This service was extended with the acquisition of an inland water steamer, the *City of Kingston* and a sternwheeler, the *State of Washington*. An associated railway venture, the Chilcoot Railway & Transport Company, designed to extend the line of communications to include the Klondike gold fields, was less successful. Dodwell Carlill & Co. invested two lots of $50,000 in the construction of a wire tramway. It took so long to build that by the time of its eventual completion, in 1899, much of the equipment and supplies had already been carried to the goldfields by human packers. Meanwhile the construction of the White Pass Railroad twelve miles to the south threatened to put the tramway out of business. The Company's investment was recovered, however, when the tramway was sold to White Pass under the threat of reducing the rate to render the railroad uncompetitive.

Dodwell's even managed to make the best out of a crushing duty of ten cents per pound imposed on tea imports by the US government. Fairfield's had just added the Guion Line *Arizona* to the NPSS fleet. With luxurious passenger accommodation, she was the largest vessel then on the Pacific. The duty was imposed, effective in thirty days, whilst she was crossing the Pacific westwards; so on her arrival in Japan she discharged her entire cargo and turned round loaded to capacity with tea, arriving at Tacoma a day before the duty came into effect, and achieved record earnings of six cents a pound.

The supply of vessels to the US military and naval authorities proved especially profitable. The outbreak of the Spanish-American War and the destruction of the Spanish fleet in Manilla Bay resulted in a frantic search by the US War Department for steamers to transport troops and supplies to capture the city of Manilla which was strongly garrisoned by 60,000 Spanish troops. Dodwell hesitated to break the neutrality laws, turning down an offer of fifteen cents per register ton daily (later increased to twenty cents) for the charter of the entire NPSS fleet. Dodwell's brother Fred, who had arrived at the Tacoma branch in 1898, by-passed the neutrality laws through the American embassy in London, by incorporating the North American Steamship Company, with a nominal capital bond issue of $1½ million, for the purchase of the NPSS fleet. Control of the fleet was maintained, for, although aliens were limited to the ownership of only 20 per cent of stock in an American corporation, the law imposed no restriction on bond issue. All the vessels were immediately chartered to the War Department, at rates varying between $250 a day for the *Batavia* and $350 for the *Victoria*. The large *Arizona*, which was too capacious for the Pacific trade, especially after the increase in the tea duty, was sold to the US War Department for $600,000. Dodwell's continued thereafter to cash in successfully on the changing economic fortunes at the Far East end of its trade. It took a financial interest in three steamers with James Chambers & Co. It helped in the creation of a new port for tea shipments from Japan, Keelung, which avoided the expense of transhipment to Amoy. And it acted as the exclusive agent for the chartering of ships by the Japanese government during the Russo-Japanese war of 1904–05. Its Japanese trading business contined to expand, with the export of coal from Japan to Singapore and Shanghai, and the shipment of Japanese straw braid from Kobe for Europe. Dodwell's also helped with the opening of a new port, Yokkaichi, for the export of Japanese porcelain. This became a direct port of call, saving transhipment from Nagoya.[34]

George Benjamin Dodwell retired from the East in 1899, to return to London and complete successfully his plan for the transformation of his business into a limited liability company. This reorganisation provides a detailed insight into the sources and nature of its capital structure and a consolidated picture of its earnings. The first register of members of Dodwell & Co. Ltd records the names, addresses and occupations of the first group of shareholders investing in the company on 17 January 1899, the first day of issue. It is clear that from the beginning existing employees of the company were responsible for a substantial amount of the capital. Of the thirty-two persons listed, twenty-two were directly associated with Dodwell's. The senior partners of the old firm became the majority shareholders: A. J. H. Carlill, Frederick D'Iffanger, Dodwell himself, Fred Dodwell, G. S. Melhuish, E. S. Whealler and G. S. Thomson, who were mainly branch managers, invested over 80 per cent of the total paid-up capital on that day. Mercantile assistants, clerks and book-keepers of the firm also availed themselves of the £25 shares. The firm's *compradore* at Hong Kong, Lim Pong Poo, purchased 100 shares, and his opposite number at Shanghai, Tong Chung Lane, bought twenty. Investors not already associated with Dodwell's were accountants, merchants and married women, who invested a total of £183. Of these initial investors, 47 per cent of the capital was derived from London, 11 per cent came from Hong Kong, 27 per cent from Shanghai, 11 per cent from Kobe and Yokohama, and the remainder from the American ports of Tacoma and Seattle. Further investments followed, so that by 23 March 1899 £47,650 of the total nominal capital of £100,000 had been paid up. The high proportion of investments from within the company itself remained. In opting for limited liability the original founders were thus not necessarily seeking to gain outside investment. The advantage of the new arrangement lay in the fact that each shareholder's liability in the event of bankruptcy was limited to his or her original investment, however large or small.

Dodwell immediately put down £1,067 and Carlill £554, giving an indication of their personal wealth, their confidence in the new firm, and their expectation of future growth and diversification.[35] This confidence was justified: that Dodwell's achieved a turnover of $90 million in its first six months has already been noted. The first year of trading of the limited company resulted in a profit of over £25,000, from which a dividend of 10 per cent was paid to shareholders.[36] This profit is especially remarkable in view of the fact that the company's branches were often run by only one or two persons, sometimes sharing an office with another firm, and helped by a few loyal *compradores* and other local labour. On its foundation in 1891 Dodwell's had similarly had only twenty full-time European employees.

The performance of the company over its first decade is analysed in table 4. The Russo-Japanese war stimulated profits at Shanghai, Hong Kong, Yokohama and Kobe: the former two ports achieved the highest totals for the decade, equalling 68 per cent of total profits. At Shanghai the main preoccupation of the branch was the export of tea and other produce, the import of Manchester piece goods, and ship's agency business, before it began, in the 1920s, dealing with machinery and electrical goods. Shipping was the principal activity of the Hong Kong office, which entered trading and agency business on a large scale in the early decades of the twentieth century, investing in local electrical and dock companies. The war with Russia doubled the profits of the Yokohama branch and increased the Kobe office's profits fivefold, especially on account of the Japanese navy's need to lay in large reserves of Cardiff coal. When hostilities ceased, these branches supplied and fitted out several tramp ships to return Russian prisoners from Japan to Odessa. The engineering concern of Mosle & Co. was acquired in 1906 as part of an unsuccessful policy of expansion,

Table 4. *Declared profit per year, before payment of dividend, of Dodwell & Co. Ltd: earnings per branch (£ sterling)*

Branch	1899	1900	1901	1902	1903	1904	1905	1906	1907	1908	Totals
Shanghai	7,391	7,677	4,987	4,459	12,187	12,375	5,729	7,092	12,187	4,010	78,094
Hong Kong	6,398	18,553	12,249	3,408	6,410	7,020	8,238	9,360	7,769	4,795	84,200
Yokohama	124*	251	3,246	6,927	5,520	14,482	8,089	5,140	2,754*	2,297*	38,480
Kobe	2,312	7,059	2,906	1,328	2,404	12,056	6,184	1,036	1,349*	4,735*	29,201
Tacoma	4,505	8,122	3,138	289	2,072	2,373	4,946	3,294	3,647	3,419	35,805
Portland	1,655	3,601	355*	–	–	–	–	–	–	–	4,901
Seattle	859*	1,164	836*	–	–	–	–	–	–	–	1,187
Victoria	77*	2,821*	546*	235*	554	338	788	1,665	1,808	1,857	3,331
Vancouver	292*	–	300	–	–	-	–	–	–	1,395*	1,387
Foochow	–	–	–	500	–	294*	3,596*	1,746	1,359	1,855*	2,140
Colombo	–	–	–	444	173	563	7,021*	2,039	1,861	2,312	371
London	2,692	7,872*	11,718	10,600*	12,582*	6,801*	2,511*	13,781*	4,075	1,944	33,718
Totals	25,319	35,734	36,807	6,520	16,738	42,112	20,846	17,591	28,603	8,055	238,325
Dividend (%)	10	10	10	10	10	10**	10	15	20	5	
Balance for next year	5,319	8,592	10,400	11,920	12,159	16,272	16,938	19,779	22,233	23,790	

*Losses **In addition, shareholders received a bonus of £2 10s per share.
Source. DOD 3/1, reports and accounts, frontispiece.

resulting in heavy losses, but these branches flourished again with the advent of the first world war.

At Foochow, where Dodwell & Co. held their only agency in the Far East for the Blue Funnel line, the export of tea was the main preoccupation: profits were accordingly reduced when public taste increasingly switched to Indian teas. The Colombo branch concentrated on the sale of Ceylon teas to Russia, and the export of cinnamon, cocoa beans and coconut products. The losses of 1905 were the result of heavy investment in the Malacca Rubber Plantations Co. Ltd, of which Dodwell himself was chairman; but the branch soon recovered and its profits rose.

In the Far East trade generally the expansion of Dodwell & Co.'s business was based mainly on the homeward-bound trades, a distinction which emerged in the discussions of the Royal Commission on Shipping Rings of 1909. The outward trade of manufactured goods from the UK employed regular liners for high-value, low-bulk goods. These items were usually sent in many small packages requiring a speedy passage. Liner services had only a limited need for the work of the shipping agent, as their lines and departures were well advertised and merchants could thus approach them direct. The greatest scope for profits for shipping agents was derived from organising whole shiploads of bulky, seasonal goods on board tramp steamers, which relied on the agent for local knowledge of commodities and merchants, for the shipment of homeward cargoes from the East.[37]

Of the Pacific branches, Tacoma made steady profits as the base of the steamship line, and especially through its association with a successful flour milling business. The Seattle office became fully established only through a huge demand for timber after the Yokohama earthquake of 1923. The Vancouver office did relatively little business in the first decade of the firm, but was to gain important shipping agencies, such as Norddeutsche Lloyd and services to South America. The Victoria branch recovered from early losses and developed a solid shipping agency business. The profits of the London branch fluctuated according to the demand for UK goods all over the world. In 1901 it reaped the benefits of the Underwood typewriter agency, which gave it exclusive marketing rights throughout China and Japan. The personnel of the London branch were well known at the Baltic Exchange, where their main occupation was to arrange tonnage to fill Dodwell & Co.'s runs on the New York berth, mainly with vessels owned by James Warrack & Co., James Chambers & Co., Barber Steamship Lines and Gellatly Hankey Sewell & Co., all companies with which Dodwell's had had a long and close association.[38] It must be emphasised that Dodwell's profits were largely derived from its function as agent only, although, as stated earlier, it did occasionally take a financial interest in a venture.

The role of George Benjamin Dodwell in the expansion of British Maritime activity in the Far East, through his capacity as a shipping agent, may be regarded as remarkable. Not only did he contribute to the increased profits of the shipping department of his firm, Adamson Bell & Co., but he played a prominent part in the shipping world as a whole, shown by his selection as a witness to the 1909 Royal Commission on Shipping Rings. He assisted in the expansion of his firm's trade with Japan, and one of his greatest achievements was the inauguration of a Pacific steamship service which was to lead to a vast business in passengers and freight from the Far East to American and Canadian ports on the Pacific. In assuming the direction of his firm after its bankruptcy, he continued expanding his activities, despite losing the CPR agency. His position as a shipping agent, rather than as a ship owner or shipbuilder, enabled him to take a short-term interest in many varied commodities and services on a surprisingly small capital base; as a constant middleman he was not tied to a particular company, port or commodity, and could spread his risks widely. As an international marketing and shipping organisation the Dodwell group today, with branches in seventeen countries, thrives on the same approach.

Notes

1 These include Kwang-Ching Lui, 'British–Chinese steamship rivalry in China, 1873–1885', in C. D. Cowan (ed.), *The Economic Development of China and Japan* (1964), pp. 49–75; G. C. Allen and A. Donnithorne, *Western Enterprise in Far Eastern Economic Development* (1954); S. Marriner and F. E. Hyde, *The Senior: John Samuel Swire, 1825–1898* (Liverpool, 1967); F. E. Hyde, *Blue Funnel: a History of Alfred Holt and Company of Liverpool, 1865 to 1914* (Liverpool, 1956), and *The Far Eastern Trade, 1860–1914* (1973); D. R. McGregor, *The China Bird: the History of Captain Killick and One Hundred Years of Sail and Steam* (1961); and M. Keswick (ed.), *The Thistle and the Jade: a Celebration of Jardine, Matheson & Co.* (1982).

2 A notable exception is P. Davies, *Henry Tyrer: a Liverpool Shipping Agent and his Enterprise, 1879–1979* (1979); a coastal trade shipping agent is discussed in S. Ville, 'James Kirton, shipping agent', *Mariner's Mirror* 67 (1981), pp. 149–62.

3 Dodwell & Co. Ltd was acquired by Inchcape & Co. Ltd in 1972, and its archives are now housed in the offices of Inchcape PLC, 40 St Mary Axe, London EC3A 8EU. There is relatively little published material relating to the history of Dodwell's, except for an in-house account, *The House of Dodwell: a Century of Achievement, 1858–1958* (1958); chapter 13 in P. J. Griffiths, *A History of the Inchcape Group* (1977), pp. 153–62; a short summary appears in A. Wright (ed.), *Twentieth Century Impressions of Hong Kong, Shanghai and other Treaty Ports, etc.* (1908); references also occur in the shipping press, e.g. *Syren and Shipping*, 3 December 1947.

4 See Cowan, *op. cit.*, and Allen and Donnithorne, *op. cit.* On Japan, see W. W. Lockwood, *The Economic Development of Japan — Growth and Structural Change, 1868–1938* (Princeton, N.J., 1954); G. C. Allen, *A Short Economic History of Modern Japan* (1962); J. R. Black, *Young Japan: Yokohama and Yedo* (1880–81); W. G. Beasley, *The Modern History of Japan* (1981).

5 McGregor, *op. cit.*, p. 66. Other shipping firms in the Far Eastern trade are discussed in G. Blake, *The Ben Line: the History of a Merchant Fleet, 1825–1955* (1956), and J. F. Gibson, *Brocklebanks, 1700–1950* (Liverpool, 1953).

6 See n. 2.

7 DOD 5/3, miscellaneous file including correspondence to and from G. B. Dodwell, 1872–1925.

8 *Royal Commission on Shipping Rings, Parl. Papers*, 1909, XLVIII, evidence of G. B. Dodwell, qq. 18872–80.

9 Allen and Donnithorne, *op. cit.*, p. 23. See also S. R. Brown, 'The transfer of technology to China in the nineteenth century: the role of direct foreign investment', *Journal of Economic History*, 39 (1979), pp. 181–97.

10 DOD 6/3, notebook of G. B. Dodwell, pp. 104–6.

11 See Kwang-Ching Lui, *op. cit.*, pp. 49–75.

12 DOD 6/3, notebook of G. B. Dodwell, pp. 120–1.

13 Arrangements were made annually in London by Adamson Bell & Co. in conjunction with the American firm Russell & Co. (later to become Shewan Tomes & Co.) with steamship owners interested in the trade from China and Japan to New York.

Dodwell's evidence, *R.C. on Shipping Rings, op. cit.*, q. 18776.

14 A. S. J. Baster, 'Origins of the British exchange banks in China', *Economic History*, III (1934), pp. 140–51.

15 See Pao Kuang Yung, 'The *compradore*: his position in the foreign trade of China', *Economic Journal*, 21 (1911), pp. 636–41; Yenp'ing Hao, *The Compradore in Nineteenth Century China: Bridge between East and West* (Cambridge, Mass., 1970); and T. Rawski, 'Chinese dominance of Treaty Port commerce', *Explorations in Economic History*, 7 (1969–70), which includes a revisionist view of *compradores*.

16 Marriner and Hyde, *op. cit.*, pp. 115–17.

17 This company, now known as Gellatly Hankey & Co. Ltd, was acquired by the Inchcape group in 1983.

18 McGregor, *op. cit.*, p. 180.

19 Allen and Donnithorne, *op. cit.*, p. 23.

20 *Japan Weekly Mail*, Shipping Intelligence at Yokohama, 1878.

21 *North China Herald*, Shipping Arrivals and Departures at Shanghai, 1883.

22 Allen and Donnithorne, *op. cit.*, p. 200.

23 *Japan Mail Summary*, Shipping Intelligence at Yokohama, 1889.

24 *Ibid.*, 1892.

25 *R.C. on Shipping Rings, op. cit.*, qq. 18787–9.

26 DOD 5/2, letters and memoirs relating to the history of the company, miscellaneous.

27 Marriner and Hyde, *op. cit.*, p. 123.

28 DOD 5/3, memo written on the death of Dodwell by A. J. H. Carlill. See G. Musk, *Canadian Pacific: the Story of the Famous Shipping Line* (Newton Abbot, 1981).

29 *R.C. on Shipping Rings, op. cit.*, qq. 18947–8.

30 DOD 5/1, letters and memoirs relating to the history of the company, miscellaneous.

31 *R.C. on Shipping Rings, op. cit.*, q. 18944.

32 DOD 5/1, memoirs of J. P. Dowling.

33 *Ibid.*

34 *Ibid.*, memoir of O. M. Poole.

35 DOD 1/24, share ledger No. 1, 1899. Dodwell's personal wealth is shown by his beneficent donations and foundations — see his obituary in the *West Herts and Watford Observer*, 12 October 1925. The Probate Registry records that he left £77,860.

36 DOD 3/1, reports and accounts from 1899.

37 A. W. Kirkaldy, *British Shipping: its History, Organisation and Importance* (1914), pp. 189–91.

38 Dodwell & Co. Ltd, *The House of Dodwell, op. cit.*, p. 14.

This article forms part of a larger study of the history of the Inchcape group of companies, to be published by Macmillan in 1986. A slightly amended version was presented at Professor T. C. Barker's seminar in Modern Economic and Social History in autumn 1984 at the Institute for Historical Research, London.

7 The depression in British shipping, 1901–11

DEREK H. ALDCROFT

EW industries have been subject to such violent fluctuations in fortune as the shipping industry. One year's trading has never been a very satisfactory guide to the next, and on balance the bad years have outnumbered the good. In the 45 years before 1914 the number of poor years exceeded the prosperous ones by two to one.[1] This may not at first seem surprising, as the period includes the years of the Great Depression (1873–96) when trade and industry were relatively depressed. The fact is, however, that nearly one-third of the bad years occurred in the early twentieth century, a time when the rest of the British economy was by all accounts fairly buoyant. Between 1901 and 1911 the shipping industry remained in a depressed state [2]—so depressed in fact that it has been referred to as the first major international shipping depression.[3] That the industry should display contrary tendencies to the rest of the economy is interesting and requires further examination and elucidation.*

Freight rates began to decline towards the end of 1900, and by 1901 many rates had fallen to 50 per cent below those ruling in the autumn of the previous year. During the next few years freights remained heavily depressed, though a very slight recovery seems to have occurred in 1906 and the early part of 1907. Then between 1907 and 1908 freights fell again, this time to the lowest level for over fifty years, and according to Angier 1908 was a year of "unexampled depression in all freights both outwards and homewards".[4] By the end of 1909 the worst was over, but in the following years freights only recovered slowly, and it was not until 1912 that they again reached the level of 1900.[5]

It is dangerous, of course, to attach too much importance to the tramp index as a measure of prosperity of the shipping industry as a whole. For one thing the Isserlis freight index, which is the only comprehensive index available for this period, does not include liner rates (both passenger and cargo) which for various reasons tended to be more stable, nor does it differentiate between outward and homeward trades. Cairncross has broken down and reworked the available indexes (namely those of Hobson, Isserlis, and the Board of Trade) so as to take some account of liner rates. It is clear from his calculations that outward freights were maintained at a much higher level than inward freights throughout these years.[6] This is largely what one would expect. The inward trades were always highly competitive, since the cargoes

---

* This is part of a longer study of the British shipping industry in the nineteenth and early twentieth centuries which is being carried out by the author.

moved in this direction have been particularly suited to the tramp vessel.[7] As a consequence liner conferences, which helped to maintain rates in the outward trades, have made little headway in the opposite direction. Secondly, it should be remembered that freight rates generally were falling almost continuously throughout the latter half of the nineteenth century, and it is not always possible to determine how far this was due to changes in the supply of and demand for tonnage and how far it merely reflected changes in the cost of transport due to technical progress. If anything, however, costs of operation seem to have been rising in the first decade of the twentieth century. Finally, it is as well to point out that freight rates had been severely depressed for most of the 1890s, so that the boom of 1899–1900 can be regarded merely as an interruption to a long period of depression. On the other hand, it is easy to explain the setback of the 1890s in terms of the general recession in the economy as a whole, whereas for the period 1901 to 1911 there is no such obvious explanation.

Shipowning was still far from being a profitable occupation in these years, even when allowance is made for the limitations of the freight index and account is taken of the fact that outward freights were fairly well maintained. The profitable operation of shipping is very much dependent upon adequate cargoes in both directions, and it is abundantly clear that a sufficient volume of cargo of a remunerative character was not forthcoming in the homeward trades at this time. Indeed, contemporaries were in no doubt as to the severity of the depression. Angier's report for 1902 noted that "the result of the past year's trade, as far as 80 per cent of British shipping is concerned, is an absolute loss to the vast majority of ships, or at best the bare covering of out-of-pocket expenses. Of the remaining 20 per cent of the tonnage, consisting of "liners" proper, only the few most favoured companies have done well—viz., those with good mail contracts.... and the small 'set' in the run of Government transport work. The balance has shown but small profits, and many are in a far from strong financial position."[8] The next two or three years were as bad, if not worse. Losses continued to be made in many trades, and in some cases freights failed to cover even operating expenses, as a result of which "the financial position of a vast number of fleets of liners as well as cargo boats is at present very weak".[9] The slight revival in 1906 proved transitory. By 1908 shipowners all over the world were said to be making losses, and much tonnage was laid up. At the end of the year between 1½ to 2 million tons gross of tonnage lay idle, over half of which belonged to Britain. One German company, the Hamburg-Amerika, had an average of 136,000 tons gross laid up during 1908. Sir Walter Runciman estimated that in 1908 dividends of British shipping companies dropped by £25 to £30 million and that shipowners were short of a living freight by £23.5 million.[10] As one shipowner put it: "The prevailing depression in shipping has reached so acute a pitch as to become a grave menace to the national prosperity, and shipowners are face to face with a serious crisis. Unless something can be done to restore a more healthy tone to trade generally, nothing can avert ruin to many".[11]

Those who hoped for a quick revival were to be disappointed. 1909 was another disastrous year, according to Sir Christopher Furness without precedent in the past twenty years.[12] Even by the autumn of that year 738,000 tons gross of shipping were still laid up at the principal ports of the United Kingdom.[13] For many cargo-boat companies it was the worst year ever experienced. The profits of the Nitrate Producers' Steamship Company were the lowest on record, 79 per cent down on 1900.[14] Forty-five of the chief cargo-boat companies paid no dividend and set nothing aside for depreciation,[15] and few companies made sufficient to cover both and make a profit. By this time the rapid fall in earning power of steamers meant that much of the tonnage was over-valued in relation to market value, up to 50 per cent or more in some cases. Second-hand tonnage was selling for a quarter of its former value in many cases, and vessels over 15 years old were now difficult to sell except to the shipbreakers. *Fairplay* maintained that, if all the cargo boat companies had been wound up and the vessels disposed of at the current market price, most companies would have incurred a heavy deficit and shareholders' capital would have been lost.[16]

The following year brought only slight improvement. In July *Fairplay* reported that freights were still not covering working expenses in all cases and that 90 per cent of the cargo boats were not worth more than half their book value, though by this time some companies had already written down their capital assets.[17] Though conditions continued to improve slowly, Angier's report for 1911 struck a dismal note: "it is very doubtful whether the industry taken as a whole has, even in the last year when freights have been on a level higher than in any year since 1900, done more than make by hard work and constant vigilance such a return on capital as could have been made by the investing of a like amount in first class securities, involving no labour or attention".[18] The period of unremunerative freights was finally broken in 1912, when they rose sufficiently to allow shipowners to make a real profit for the first time for more than a decade.

Unfortunately comprehensive profit figures for shipping companies are not available to substantiate the statements above. Many companies did not publish accounts, and those that did often framed them in such a way as to render them almost incomprehensible.[19] Figures in the published accounts require therefore to be handled with a great deal of care. The best data available is that for the earnings (before depreciation) of the principal cargo-boat companies collected by *Fairplay* from 1904 onwards. Nearly 100 companies, owning in all about 1.67 million tons gross (average of the years 1904–14), were covered in the survey. It was found that when allowance was made for depreciation at 5 per cent. and dividends these companies were running at a loss in every year between 1904 and 1911. Even in 1911 over a third of the companies were paying no dividend and setting aside nothing for depreciation. If the analysis is extended to the years 1912 and 1913 the effect of the improvement in freights is at once apparent. In the ten years 1904–13 these companies earned a total of £15,944,843, nearly two-thirds of which was made in the last two years when depreciation was being written off at more than twice the normal rate.

Even so, by the end of 1913 there was still a deficiency of over £1 million on the depreciation account of these companies, and on this basis *Fairplay* estimated that the deficiency for the whole of the cargo-boat fleet was in the region of £7.3 million.[20] If anything, therefore, the selection taken represents the best companies.

No sample analysis has been made for liner company earnings, but data for six companies has been extracted from the published accounts and presented in Table 1. As might be expected, profits (before depreciation) of liner companies were maintained somewhat better than those for cargo boats, though it is quite evident that earnings were depressed during the period in question. Powers of resiliency, however, varied a great deal from company to company, as the profit figures show. Whilst the P. & O. and Cunard to a lesser extent showed fairly high profits, other liner concerns, particularly the Indo-China and the Houlder Line, experienced a dramatic slump in profits. In fact the latter's profits fell continuously from 1900, and in 1907 the company made an absolute loss of £5,155. The financial position of the company was so poor that for six consecutive years (1906–11) it failed to pay a dividend or transfer anything to depreciation.

Total earnings of course tend to give an unduly favourable picture of the shipping companies' fortunes, since they take no account of the expansion in the size of fleets.

TABLE I

Earnings of Selected Liner Companies (£)

	Houlder line	Indo-China Steam Navigation Company.	Cunard	Orient Steam Navigation Co.	P. & O.[b]	Prince Line [c]
1898		112,400	249,406			111,074
1899	82,419	104,792	279,554	102,283		147,893
1900	97,194	188,816	538,080	51,730	900,411	155,886
1901	62,094	148,061	195,849	134,429	520,537	81,604
1902	64,480	59,912	247,150	50,905	848,345	51,189
1903	23,964	38,017	248,563	48,314	828,545	82,435
1904	23,079	120,492	61,588	59,371	758,242	82,287
1905	30,458	106,051	308,182	60,327	808,251	80,267
1906	12,163	5,500	553,193	75,305	733,034	102,569
1907	—5,155	24,226	554,794	90,542	738,655	90,037
1908	9,357	7,489	172,971	69,780 ᵃ	686,239	77,478
1909	21,236	66,565	649,416		655,780	74,362
1910	16,702	88,852	958,158		783,244	135,073
1911	18,500	82,469	815,724		831,776	225,646
1912	91,238	107,177	1,154,197		798,685	443,281
1913					1,014,661	

(a) Basis of calculation changed after 1908.
(b) Year ending 30 September.
(c) Year ending 30 June.

This is particularly so in the case of liner companies, whose fleets expanded rapidly in this period. The P. & O., for example, increased its tonnage by about 150,000 tons in the years 1900 to 1911, and if earnings are divided by the tonnage employed the profitability of the company is much reduced. Earnings per gross ton of the P. & O. fell continuously from the turn of the century until 1909, and even in 1913 they only reached 80 per cent. of the 1900 figure. Table 2 gives an index of earnings per ton for four companies, two liner and two cargo-boat. It will be seen that none of the companies managed to regain their base-year earnings, and in two cases, White Star and the Mercantile Steamship Company, earnings in 1908 were less than 20 per cent. of the 1900 level.

Despite the absence of complete profit data, there seems little doubt that shipping was seriously depressed in this period. As one might expect, the problem was most acute in the cargo section of the industry though some of the passenger liner companies did not escape unscathed. The depression was not confined to this country;

TABLE 2

Index of earnings per ton of four companies

(1900–01 = 100)

	P. & O. Co. (a)	White Star Line	Nitrate Producers' Steamship Company (b)	Mercantile S. S. Co.
1898	64.07	96.65	47.58	78.80
1899	76.34	51.12	66.37	81.42
1900	100	100	53.24	100
1901	62.87	46.08	100	78.14
1902	100.29	53.34	56.20	40.14
1903	87.29	47.89	38.27	21.14
1904	82.63	34.60	25.34	25.41
1905	78.44	49.71	29.82	29.66
1906	69.91	57.74	25.24	29.21
1907	70.80	57.83	22.75	29.92
1908	64.22	18.35	24.82	14.03
1909	60.32	37.57	21.03	16.38
1910	65.12	64.81	25.34	27.55
1911	67.21	58.60	30.00	37.29
1912	64.07	48.08	36.72	75.77
1913	80.09	57.64	78.79	84.80
1914	57.03	45.31	71.55	

Note: P. & O. and White Star per ton gross;
          Mercantile and Nitrate Producers' per ton deadweight.

(a)   year ending 30 September.
(b)   year ending 30 April.

Source: *Fairplay*, 24 Dec. 1914, 1040, and F. C. James, *Cyclical Fluctuations in the Shipping and Ship-building Industries* (1927), 78, Table 1.

as pointed out earlier, it was international in scope. However the evidence, meagre as it is, does suggest that other countries fared less badly and that Britain bore the brunt of the burden. This is by no means an unreasonable assumption, since as she owned the largest mercantile marine it can be argued that Britain had more to lose. Moreover, Britain had a greater proportion of tramp tonnage than other countries, and this section of the industry came off the worst. Finally, it is important to note that British trade, particularly the import component, was growing less rapidly than that of other countries, particularly Germany, the second largest shipowner.

Basically the depression in shipping was due to an imbalance between the available carrying capacity and the volume of world trade. The most pertinent question to answer is how this situation arose.

In the first decade of the twentieth century world tonnage increased at a faster rate than in any decade of the nineteenth century, from 29 million tons gross in 1900 to 41.9 in 1910, an increase of 45 per cent. By 1914 the world fleet was 70 per cent. greater than in 1900, compared with an increase of 62 per cent. in the volume of world trade. Two factors account for this. First, the Spanish-American and Boer Wars gave an artificial stimulus to the industry. Large amounts of shipping were chartered for Government transport service—some two million tons gross by the British Government alone—and this greatly stimulated the demand for new orders. But the extraordinary demands of war had already passed away by the time the new tonnage was completed. As so often happens, "overproduction of tonnage, started in the years of prosperous trade, retains the impetus given to it long after the reaction of the boom has set in, and the effect of the continued overproduction is greatly exaggerated by the ever slow and gradual restriction of trade following the booming times".[21] The net additions to world tonnage continued at a high level during the next few years, since it was at this time that Germany and Japan were rapidly building up their fleets and Britain was renewing her own. Thus the world was already overstocked with tonnage when the crisis of 1907–8 brought an appreciable drop in the volume of trade and passenger traffic. The latter suffered the more severe decline. Between 1907 and 1908 the number of passengers crossing the Atlantic from British and European ports fell from 1,725,736 to 688,885.[22] This was particularly serious for the large liner companies such as Cunard, White Star, and Hamburg-Amerika, which concentrated on the North Atlantic passenger trade. Passenger traffic of the Hamburg-Amerika company dropped from 470,290 to 280,404, and its profits were halved.[23] Cunard lost nearly half its passengers, with an even greater reduction in total earnings.

The crisis did at least bring a halt to the shipbuilding boom, and until 1911 net additions to new tonnage were comparatively moderate. But the damage had already been done. The new tonnage in itself might not have been so bad had it not been for the fact that much of it was far superior to anything which had been built before. The couple of decades before 1914 had seen the completion of the technological revolution in shipping. During that time the bulk of the British fleet was rebuilt.

Of the tonnage on the register in 1913, 85 per cent. had been built since 1895 and 44 per cent. since 1905. These vessels consisted of the largest and most efficient types of ships and were capable of carrying more per ton than the ones they replaced. Hence there would still have been an increase in total carrying capacity had the size of the fleet remained constant. For the fifteen years ending in 1908, Sir Norman Hill estimated the increase in carrying power of the net ton to be in the region of 14 per cent.[24] A rough estimate would suggest therefore that the total carrying capacity of the British fleet was 38 to 40 per cent. greater in 1908 compared with 1900, whilst during the same period the volume of British trade increased by only about 21 per cent.[25]

It can of course be argued that it was the demand rather than the supply side of the equation which was the crucial factor. The imbalance between the carrying capacity and the volume of cargo to be carried was partly a reflection of the uneven growth in British trade. Though trade expanded fairly rapidly, imports increased much more slowly than exports; by 1910 the volume of British imports was only 15 per cent. greater than in 1900, compared with a rise of about 50 per cent. for British exports.[26] In other words outward cargoes were growing far more rapidly than inward ones, a point which is reflected in the index of freight rates. Hence the deficiency in the volume of inward cargoes depressed profit margins. Moreover, there is a further point to bear in mind. The relative ease with which outward cargoes could be obtained encouraged shipowners to keep their vessels running in the hope of acquiring homeward cargoes. This of course only served to worsen the situation by depressing the market even further.

The crisis was aggravated by a number of minor, though not unimportant, factors. For one thing profit margins were squeezed because costs of operating vessels, which had risen sharply at the turn of the century, did not decline with the fall in freights. No satisfactory data is available on costs, but by all accounts coal prices, wages, and insurance premiums remained at a high level compared with freights throughout this period.[27] Intermittent rate wars also reduced earnings in some cases. Despite the existence of freight conferences and passenger pools, rate wars were not uncommon, and according to one author they "sprang up with renewed vigour" in the early twentieth century.[28] Some of them were disastrous to the profits of the companies concerned. The Union-Castle company's profits were seriously depleted when a rate war lasting 18 months broke out in the South African trade in July 1902.[29] One of the most serious of all rate wars occurred in the North Atlantic passenger trade in May 1903 as a result of Cunard's withdrawal from the passenger pool. By 1904 steerage rates had been reduced by two-thirds. Peace was eventually restored in October 1904, though not before the companies concerned had sacrificed most of their profits for that year: Cunard's earnings, for example, dropped from £248,563 to £61,588 in 1904. Altogether it has been estimated that the crisis cost the participant companies nearly £1 million.[30]

Finally the revision of the *Freeboard Rules and Tables* in 1906 added some 1½ million tons of shipping to an already depressed market, though in 1909 it was counter-balanced to some extent by the withdrawal from the market of a certain amount of tonnage due to the adoption of an international load line.[31]

*

Shipowners burned their fingers badly in the depression, yet few lessons were learnt. Certainly after the depth of the crisis (1908) investment in ships was checked and shipowners adopted a more cautious financial policy. The book values of fleets were reduced drastically—up to half in some cases—and the fancy dividends of the boom years 1899–1900 were slashed. Moreover, it seems probable that owners paid more attention to building up depreciation funds in later years. Yet the experience was soon forgotten. Even by the end of 1910 it was said that some were "at the old game of paying dividends which, regard being had to the depreciation of the proper-ty, most certainly have not been earned".[32] During and shortly after the First World War speculation was again rife, and excessive optimism in the boom of 1919–20 produced disastrous results once again.[33] As Gregg observed: "Shipping men, it seems, have never been able to persuade themselves in periods of prosperity that good times would not last always. Overbuilding of tonnage has continually recurred, sometimes coincident with a falling off of the amount of cargo shipped".[34]

One good result of the depression was that it strengthened the inclination of shipping concerns everywhere to compromise and eliminate competition.[35] Sir Christopher Furness, speaking at the annual meeting of Manchester Liners Ltd. in October 1909, felt the time had arrived "when cut-throat competition shall come to an end and reasonable freights be earned on the large amount of capital employed in ships flying the British flag".[36] Other important shipowners such as Booth of Cunard and Ballin of the Hamburg-Amerika endorsed this view, but few were prepared to take positive action on the matter. A strengthening of the conference system is all that seems to have taken place, for attempts to extend the boundaries of co-operation failed. Numerous suggestions were put forward to regulate freights and tonnage, but none were implemented. In October 1907 suggestions for a freight union among tramp owners failed to get widespread support, partly because many tramp owners were also merchants and freight contractors which resulted in a certain conflict of interests in the dual capacity.[37] The most ambitious scheme for regulating tonnage on an international basis was drawn up by J. H. Welsford, a member of the Liverpool Steam Ship Owners' Association. Briefly the proposal was that all surplus tonnage be laid up and financed out of a levy on shipping in full work.[38] Welsford's scheme was of necessity based on voluntary action, and in the absence of general support from shipowners in this country and elsewhere the Association recommended that no action be taken.[39]

One of the most notable features of this period was the number of combinations or mergers which took place among shipping companies. How far this was due to the depression is difficult to say, but there is no doubt that the unfavourable conditions encouraged firms to combine, and Sturmey attributes the numerous mergers of 1912–14 to the lagged responses to the depression.[40] The amalgamation movement seems to have begun in earnest around the turn of the century when two well-established lines, the Union Steamship Company and the Castle line, merged their interests after a period of intense rivalry. Two years later Blue Funnel acquired a controlling interest in China Mutual, their former competitors in the Eastern trade. During the next few years most of the larger liner companies such as P. & O., Cunard, Royal Mail, and Furness Withy were rapidly absorbing other companies. Cunard acquired a large interest in the Anchor line (1911), Furness Withy secured Houlder Brothers (1911) and the Warren Line (1912), whilst in 1914 P. & O. made a still larger catch when it absorbed the British India Steam Navigation Company. The combined group had a capital of £15 million and controlled nearly 1¼ million tons gross of shipping. Perhaps most spectacular of all however was the Royal Mail grouping. In 1903 Sir Owen Philipps, already an established figure in British Shipping, became chairman of the Royal Mail Steam Packet Company, the oldest British steamship line trading to South America. He rapidly raised the line to pre-eminence in the shipping world and brought many other companies within the Royal Mail group. His acquisitions included such notable concerns as Elder Dempster, the Pacific Steam Navigation Company, Union-Castle, and the Glen, Shire and Nelson lines. By 1914 Philipps, who by then was known in shipping circles as the "Colossus of the Seas", controlled one of the largest shipping groups in the world. The amalgamation movement accelerated during and early after the First World War, when many firms were acquired at inflated prices. By the early 1920s about one quarter of the U.K. tonnage was owned and controlled by one of the "Big Five" groups—P. & O., Royal Mail, Cunard, Ellerman, and Furness Withy—whilst about three-quarters of the British liner tonnage was owned by seven large shipping companies.

*

In concluding, perhaps two points might be raised. In the author's opinion the material presented in this paper casts some doubt on the relative severity of the Great Depression (1873–96), at least as far as shipping is concerned. During the first decade of the twentieth century British shipping was more depressed than at any time during the last quarter of the nineteenth century. Admittedly the statistical data on which this conclusion is based is very weak, but what evidence there is does suggest that shipping fared better before 1900 than afterwards. The second point arises from this. As regards the profitability of ship operation, either before or after 1900, we are still groping in the dark, and until more case studies of individual firms are produced we shall continue to do so. So far only one really first-class study of a shipping firm has been produced, namely Professor Hyde's *Blue Funnel*. Surely Britain's nineteenth-century mercantile supremacy deserves a larger contribution than this?

NOTES

1. E. S. Gregg, "Vicissitudes in the Shipping Trade, 1870–1920", *Quarterly Journal of Economics*, Aug. 1921.

2. Cf. F. C. James, *Cyclical Fluctuations in the Shipping and Shipbuilding Industries* (Philadelphia, 1927), 24.

3. Sturmey refers to the period 1904 to 1911: S. G. Sturmey, *British Shipping and World Competition* (1962), 50, n. 1.

4. E. A. V. Angier, *Fifty Years' Freights*, 1869–1919 (1920), 126.

5. This summary is based on the tramp index constructed by Isserlis: L. Isserlis, "Tramp Shipping Cargoes and Freights", *Journal of the Royal Statistical Society*, Part I, 1938, 122.

6. A. K. Cairncross, *Home and Foreign Investment*, 1870–1913 (1953), 174–76.

7. If the figures of vessels sailing in ballast are anything to go by, it would appear that cargo was much easier to obtain in the outward direction. In 1913 the proportion of British vessels clearing in ballast was only half that for those entering: H. Leak, "The Carrying Trade of British Shipping", *Journal of the Royal Statistical Society*, Part II, 1939, 233.

8. Angier, *op. cit.*, 107.   9. *Ibid.*, 111.   10. *Fairplay*, 21 Jan. 1909, 91.

11. *Ibid.*, 3 Sept. 1908, 324.   12. *Ibid.*, 21 Oct. 1909, 564–5.   13. *Ibid.*, 21 Oct. 1909, 564.

14. *Ibid.*, 24 Dec. 1914, 1040.   15. *Ibid.*, 30 Dec. 1909, 927–98.

16. *Ibid.*, 30 Dec. 1909, 927–32.   17. *Ibid.*, 28 July 1910, 109.   18. Angier, *op.cit.*, 132.

19. *Fairplay* maintained that it surpassed the wit of man to arrive at the profit and loss account on shipping: *ibid.*, 13 Jan. 1910, 34.

20. *Fairplay*, 26 Dec. 1912, 1022, and 24 Dec. 1914, 1041.

21. Angier, *op.cit.*, 107.

22. E. Murken, *Die grosse transatlantischen Linienreederei-Verbände, Pools und Interessengemeinschaften bis zum Ausbruch des Weltkrieges — ihre Entstehung, Organisation und Wirksamkeit* (Jena, 1922), 693–97.

23. F. B. Herschel, *Entwicklung und Bedeutung der Hamburg-Amerika-Linie* (Berlin, 1912), 99; cf. P. Lenz, *Die Konzentration im Seeschiffahrtsgewerbe* (Jena, 1913), 91.

24. *Annual Report of the Liverpool Steam Ship Owners' Association for 1909*, 5–6; *Shipping World*, 30 Oct. 1909, 377.

25. Compiled on the basis of information given in *Fairplay*, 25 Dec. 1913, 1066–9. The calculation does not of course include passenger traffic.

26. See A. H. Imlah, *Economic Elements in the Pax Britannica* (1958), 97–8.

27. Angier, *op.cit.*, 124 and 129.

28. E. A. Saliers, "Some Financial Aspects of the International Mercantile Marine Company", *Journal of Political Economy*, Nov. 1915, 921.

29. M. Murray, *Union-Castle Chronicle 1853–1953* (1953), 148.   30. Murken, *op.cit.*, 278.

31. D. H. Robertson, *A Study of Industrial Fluctuations* (1915), 34, n. 4.

32. *Fairplay*, 29 Dec. 1910, 909.

33. See the author's "Port Congestion and the Shipping Boom of 1919–20", *Business History*, June 1961.

34. Gregg, *loc.cit.*, 617.   35. B. Huldermann, *Albert Ballin* (1922), 112.

36. *Fairplay*, 21 Oct. 1909, 565.   37. *Ibid.*, 3 Oct. 1907, 485.

38. *Annual Report of the Liverpool Steam Ship Owners' Association for 1909*, 3–5.

39. *Minutes of the General Meeting of the Liverpool Steam Ship Owners' Association*, 16 Nov. 1909.

40. Sturmey, *op.cit.*, 365.

8 Maritime activity and port development in the United States since 1900: a survey

R. W. BARSNESS

O NE of the most neglected aspects of American transportation history is the development of the nation's seaports. This neglect is both surprising and unfortunate, for ports have played a vital role in the nation's history since colonial days and knowledge of their development can add to our understanding of both ocean and inland transportation as well as regional economic development. Moreover, the handful of books and articles which historians have written about ports pertain largely to the eighteenth and nineteenth centuries.[1] Twentieth-century developments have been left almost entirely to economists and geographers interested in relationships between ports and their hinterlands. Some of these economic and geographical analyses are of excellent quality,[2] but they are not a substitute for history, nor do they purport to be.

The purposes of the present paper are first to call attention to this historical neglect of the nation's seaports in general and twentieth-century developments in particular, and secondly to make a modest start towards remedying this situation by sketching out the broad trends which have characterized port development since the turn of the century. Hopefully, other scholars will become sufficiently interested to undertake detailed investigations of these trends and their components in the near future

CHANGING TRAFFIC PATTERNS

Despite significant short-term fluctuations caused by war, economic depression and extended labour stoppages, the average annual flow of commerce through American ports has increased tremendously since 1900.[3] At the same time, equally significant changes have occurred in the composition of the nation's maritime commerce.

One of the most dramatic reversals to occur during the twentieth century involves ocean passenger service. The coastwise segment of this business began to encounter serious competition from the nation's growing railroad network by the middle of the nineteenth century, and intercoastal passenger service (both via Cape Horn and the Isthmus of Panama) experienced a similar challenge from transcontinental railroads during the late nineteenth century.[4] Nevertheless, combination passenger and package freight vessels were still an important means of transportation between many coastal

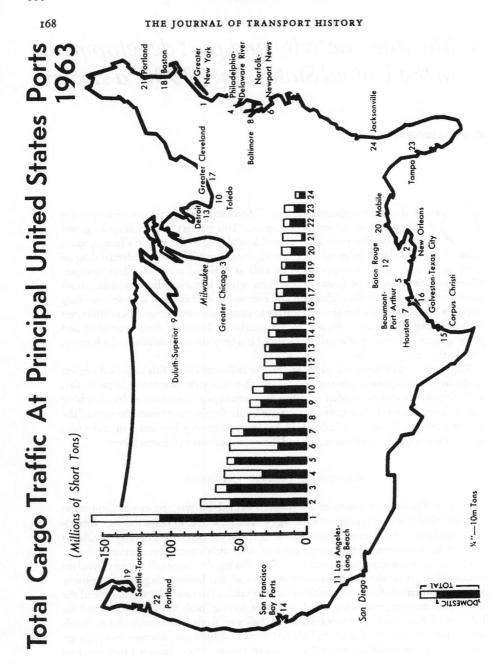

Total Cargo Traffic At Principal United States Ports 1963

(Millions of Short Tons)

¼"—10m Tons

cities at the turn of the century, and remained so until about the First World War or slightly later, when they succumbed to a combination of new federal regulatory legislation, improved railroad passenger and freight service and the rapid development of inter-city motor vehicle transportation.[5] On the Pacific Coast, where nature placed coastal shipping on approximately equal geographical footing with interior railroads, passenger and package freight vessels continued to flourish during the 1920s. However, rising costs and vigorous intramodal and intermodal competition left coastal operators financially weak, and unable to withstand the Great Depression and labour problems of the 1930s.[6] Intercoastal passenger services, which had revived following the First World War because of the presence of the Panama Canal, also became a casualty in 1938.

Overseas passenger service at the turn of the century was dominated by immigration traffic and was heavily concentrated at three American ports – New York, Boston and San Francisco. New York was easily pre-eminent by virtue of the heavy flow of emigrants from Europe (which increased from about 500,000 annually during the 1890s to 1 million annually in the decade prior to the First World War).[7] When wartime disruptions and post-war restrictive immigrant legislation curtailed this traffic, the ocean passenger business became increasingly oriented towards business and pleasure travel. The number of passengers travelling in higher classes rose substantially during the 1920s, and a much better balance was achieved between inbound and outbound traffic.

Ocean shipping in general suffered severely during the Great Depression and passenger traffic was no exception; for example, the number of transatlantic passengers carried by members of the Atlantic Passenger Steamship Conference declined from about 1·1 million in 1929 to only 500,000 in 1933. Yet overseas passenger operators were still better off than their domestic brethren, for the overseas market was not yet subject to intermodal competition. Trans-Pacific and transatlantic air service did begin shortly before the Second World War, but these services were so limited at first that they represented no immediate threat to ocean carriers.

Ten years later circumstances had changed dramatically, for the development of long-range aircraft, improvements in navigational equipment, and increased public confidence in air transportation allowed international air carriers to compete directly with passenger ships. The decade of the 1950s was decisive. In 1950 sea passengers and air passengers bound to or from the United States totalled about 1·1 million for each mode. By 1959 international air passengers had nearly quadrupled to 4·3 million while sea passengers increased only about 25 per cent, to 1·4 million.[8] The dominance of air transportation varied widely from route to route, and on the North Atlantic, where ocean passenger service was particularly well established, the number of air passengers did not surpass the number of sea passengers until 1958. About 80 per cent of the latter moved through the Port of New York.

The relative decline of ocean passenger service during the 1950s became absolute during the 1960s, when ageing, labour-intensive ships were forced to compete against the superior economics and other attractions of commercial jet aircraft.[9] Government operating subsidies and corporate profits from freight operations were no longer adequate to offset passenger ship losses, and firms of all nationalities began to sell, lay up or scrap their older vessels. Ships which remained in service, plus a handful of new vessels, were devoted primarily to cruising services. In fact, by the end of the decade scheduled passenger services had largely disappeared from American ports except for a summer service across the North Atlantic.

Another historic mainstay of port activity which has declined since the turn of the century is domestic general cargo traffic. Intercoastal general cargo movements have fluctuated more than coastwise traffic (primarily because of the opening of the Panama Canal), but ultimately both domestic trades succumbed to similar adverse circumstances. Domestic shipping operators have been protected by law against foreign flag competitors since since the early days of the Republic; however, no protection existed against competition from other modes of domestic transportation. Chronologically, railroads were the first of these competitors to develop, followed by pipelines and motor trucks. Yet the competitors were not always anxious to compete, as evidenced by the fact that between the Civil War and the First World War railroads repeatedly used their superior financial resources to purchase, lease, or otherwise neutralize both inland and ocean competition. This situation was terminated by the Panama Canal Act of 1912, which made it illegal for railroads to own or control inland, coastwise or intercoastal water carriers with which they did or might compete.[10] The Panama Canal Act was welcomed by mercantile interests in many American port cities, but the results were not always those which proponents of the legislation had predicted, for when forced to compete with water carriers, the railroads did so vigorously with selective rate reductions, reluctance to interchange traffic, and other measures designed to make life difficult for the water carriers.

Two additional factors hastened the secular decline of coastwise and intercoastal general cargo traffic. The first of these consisted of disruptions resulting from two world wars. A severe shortage of shipping capacity at the start of both conflicts necessitated large-scale diversion of vessels from domestic to overseas service, and also during the Second World War scores of domestic vessels were sunk by German submarines. With normal coastwise and intercoastal services either sharply curtailed or suspended, traffic was forced to move by other modes especially rail, where in many cases it remained when peace returned.[11] Paradoxically, emergency shipbuilding measures during the latter stages of the First World War created severe overcapacity in the interwar domestic fleet which, together with the depression of the 1930s, led to such a sharp reduction in freight rates that many coastal operators found it impossible to survive.[12]

The second factor has been the dismal state of labour-management relations which has existed in the American maritime industry since the early 1930s. Unlike the railroad industry, where massive strikes in recent decades have been both relatively infrequent and of short duration, the maritime industry has suffered repeated shutdowns of much of the fleet and entire coastal areas for extended periods of time.[13] Exporters and importers have been able to avoid strike-prone American flag vessels by using foreign flag carriers, but have not been able to avoid using American ports on any significant scale. Thus, strikes by longshoremen have served more to interrupt and defer foreign commerce than to drive it away from American ports. Coastwise and intercoastal shippers, on the other hand, have been able to minimize disruptions from maritime work stoppages by turning to other modes of transportation.[14] And since the railroad, pipeline and motor carrier industries proved more effective than the domestic maritime industry in offsetting cost increases with gains in productivity, traffic diversions caused by labour disputes often became permanent.

Between 1939 and 1949 the number of dry-cargo vessels operating in coastal service declined from 235 to 78, while between 1935 and 1952 the number of vessels operating as intercoastal common carriers decreased from 180 to 60.[15] Both trades continued to decline during the 1950s, but the intercoastal segment began to revive during the subsequent decade as a result of containerization. Containers were simply large steel cargo boxes which were designed to carry their contents undisturbed from shipper to consignee, and whose standardized dimensions permitted them to be loaded, stowed and unloaded easily by all modes of transportation and to be transferred readily from one mode to another.

Economically containerization provided a classic illustration of the substitution of capital for labour and the exploitation of scale economies. The costs of building new container ships, specialized terminal facilities and a large supply of containers were more than offset by dramatic reductions in cargo pilferage, damage and handling costs, and lower unit costs resulting from the larger size of container ships and their faster turn-around time and cruising speeds compared to traditional breakbulk freighters.

The first modern all-container ships were introduced during the late 1950s by carriers in the 'offshore' trades between East Coast ports and Puerto Rico and West Coast ports and Hawaii and Alaska.[16] In the early 1960s all-container vessels were placed in service on intercoastal routes where they quickly demonstrated their ability to compete successfully against long-haul motor carriers and the railroads.[17] The striking success of domestic container lines together with the rapid evolution of container technology led in turn to the widespread adoption of container service on foreign trade routes as well. By the early 1970s virtually all American ports were handling containers, although traffic was admittedly highly concentrated at a small number of major ports due to the economics of the system. New York, Los Angeles-Long Beach and Oakland were particularly important, for in addition to playing leading roles in foreign commerce, they also dominated the offshore and intercoastal trades.

Coastwise and intercoastal movements of bulk cargo present a mixed picture during the twentieth century. Lumber and coal were the principal commodities moving in shipload lots at the beginning of the period, and in each case the flow was primarily coastwise rather than intercoastal.[18] As the century wore on, lumber traffic on both the Atlantic and Pacific coasts suffered a gradual decline (first relatively, then absolutely) as a result of the changing geography of the lumber industry and increased competition from the railroads.[19] Coal traffic, which moved from Middle Atlantic ports such as Norfolk-Newport News and Philadelphia to other coastal points, began to decline during the 1920s as a result of the growing use of petroleum, and the situation grew worse with each passing decade.

Petroleum companies had begun to ship crude and refined products by coastal tankers around the turn of the century,[20] but this commodity did not dominate coastwise and intercoastal bulk traffic until after the First World War. Several factors were responsible. On the supply side, the production of crude oil expanded prodigiously with the opening of new fields in Texas, California and other areas far removed from the principal markets. Demand also increased at a phenomenal rate due to the rapid growth of highway and motor vehicle transportation, and the growth in the use of fuel oil for home heating, industrial purposes, and ships' bunkers. Finally, the development of larger, safer and more economical ocean tankers made it feasible to link producing areas in the south-western and western United States with major markets in the north-east.

The largest single flow of bulk petroleum moved from Texas and Louisiana ports to New York and Philadelphia. Another important flow occurred on the Pacific Coast, where vessels carried much of California's large crude oil production to refineries near San Francisco and Los Angeles, as well as refined products from these centres to Seattle, Tacoma, Portland and other coastal points. In addition, surplus production in southern California plus the presence of the Panama Canal led to substantial intercoastal shipments of both crude and refined products during the 1920s and 1930s. Both shipping and receiving ports on all coasts found it necessary to help petroleum companies to develop local pipeline networks, tank farms for storage, and other terminal facilities to accommodate the special requirements of this new traffic.

During the Second World War German submarines operating along the Atlantic Coast gave priority attention to tankers and caused such losses that coastal service was first severely crippled and then suspended. Petroleum traffic was diverted primarily to the nation's railroads, which performed heroically despite a serious shortage of tank cars. In the post-war period, long-distance pipelines have replaced the railroads as the prime competitor for petroleum traffic. When a large, steady flow of products can be assured over a long period of time, pipelines provide an extremely economical means of transportation. They have also proved relatively invulnerable to labour disputes. On the other hand, since tankers require much less capital than pipelines and offer greater flexibility, several dozen vessels have remained active in the post-war domestic petroleum trade, especially between the Gulf Coast and north-eastern United States.

Broadly speaking, America's foreign commerce during the twentieth century has been marked by sharp fluctuations during the early decades, attainment of a position of world leadership during the 1940s, and strong continued growth since the Second World War. Throughout the century the basic pattern and character of the nation's foreign trade have remained remarkably stable, with exports dominated by agricultural commodities and capital goods and imports consisting largely of consumers' goods, tropical agricultural commodities and selected raw materials. Agricultural exports and raw material imports (both of which have relatively low average values per ton) have grown particularly rapidly since the Second World War and have contributed to a sharp decline in the average value per ton of commerce. For example, although the nation's total ocean-borne trade increased from approximately 142·2 million long tons valued at $20·2 billion in 1947 to 404 million long tons valued at $36·1 billion (in constant dollars) in 1966, the average value per ton declined 37 per cent.[21]

The striking growth in raw material imports has been closely related to technological change,[22] the gradual depletion of domestic resources, and liberalization of world trade policies. The principal commodities imported include iron ore, bauxite, chrome, and non-ferrous ores, and above all petroleum. In fact, post-war increases in the consumption of gasoline and other petroleum products such as home heating oil and diesel fuel, coupled with the development of more economical sources of supply in South America and the Middle East, changed the United States from a net exporter to a net importer of petroleum by the late 1940s. Concurrently, petroleum became the leading foreign trade commodity by volume at most American ports. For example, at the Port of New York imports of crude and refined products increased from 13·9 million long tons in 1950 to 24·5 million in 1960 and 38·3 million in 1970. Meanwhile, total general cargo imports at the Port of New York remained essentially unchanged during the 1950s and increased from 7·7 million long tons in 1960 to 9·9 million in 1970.[23] The four principal exceptions to petroleum dominance of ports have been Mobile and Baltimore with large imports of bauxite and iron ore respectively, Norfolk-Newport News, which developed a large export trade in coal following the Second World War, and Galveston, which has specialized in agricultural commodity exports.

Another major change in America's post-war foreign commerce has been the development of large-scale trade with Japan. Significant commercial relations between the United States and Japan began early in the century with Japanese exports of raw silk, and acquired an added dimension during the 1920s and 1930s when Japan imported large quantities of raw materials, including strategic commodities such as petroleum and scrap iron.[24] Nothing in the pre-war picture, however, suggested the volume of trade which was to occur in the post-war period. By 1965 Japan had moved from its traditional deficit position to a surplus in trade with the United States, and ranked second only to Canada in total trade with the United States. Moreover, the steady post-war decline of the American merchant marine meant that trade with Japan moved increasingly in Japanese vessels.[25] The latter became a familiar sight in both major and minor American ports as they unloaded cargoes of motor vehicles, steel products, textiles, electronic and optical equipment, and other consumer goods, and loaded raw materials and agricultural commodities bound for Japan. In some instances new port facilities were built to handle these bulk cargo exports, especially where Japanese purchasers entered into large-volume, long-term contracts with American suppliers.[26]

TECHNOLOGICAL CHANGE

Ocean transportation technology has changed significantly since the turn of the century, starting with the means of propulsion. Sailing vessels still constituted about 20 per cent of the world's merchant tonnage in 1900,[27] but the era of sail was effectively over, and most remaining sailing vessels were replaced by coal-burning steamships by the First World War. The latter in turn soon fell victim to the superior efficiency of oil-burning steamships and motorships. In 1914 oil-burning steamships and motorships comprised only 3·4 per cent of the world's non-sail merchant tonnage, but this increased to 54·7 per cent in 1939 and an overwhelming 95·9 per cent in 1961.[28] The change in power plants had important implications for ports as well as vessel operators, since most American ports did not have equally good access to coal and oil. For example, the Port of Los Angeles, which was handicapped for decades by the lack of economical bunker coal, became a magnet for oil-burning vessels because it had few peers in the world as a port of call for bunker fuel.

Another important change has been a tremendous increase in the average size of oceangoing vessels, especially since 1945. In 1939 most tankers had a capacity of 10,000 to 12,000 deadweight tons, and supertankers about 16,000 tons.[29] Thirty years later tankers of 16,000 tons were considered uneconomic, tankers of 60,000 tons were common and most new construction involved supertankers ranging between 150,000 and 300,000 deadweight tons. Dry bulk carriers did not keep pace with tankers, yet those constructed after the Second World War were also huge, often ranging between 50,000 and 80,000 deadweight tons. In terms of general cargo, the average dry-cargo freighter of 1939 was less than 9,000 deadweight tons, while the container ships which came to dominate this trade during the 1960s typically ranged from 20,000 to 30,000 deadweight tons.

Since relatively few natural deep water harbours existed in the United States, increases in the average and maximum size of cargo vessels required commensurate improvements in approach channels, turning basins, docks, wharves and terminal facilities. At the turn of the century channels 30 ft deep were adequate for virtually all ships in the world.[30] In subsequent decades minimum harbour depths had to be increased to 35, 40 and 45 ft, and even the latter was inadequate to handle some of the largest post-war tankers fully loaded. The cost of breakwaters, channel improvements and related navigation features has usually been borne by the federal government under rivers and harbours legislation, but docks, wharves and terminal facilities have always been the financial responsibility of individual ports and their users. The economic feasibility of port improvements to keep pace with the changing demands of ocean shipping has varied widely from one location to another, but in general even in doubtful cases both the federal government and state and local interests have proved remarkably willing to spend large sums both to help older ports keep pace and to develop modern new ports from scratch.[31]

Finally, significant changes also have occurred during the twentieth century in the handling and carriage of ocean cargo. Most of these changes have sought to improve the efficiency of the ocean transport system (ships, ports and inland transport connections) by making the system more capital-intensive and less labour-intensive.[32] In particular, small and medium-sized general purpose freighters which carried cargo in boxes, crates, barrels, sacks, bales and other packaged forms have been increasingly replaced by large, automated cargo vessels designed to carry a single commodity or narrow range of relatively homogeneous commodities in bulk. For example, in addition to shipload movements of petroleum, coal, iron ore and grain, specialized vessels have been designed to carry bananas, molasses, edible and non-edible oils, steel products, automobiles, liquefied petroleum gases, liquefied sulphur and even wine. And, of course, for all practical purposes general cargo moving in containers is bulk traffic, for container ships and terminal facilities are every bit as specialized as those handling iron ore or petroleum.

The trend toward larger and more specialized vessels has had important implications for American ports. First, as noted above, port officials have been under continuing pressure to widen and deepen navigation channels and enlarge terminal facilities. Secondly, individual ports have found it necessary to build specialized terminals to load, unload, transfer and store large quantities of specific commodities. This situation has frequently presented a dilemma, for specialized terminals are typically both expensive and inflexible and therefore justifiable only when a reasonably steady flow of traffic is assured. Ports lacking specialized terminals have found it difficult to compete for specific types of traffic, yet the presence of such facilities has not guaranteed that traffic will flow, for other factors also are important, especially inland transport routes and rates and the new economics of large specialized ocean vessels.[33]

PORT COMPETITION

Since the turn of the century the distribution of ocean-borne commerce among the nation's ports has been affected by several major developments. First, the tremendous growth of total commerce made it possible for new ports to develop at the same time that older ports continued to prosper. Second, regional economic development in the south-east, south-west and far west caused port activity in those areas to increase faster than the national average. Third, completion of the St Lawrence Seaway in 1959 transformed several major Great Lakes ports into ocean ports as well and attracted cargo which previously moved through other coastal gateways. Finally, on a coastal basis, new concentrations of population and economic activity together with changes in maritime technology, generous expenditures of public funds, and vigorous promotion have made it possible for rival ports to reduce the historic superiority of New York on the Atlantic and New Orleans on the Gulf and actually displace San Francisco as the leading maritime centre on the Pacific Coast.

Although New York has retained its leadership among American ports, its share of total commerce, both foreign and domestic, has undergone a secular decline for nearly a century. For example, in 1870 New York handled 57 per cent of the value of the nation's foreign trade.[34] This declined to 50 per cent in 1900 and 42 per cent in 1922. By the late 1950s New York's share of the value of water-borne foreign trade had dropped to 37 per cent.[35] In terms of the volume of commerce, New York's leadership has always been less pronounced, both nationally and on the Atlantic Coast. Locational and railroad rate advantages, together with other factors, have allowed Philadelphia, Baltimore and Norfolk-Newport News to compete successfully with New York for bulk commodity traffic, and during the 1950s Philadelphia and Norfolk-Newport News occasionally matched or surpassed New York's volume of foreign commerce. But none of these ports has ever matched New York's aggregate foreign and domestic commerce nor effectively challenged its pre-eminence in general cargo. (For the distribution of water-borne commerce by volume among United States ports in 1963, see the accompanying map.) In fact, the greater frequency and range of direct sailings at New York, plus superior banking, insurance, brokerage, and other ancillary services have strengthened its general cargo leadership over rival areas such as New England, where the Port of Boston has essentially marked time during the twentieth century.[36]

On the Gulf Coast several new ports joined nineteenth-century rivals such as Mobile and Galveston to provide additional competition for the Port of New Orleans. The new competitors included Tampa, Baton Rouge, Port Arthur, Beaumont, Texas City, Houston and Corpus Christi. Several of these ports developed along artificial deep-water channels or improved rivers rather than on the coast proper, and all handled primarily bulk cargo, especially petroleum. For example, Houston, the most important of these new ports, developed at the end of the Houston Ship Channel, a 50-mile-long deep-water channel which was completed in 1914.[37] Although Baton Rouge was located upstream from New Orleans on the Mississippi River, and all other Gulf Coast ports had access to the Mississippi waterway system through the Gulf Intracoastal Waterway, the intersection of these two systems at New Orleans helped the city to retain its historic leadership in the trans-shipment of cargo between inland and deep-water vessels.[38] New Orleans has also benefited significantly from excellent railroad connections with a broad hinterland.

The challenge to the established maritime order on the Pacific Coast bore a strong resemblance to events on the Gulf Coast, except that on the Pacific Coast the challenger ultimately prevailed. Phenomenal population and economic growth, rich oil discoveries, and large-scale artificial harbour development during the early decades of the twentieth century allowed the contiguous ports of Los Angeles and Long Beach on San Pedro Bay to match the tonnage of San Francisco Bay ports prior to the Second

World War, and to surpass the latter in both tonnage and value during the post-war period.[39] Most of southern California's post-war maritime growth occurred at Long Beach, where royalties from oil production at the harbour provided port officials with unprecedented capital resources and made it possible to build virtually any port facility they desired, including many specialized terminals. Other historic centres of Pacific Coast shipping activity such as Seattle, Tacoma, Portland and San Diego have grown gradually since the turn of the century, but continue to rank far behind Los Angeles-Long Beach and the ports of San Francisco Bay.

In addition to changes in the regional and coastal distribution of ocean-borne commerce, important changes also have occurred in the location of waterfront activity within port areas. At the turn of the century, when traffic consisted of passengers, package freight, and moderate-sized shipments of general cargo and bulk commodities, port facilities were generally simple and unspecialized and located as near as possible to the central business district of the port city. However, in subsequent decades increases in the total volume of commerce, the proportion of cargo moving in bulk and the size of individual shipments gradually required the relocation of older terminals and the development of new ones in outlying areas where more land was available for transfer, storage and processing facilities, and where rail, highway and barge connections were less congested.[40] In some instances these outlying locations offered better access for ocean vessels, too. For example, activity at the Port of New York has gradually shifted from crowded Manhattan Island to spacious new terminals on the New Jersey shore. At the Port of New Orleans bulk commodity terminals and related industrial facilities have spread from historic waterfront areas to points both upstream and downstream from the city. On the Pacific Coast the Port of San Francisco's location on the doorstep of the business district proved ideal in the nineteenth century but a liability in later decades because of lack of land for waterfront expansion and satisfactory rail and highway access. As a result, port development during the current century has occurred largely at Oakland and Richmond on the east side of San Francisco Bay, and at inland ports such as Stockton and Sacramento.[41]

As statements above have already suggested, competitive relationships among American ports have been influenced by many factors including ease of access for both ocean and inland carriers, frequency and range of direct sailings, availability of both general cargo and specialized terminal facilities, local labour-management relations, adequacy of commercial services such as customs brokerage, insurance, and export-import financing, the level of port charges, and the effectiveness of port promotion by local interests. This last aspect includes advertising, traffic solicitation, public relations and other activities designed to attract cargo to a particular port.[42]

The significance of all these factors has been enhanced by the fact that the most important potential aspect of port competition, ocean and inland freight rates, has been minimized during the twentieth century by the principle of equalization. The objective of this policy has been to equalize total transportation costs (inland plus ocean) between North American and overseas points, no matter which port in a given region handled the traffic. Equalization had its origin in 1877 when major east-west rail-roads sought to avoid excessive competition and arrange an equitable distribution of traffic moving between mid-west origins and North Atlantic ports.[43] Rates to Baltimore were set three cents and those to Philadelphia two cents per hundred pounds lower than to New York and Boston, not so much because Baltimore and Philadelphia were closer to the interior as to offset the higher ocean rates prevailing at those ports. This arrangement essentially stabilized competitive relationships until the turn of the century when ocean carriers adopted equal overseas charter rates for all North Atlantic ports. The rail export differentials designed to equalize total transport costs were narrowed, but not eliminated, thereby giving Philadelphia, Baltimore and Norfolk (which had been awarded the same rates as Baltimore) a rate advantage on shipload movements.

Rail differentials on import traffic varied in detail from export differentials, but had the same broad objective – to offset some of the rate and other maritime advantages enjoyed by New York, and to a lesser extent by Boston. New York and Boston continued to enjoy more favourable berth or liner rates on some traffic movements until the 1930s (when ocean rates to and from all ports in the North Atlantic range were made uniform), but Boston did not really enjoy full parity with New York, for it lacked many of the latter's non-rate attractions.[44] Commercial interests in New York, however, dwelled less on their continuing maritime advantages than on the handicaps which resulted from the rail rate differentials. Consequently, they began a lengthy campaign to eliminate the differentials and re-establish 'true' equalization. After decades of complex litigation, New York and New England interests won their point before the United States Supreme Court in 1963.[45] However, subsequent decisions by the Interstate Commerce Commission appear to have reopened the issue.[46]

Blanket ocean and export-import rail rates also have been adopted during the twentieth century for South Atlantic ports, Gulf ports, and Pacific Coast ports. Moreover, so that railroads, ocean carriers and ports in these different regions would have reasonably equal opportunity to compete for inland traffic, differences in total transportation costs for most overseas traffic have been minimized among these regional groups.[47] As part of this arrangement, the nation's railroads adopted special export-import rate structures which allowed overseas traffic to move at lower rates than domestic traffic between the same pairs of cities.[48]

In some instances equalization has allowed smaller ports (both old and new) to gain traffic because they enjoyed rail and ocean rates which were competitive with larger rivals. In other instances equalization has caused traffic to follow longer routings through larger ports because the minimization or neutralization of rate competition has increased the importance of non-rate factors, and these typically are more favourable at larger ports. Interests seeking to promote or protect traffic at particular ports have complained throughout the twentieth century about specific applications of blanket rates and equalization, yet complaints about disadvantages in specific instances has not meant opposition to carriers these general principles, for and port interests alike have preferred stability to instability and uncertainty in their competitive relationships, and have found a sympathetic audience among federal regulatory agencies for this viewpoint.

Finally, port competition also has been influenced by the wide variety of administrative arrangements adopted at American ports. The public character of port functions and activities was recognized long before the turn of the century,[49] but except for the federal government's uniform jurisdiction over navigable waters, governmental intervention during the nineteenth century was minimal at most ports. Comprehensive public control was established by the State of California over the Port of San Francisco in 1863,[50] but in most coastal cities both ownership of port facilities and effective control of port operations remained in private hands, usually those of the railroads.

Real and imagined abuses of railroad control over ports, together with anti-corporate sentiment generally during the Progressive Era, caused business, agricultural and labour groups in many coastal states and cities to demand that port administration be placed in the hands of public authorities. Some business and civic groups sought merely to increase public regulation of port activities, leaving ownership and operation largely in private hands. Other groups argued that the public character of port facilities and the superior financial resources of government for future development made public ownership the only appropriate solution. Among the latter group, opinion was divided over whether public bodies should operate port facilities directly or lease them under suitable conditions to private parties.

Since decisions regarding port administration ultimately rested with state and local governments, a wide variety of new arrangements emerged during the first quarter of the twentieth century. Some port agencies were organized as a unit of municipal government; for example, the Board of Harbour Commissioners of Milwaukee and the Bureau of Port Operations in Philadelphia. Other agencies, such as the Port of Seattle and the Harris County-Houston Ship Channel Navigation District, were established as public corporations or independent commissions with authority to levy district-wide taxes. Many other port agencies enjoyed substantial independence as a public authority or corporation, but lacked the power to levy taxes. The latter category included units with bi-state jurisdictions such as the Port of New York Authority, statewide jurisdictions such as the Virginia State Ports Authority, and local jurisdictions such as the Board of Commissioners of the Port of New Orleans.[51]

Relationships between administrative arrangements and twentieth-century port development and competition have been complicated by the fact that quite apart from the diversity of administrative structures and political jurisdictions, important differences have also existed in the extent of public ownership and operation of port facilities, in regulatory authority over private facilities, and in the financial capabilities of port agencies. Moreover, at some major ports such as New York, Philadelphia and Chicago administrative authority has been divided for decades between two separate and unrelated port agencies.

CONCLUSION

Port development has been a neglected area of American historical research. To help correct this neglect, this paper has sought to provide an overview of port development in the United States during the twentieth century. These developments have included large-scale growth in total commerce (especially foreign commerce since 1945), important changes in the composition of maritime commerce such as the decline of ocean passenger traffic and growth of petroleum traffic, dramatic technological changes in merchant vessels and cargo handling systems, the appearance of endemic labour-management strife since the 1930s, and increased competition among the nation's ports as a result of regional economic development, construction of new artificial harbours, adoption of the principle of equalization in ocean and inland freight rates, and diverse approaches to port administration and financing. Hopefully these factors as well as others will be the subject of detailed historical research in the near future so that a definitive account of the nation's port development will be possible before long.

NOTES

1. The best bibliographical guide to maritime research is Robert Greenhalgh Albion, *Naval and Maritime History: An Annotated Bibliography*, 3rd edn with supplements (Mystic, Conn., 1963-8).

2. Four good examples of such studies are: Donald J. Patton, *Port Hinterlands: The Case of New Orleans* (College Park, Maryland, 1960); Warren Rose, *Catalyst of an Economy: The Economic Impact of the Port of Houston, 1958-63* (Houston, Texas, 1965); Stanley J. Hille and James E. Suelflow, *The Economic Impact of the Port of Baltimore on Maryland* (College Park, Maryland, 1969); Eric Schenker, *The Port of Milwaukee: An Economic Review* (Madison, Wisc., 1967).

3. Even when figures are available, it is often difficult or impossible to compare port statistics for earlier decades with those for recent decades. Statistics for earlier decades are frequently unclear about the unit of volume employed (long tons, short tons, metric tons or net tons), on the relevant geographical area (individual port, group of adjoining ports or customs district), or the method for determining the value of commerce (especially the impact of price changes). Both foreign and domestic water-borne commerce have their own statistical pitfalls, many of which are discussed in Roy S. MacElwee, *Port Development* (New York, 1926), 109-22.

4. More often than not railroads enjoyed both shorter distances and faster average speeds between coastal cities. To some extent coastwise and intercoastal vessels were able to offset the time advantage of the railroads by charging lower fares or offering greater passenger comfort and service (especially outstanding cuisine) for comparable fares. Neither mode could boast much about safety or reliability. A delightful pictorial history of one segment of the coastwise passenger trade is George W. Hilton, *The Night Boat* (Berkeley, Cal., 1968).

5. For an excellent account of coastwise shipping which held its own against all-rail competition but could not do so against the motor truck, see William Leonhard Taylor, *A Productive Monopoly: The Effect of Railroad Control on New England Coastal Steamship Lines, 1870-1916* (Providence, R.I., 1970).

6. Giles T. Brown, *Ships That Sail No More* (Lexington, Kentucky, 1966), 181-241. This account of coastwise service on the Pacific Coast from 1910 to 1940 is focused on the Admiral Line, which was the leading carrier during those decades.

7. Gunnar Alexandersson and Goran Norstrom, *World Shipping* (New York, 1963), 47.

8. Air Transport Association, *Air Transport Facts and Figures, 1960* (Washington, D.C., 1960), 21. The figures exclude travel over land borders (except Mexican air travel), crewmen, military personnel, and travellers between the continental United States and its possessions.

9. Overseas passenger traffic reached a peak at the Port of New York during the early 1960s, then declined sharply. For example, the total number of passengers was 1,008,143 in 1963 and 1,039,838 in 1964, but dropped to 842,725 in 1969 and 724,101 in 1970. The proportion of total traffic moving on regularly scheduled vessels also declined while the cruise share increased. See Port of New York Authority *The Port of New York Foreign Trade,1971* (New York, 1971), 26.

10. 37 *Statutes at Large* 560.

11. John L. Hazard, *Crisis in Coastal Shipping* (Austin, Texas, 1955), 13–14. This monograph, one of the few which has been written on coastal shipping, is an excellent analysis of Atlantic–Gulf common carrier service.

12. The plight of domestic ocean shipping between the wars is analysed in U.S. Maritime Commission, *Economic Survey of Coastwise and Intercoastal Shipping* (Washington, 1939).

13. One of the most important factors contributing to the distressed state of maritime labour–management relations has been the historically casual nature of maritime employment. Both ship operators and longshore employers have sought to offset their susceptibility to short-term fluctuations by drawing workers as needed from labour pools sufficient to cover peak requirements. For individual workers, both afloat and ashore, this has meant an environment of uncertain employment opportunities, extended periods of unemployment, casual relationships with specific employers, and relatively little incentive not to go out on strike. Joseph P. Goldberg, *The Maritime Story* (Cambridge, Mass., 1958), is an outstanding account of twentieth-century labour–management relations involving seagoing unions, while Maud Russell, *Men Along the Shore* (New York, 1966), is a good popular history of the International Longshoreman's Association. Also helpful because of its highly critical approach is Joseph H. Ball, *The Government-Subsidized Union Monopoly: A Study of Labour Practices in the Shipping Industry* (Washington, 1966).

14. The distressed state of maritime labour-management relations on the Pacific Coast during the 1930s and 1940s is examined in Wytze Gorter and George H. Hildebrand, *The Pacific Coast Maritime Shipping Industry, 1930–1948*, 2 vols (Berkeley, Cal., 1952–4). After additional years of fruitless conflict, labour and management on the Pacific Coast reached an historic "Mechanization and Modernization Agreement" in 1960, which was designed to facilitate technological change at the same time that it stabilized employment opportunities for longshoremen. See Paul T. Hartman, *Collective Bargaining and Productivity: The Longshore Mechanization Agreement* (Berkeley, Cal., 1969), 82–109.

15. D. Philip Locklin, *Economics of Transportation*, 6th edn (Homewood, Ill., 1966), 714–15.

16. For helpful background regarding both foreign and domestic aspects of this new intermodal transportation system, see Robert F. Church, *Background Note on the Development of Containerized International Shipping* (Evanston, Ill., 1968), 1–24.

17. The restoration of intercoastal traffic occurred despite the fact that maritime labour unions (especially longshore unions) prevented the full labour-saving possibilities of containerization from being realized. Whether this opposition can be overcome in the future remains problematical.

18. Intercoastal shipments of lumber were unnecessary during the early decades of this century because regional supplies were reasonably adequate. Coal was relatively scarce on the Pacific Coast, but given the lack of an isthmian canal, it was more economical for Pacific Coast residents to buy coal from British Columbia or Australia than from the eastern United States.

19. Alexandersson and Norstrom, *op. cit.*, 314.

20. Gerald T. White, *Formative Years in the Far West: A History of Standard Oil Company of California* (New York, 1962), 151, 154–7.

21. U.S. Senate, Committee on Commerce, *Hearings on United States Maritime Policy*, 90th Cong., 1st Sess., Serial 90–44 (Washington, 1967), 20.

22. In this context the role of technological change has been multifaceted. In addition to the development of new products requiring new combinations of raw materials, technology also has made it possible to locate and exploit hitherto untapped resources elsewhere in the world and to transport large quantities of these raw materials over previously uneconomic distances.

23. Port of New York Authority, *Foreign Trade, 1971*, 13–22.

24. Walter A. Radius, *United States Shipping in Transpacific Trade, 1922–1938* (Stanford, Cal., 1944), 86–142. Radius' book deals with Asiatic trade from all three coasts of the United States. An excellent contemporary volume which emphasizes the Pacific Coast is Eliot G. Mears, *Maritime Trade of the Western United States* (Stanford, Cal., 1935).

25. Total overseas traffic carried by American flag vessels declined from 81·9 million long tons in 1947 to 29·1 million in 1966. On a percentage basis, American flag vessels carried 57·6 per cent of American ocean-borne foreign trade in 1947 and only 7·2 per cent in 1966. The privately-owned American merchant fleet declined from 1,149 vessels in 1948 to 955 vessels in 1966. Because vessels constructed after the war were larger than those taken out of service, the total carrying capacity of the fleet actually increased slightly from 13,638,000 deadweight tons to 14,766,000. Yet since the rate of new construction was limited, the average age of vessels in the active fleet continued to increase, reaching 17·8 years in 1966. This had many adverse implications in terms of speed, reliability, efficiency, insurance costs, and other competitive features. See U.S. Senate, Committee on Commerce, *Hearings on United States Maritime Policy* (1967), 1–14. For an excellent analysis of the problems plaguing the American maritime industry since the 1930s see Samuel A. Lawrence, *United States Merchant Shipping Policies and Politics* (Washington, 1966).

26. For example, when Japanese interests contracted to buy 1,000,000 tons of southern California iron ore annually for a period of ten years, the Port of Long Beach built a special bulk loader to accommodate this traffic. Unit trains carried the ore from Eagle Mountain to the port. See Port of Long Beach, *Port Ambassador*, 1 no. 3 (1964), 2.

27. Alexandersson and Norstrom, *op. cit.*, 29. Within the American maritime industry, sailing vessels, especially schooners, continued to flourish in the coastal trades for some years after the turn of the century One estimate suggests that two-thirds of the Atlantic coastal tonnage in 1902 consisted of sailing vessels. See Hazard, *op. cit.*, 5–6.

28. Alexandersson and Norstrom, *op. cit.*, 29.

29. J. Bes, *Tanker Shipping* (New York, 1963), 23–5.

30. MacElwee, *op. cit.*, 186–7.

31. Estimates of capital expenditures at individual ports for portions of the twentieth century may be found in United States Department of Commerce, Maritime Administration, *The Economic Impact of United States Ocean Ports* (Washington, 1966), 14–27.

32. Many different parties have contributed to the process of technological change including owners of private (industrial) and common carrier vessels, large shippers, shipbuilders and equipment manufacturers, the U.S. Maritime Administration, and the Department of Defense. The latter has owned and operated some merchant ships since the Second World War as well as provided the largest single source of traffic for the regular merchant fleet. Institutional obstacles to technological change have consisted primarily of labour unions and federal regulatory agencies.

33. Breakbulk vessels during most of the twentieth century typically spent one day in port for every day at sea. Port time was a product of multiple stops on most voyages and relatively slow loading and unloading techniques for general cargo. In contrast, large specialized post-war vessels have had to spend a much higher proportion of their time at sea, for in addition to representing relatively greater capital investment, the limited flexibility of specialized vessels often necessitates backhaul voyages in ballast. To minimize time in port and maximize time at sea, vessel operators have preferred to call at as few ports as possible, ideally loading the entire cargo at a single port and discharging it without delay at a single destination.

An interesting question is whether this preference among shipping operators has had an appreciable effect on the distribution of traffic among American ports. It would be easy to assume that traffic has become increasingly concentrated at a few major ports, yet it may be that specialized facilities have simply provided new ways of handling traffic flows which already were highly concentrated. Moreover, smaller ports have been able to participate to some extent in specialized traffic movements (albeit not involving the largest ocean vessels) as a result of local resources or industrial development together with suitable inland transport rates.

34. Erich W. Zimmerman, *Zimmerman on Ocean Shipping* (New York, 1921), 103; MacElwee, *op. cit.*, 111.

35. Alexandersson and Norstrom, *op. cit.*, 279; Benjamin Chinitz, *Freight and the Metropolis* (Cambridge, Mass., 1960), 18–20.

36. For example, in 1939 some 39 oceangoing steamship lines called regularly at the Port of Boston, but by 1950 only 20 lines offered regular service. See John I. Griffin, *The Port of New York* (New York, 1959), 125–6. An excellent technical analysis of problems affecting the Port of Boston around the turn of the century is Edwin J. Clapp, *The Port of Boston* (New Haven, Conn., 1916). For an interesting non-technical history of the port, including good material on the twentieth century, see Works Projects Administration, *Boston Looks Seaward: The Story of the Port, 1630–1940* (Boston, Mass., 1941).

37. Marilyn McAdams Sibley, *The Port of Houston: A History* (Austin, Texas, 1968), 121–45.

38. After many years of decline and stagnation, river transportation began to revive during the 1920s and became more important with each passing decade. Several factors contributed to this revival including regional economic development, toll-free navigation improvements, minimal federal economic regulation of barge traffic, and dramatic improvements in barge and tow-boat technology.

39. Three articles pertaining to various aspects of twentieth-century developments at San Pedro Bay are: Richard W. Barsness, 'Railroads and Los Angeles: The Quest for a Deep-Water Port', *Southern California Quarterly*, XLVII (1965), 379–94; John H. Krenkel, 'The Port of Los Angeles as a Municipal Enterprise', *Pacific Historical Review*, XVI (1947), 285–97; John H. Krenkel, 'The Development of the Port of Los Angeles', *The Journal of Transport History*, VII no. 1 (1965), 24–33. Helpful references on San Francisco Bay are: Edward Morphy, *The Port of San Francisco* (Sacramento, Cal., 1923); Henry F. Grady and Robert M. Carr, *The Port of San Francisco: A Study of Traffic Competition, 1921–1933* (Berkeley, Cal., 1934); California Legislature, Senate Fact-Finding Committee on San Francisco Bay Ports, *Final Report: Ports of the San Francisco Bay Area: Their Commerce, Facilities, Problems, and Progress* (Sacramento, Cal., 1951); John Haskell Kemble, *San Fransicso Bay: A Pictorial Maritime History* (New York, 1957).

40. The development of the trucking industry has been particularly significant in regard to general cargo traffic. For example, by 1954 no less than 58 per cent of the overseas general cargo passing through the Port of New York was shipped to or from inland points by truck. See Chinitz, *op. cit.*, 41.

41. Other ports, both coastal and inland, have experienced similar relocations. For example, the Port of Chicago's extensive commerce was originally handled along the Chicago River, which joined Lake Michigan in the heart of the business district. At the turn of the century new terminals began to be built along the Calumet River which flowed through a new heavy industrial district about 12 miles south of the Loop. By the Second World War most of the city's shipping had moved to the Calumet area, leaving only scattered operations along the Chicago River and at Navy Pier. See Harold M. Mayer, *The Port of Chicago and the St. Lawrence Seaway* (University of Chicago, Department of Geography, Research Paper No. 49, 1957), 11–13.

42. During the twentieth century many American ports, both large and small, have undertaken organized promotional programmes, including the establishment of offices in selected American and foreign cities. See Marvin L. Fair, *Port Administration in the United States* (Cambridge, Maryland, 1954), 169–79, and Austin J. Tobin, 'A Port's Foreign Representative—What is His Field?', in International Association of Ports and Harbors, *Fourth Conference Proceeding* (Tokyo, 1965), Vol. II, 46–56.

43. At the time export shipments of grain comprised more than 70 per cent of the eastbound tonnage which trunk railroads carried to Baltimore, Philadelphia, New York and Boston. Clapp, *op. cit.*, 85–94.

44. Boston shared New York's proximity to Europe, but suffered along with other Atlantic and Gulf Coast competitors from a heavy excess of exports over imports. This made the port less attractive to ocean carriers than New York and also resulted in a heavy movement of empty railroad cars westward to interior points. See Clapp. *op. cit.*, 98–108, and Griffin, *op. cit.*, 116.

45. Boston & Maine Railroad *v.* United States, 373 U.S. 372 (1963).

46. *Wall Street Journal*, 27 Dec. 1966.

47. MacElwee, *op. cit.*, 250–72. The development of trucking and modern barge service has complicated the rate situation during the twentieth century. Trucking costs are much more sensitive to distance than rail costs, thereby making it difficult for trucking firms to apply blanket rates over equally broad areas. Barge service to inland points has been heavily concentrated at Gulf Coast ports, but wherever it has existed it has had an important impact on railroad rates, especially since most barge rates are exempt from federal economic regulation.

48. Since the opening of the St Lawrence Seaway in 1959, commercial interests in Great Lakes states have waged a largely unsuccessful struggle to get similarly attractive export–import rates established for Great Lakes ports. Opposition has come both from commercial interests associated with Atlantic and Gulf ports, and from the railroads which enjoyed long-haul revenues to those gateways. See U.S. Senate, Committee on Commerce, *Hearings on Great Lakes–St Lawrence Seaway Transportation*, 88th Cong., 2nd Sess. (Washington, 1964), 16–22.

49. J. Grosdidier de Matons, 'Ports as a Public Service: The Evolution in France and in the United States', *Journal of Maritime Law and Commerce*, II (1971), 582–92, 598–603.

50. Gerald D. Nash, *State Government and Economic Development* (Berkeley, Cal., 1964), 106–18. Over a century later, in 1969, control of the then obsolescent port was transferred from the state back to the City of San Francisco. See *Wall Street Journal*, 28 June, 1971.

51. Fair, *op. cit.*, 41–71. This volume is the best single source of information about administrative structures and practices at American ports.

9 The development of the port of Lagos, c. 1892–1946

AYODEJI OLUKOJU

Ports play a crucial role in the conduct of the external trade of any nation that adjoins the sea. This is demonstrated by Africa where 94 per cent of the foreign trade of African countries in 1970 passed through their seaports, a trend that had been sustained since the beginning of the century.[1] Recognising the importance of seaports, scholars have devoted considerable attention to them, producing impressive studies of different dimensions of the subject.[2] Although Lagos, the premier port, occupies a central place in the literature on Nigerian ports and maritime trade,[3] there is as yet no specific in-depth study of the development of the port up to 1950. Only passing reference is made to the earlier period in a study of the progress of the port in the 1950s.[4] Yet recent developments can be appreciated only against the background of the economics and politics of the port during those years.

The port of Lagos, located along the extreme western portion of the Nigerian coastline (see the map), was an infamous outlet for the slave trade of the Yoruba hinterland at the height of the transatlantic traffic. The British occupied it in 1851 with the declared aim of using it as a base from which 'legitimate' trade in forest products could be established in the hinterland.[5] The export trade of the port then comprised essentially palm kernels, palm oil and rubber from the adjoining hinterland. The extension of the Lagos Railway to the important commercial centre of Kano, some 800 miles inland, in 1911, expanded the scope of Lagos exports by the inclusion of groundnuts, cotton, tin, hides and skins.[6] From the mid-1910s cocoa from the densely populated and rich Yoruba hinterland was added to the list of exports. Lagos imports consisted of a wide variety of manufactured goods such as textiles, tobacco, salt, liquor, motor spirit, cigarettes, matches, paraffin and a few non-manufactured items like kola nuts. With the exception of the Gold Coast, from which kola nuts were imported, the suppliers of Lagos imports and recipients of her exports were Asian, European and American

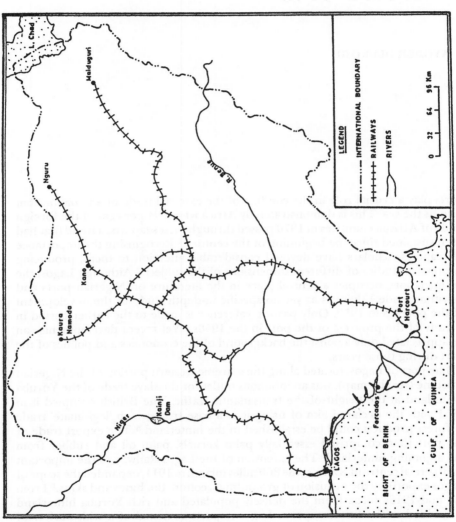

Fig. 1. The port of Lagos and its hinterland

nations. Chief among them were the United Kingdom (the colonial power and chief trade partner), Germany, France, Holland, the United States and Japan.

The value of the import and export trade of Lagos in the period from 1892 to 1914 was substantial, representing on average some 60 per cent of Nigeria's total trade. From 1893 to 1901 the total value of Lagos trade stagnated, being £1,430,651 in the former year and £1,484,402 in the latter. From 1905 rapid growth ensued, the trade increasing from £1,886,636 in 1905[7] to £4,045,609 in 1910.[8] As early as the last date it was observed that 'Immediately on landing at the wharf the stranger who visits Lagos for the first time becomes forcibly conscious of being in the midst of the commercial activities of the country.'[9] As Lagos provided the only natural doorway to the hinterland for over 100 miles of the south-western Nigerian coastline the colonial government decided to develop the port to make it play the leading role in the conduct of Nigeria's maritime trade. This article examines the development of the port in the context of Nigerian economic development. It highlights the dialogue between expatriate business interests and the colonial state in the formulation of port policy,[10] the problems of port working such as slow shipping turn-round and the character of shipping in relation to port development. It sheds light on some aspects of the economic history of Lagos in the first half of this century. For the economic fortunes of the city and the hinterland have varied with the character and volume of the shipping and maritime trade of the port — which were determined to a great extent by physical conditions in the port during this period.

The port of Lagos up to the end of the First World War

Most West African ports lacked natural harbours, as they had shallow entrances, narrow and difficult channels and long approaches from the sea.[11] Given the role of ports in economic relations between colonies and the 'mother' country, the colonial powers formulated policies to improve port facilities in their own economic interest. Such a step was particularly imperative in respect of Lagos, which had a shallow entrance and inconvenient landward access.

The bar at the mouth of the harbour had been the scourge of shipping since Lagos became prominent on the Guinea Coast in the sixteenth century. As early as 1505 Duarte Pacheco Pereira, who called the bar the 'Bugbear of the Bight', had commented upon its adverse effects on the shipping and trade of the town.[12] It continued to hamper trade to the point where navigation through it was temporarily suspended in 1895. The shallowness at the harbour mouth was compounded by silting which reduced freeway to a mere 10 ft in 1899.

The shallow depth of the port entrance, not unexpectedly, greatly endangered shipping. Thus in 1895 alone three steamers — the *Sparrow*, the *York* and the *Lagoon* — were wrecked on the bar to the point of total disablement. The *Gaiser*, another bar steamer, damaged her sternpost and ended up as a hulk in the harbour. These disasters underlined the need for action. Governor George Denton stated in correspondence to the Secretary of State for the Colonies that the record of disasters 'speaks for itself and points out distinctly that if Lagos is to be the port of the future for this part of Africa an improvement in the entrance to the Harbour is a necessity'.[13] He noted that an alternative course of action would be to make Forcados the port of the colony and connect it with Lagos by a railway line. However, the line would have traversed sparsely populated and economically underdeveloped territory. Denton suggested that it would be 'better to spend money on opening the Bar than in building the railroad'.[14]

Earlier, in 1892, the firm of Coode Matthews Fitzmaurice & Wilson had furnished a general description of the port and entrance channels to show how much work was required to produce a minimum depth at the entrance of 21–3 ft at high water. In a subsequent report in 1898[15] the consulting engineers recommended that the harbour works should consist of stone moles or breakwaters of *pierre perdue* construction each side of the harbour entrance and minor subsidiary works. The entire scheme was expected to cost some £897,000. It would involve deepening the entrance channel and portions of the harbour, the extension and strengthening of the existing Customs wharf; the construction of a branch line to Apapa (since the Apapa wharf would deal with stone traffic, railway construction materials, coal and materials for the Lagos waterworks scheme); the erection of quays for ocean steamers and the extension of the railway from Iddo to Lagos Island and Wilmot Point. The first two parts of the scheme were expected to be financed locally, the others by loans guaranteed by the revenue of the colony.

While these long-term plans were being laid the trade of the port of Lagos was being transhipped through Forcados, some 190 miles to the east, in the Niger delta. This, however, was a costly and hazardous business, as it endangered lives and damaged cargo through exposure and poor handling. A citizen of Lagos who later recalled the experience of transhipped passengers during this period remarked that 'Crossing the bar was enough to make the stoutest heart tremble in the old days, and the thought of transhipment was sufficient to give shocks to the strongest nerves'.[16] In addition, transhipment added to the cost of shipping: in 1907 it was said to have increased the freight by 'no less than 12*s* 6*d* a ton'.[17] This was, therefore, considered sufficient justification for 'the steady pushing on with the . . . Scheme for the improvement of the entrance and removal of the Bar which, when effected, will make Lagos one of the most convenient, safe and capacious harbours in the world'.[18]

The proposals submitted by the consulting engineers were, however, considered expensive and, therefore, beyond the means of the colony of Lagos. It was not until 1906 that the Secretary of State provisionally approved the scheme. The first instalment of the works was to be undertaken by the Harbour Department. In May 1907 the dredger *Egerton* arrived and work started on the bar on 30 June

1907. A second dredger, the *Sandgrouse*, which had a lifting capacity of 1,800 tons and a draught of 14 ft, arrived from England in August 1909.

The dredging operations were intended to raise what was called the 'official bar draught' — the maximum draught on which a vessel was permitted to navigate the entrance of the port at high water in clement weather. Rains adversely affected conditions on the bar, as they encouraged shoaling rather than deepening. Moreover, the height of the rains, from June to August, were 'bad bar' months when dredgers could not operate in the vicinity of the bar.[19] On the whole, as is indicated in table 1, there were fluctuations in the Lagos bar draught from 1877 to 1907, when dredging operations started in earnest, but it rarely exceeded 11 ft.

Table 1. *The official bar draught in Lagos, 1877–1907*

Year	Draught	Year	Draught
1877	10 ft–11 ft	1891	10 ft 6 in–11 ft
1884	12 ft	1894	9 ft 6 in–10 ft
1887	12 ft	1895	9 ft–11 ft
1888	12 ft	Jan.–March 1896	9 ft 6 in.–10 ft 6 in.
Feb.–March 1889	13 ft	1897	9 ft 6 in.–10 ft
April 1889	12 ft 6 in.	June 1904	10 ft
Dec. 1889	9 ft 6 in.	July 1905	10 ft
1890	10 ft	Dec. 1905	9 ft 9 in.
Oct. 1890	10 ft 6 in.–11 ft	July 1907	11 ft

Source. N.A.I. CSO 26/1 09896 vol. 1, 'Lagos Harbour Survey, Southern Nigeria', enc. Abridged Report by Mr Coode, dated 24 December 1910, p. 36.

The direct consequence of the shallow depth over the bar was that the port could not be visited by big vessels. Smaller vessels called 'branch boats' were used to convey goods and passengers across the bar. The big mail steamers stood outside the harbour or called at Forcados, from where their cargoes were transhipped to Lagos. The variety of vessels that called at Lagos during this period can be seen in table 2. The branch steamers which actually crossed the bar did not exceed a loaded draught of 13 ft. Indeed, the average draught was much less, given that the official bar draught did not exceed 13 ft before 1907.

In the meantime the expense of dredging the harbour was straining the lean finances of the colony. Expenditure on the scheme up to 31 December 1908

64

Table 2. *Vessels visiting the port of Lagos in the early twentieth century*

| Vessel | Length | | Beam | Depth | Draught | | Tonnage | |
	Overall	Between perps			Loaded	Light	Gross	Net
Mail steamers								
Falaba	392 ft	380 ft	47 ft 6 in.	34 ft 0 in.	22 ft 6 in.	14 ft 0 in.[a]	4,806	3,011
Karina		370 ft	46 ft 3 in.		23 ft 3 in.	15 ft 0 in.[a]		2,538
Burutu		360 ft	44 ft 3 in.		23 ft 3 in.	14 ft 7 in.[a]		2,441
Max Brock	400 ft	385 ft	51 ft 6 in.	28 ft 9 in.	24 ft 6 in.		4,626	2,896
Lucie Woermann	384 ft	365 ft	47 ft 0 in.	28 ft 0 in.	21 ft 0 in.		4,630	2,861
Cargo steamers								
Salaga	397 ft	360 ft						
Benue		360 ft	48 ft 3 in.	23 ft 6 in.	21 ft 9 in.	9 ft 0 in.		
Branch steamers								
Uromi		225 ft	36 ft 3 in.		13 ft 0 in.			554
Gouverneur von Puttkamer		214 ft	30 ft 6 in.		11 ft 3 in.			464
Porto Novo		202 ft	30 ft 0 in.		9 ft 9 in.			328
Lagos		170 ft	26 ft 0 in.		8 ft 6 in.			187
Ogun		153 ft	24 ft 0 in.		10 ft 6 in.			203

Note. *a* These vessels drew 16 ft 16 in.–17 ft 6 in. at Forcados after cargo had been discharged.
Source. CSO 26/1 09896 vol. 1, *op. cit.*, p. 41.

amounted to £100,745, with an additional sum of £51,822 the next calendar year. The combined figure of £152,567 was more than half the total sanctioned expenditure of £300,000.[20] Even then, little progress seemed to have been recorded on the bar for, despite these efforts, in April 1910 the SS *Ilorin* was wrecked there. This incident led the *Lagos Weekly Record* to conclude, later in the year, that 'after an expenditure of nearly £200,000 the problem of the Bar remains almost where it was at the start'.[21] The newspaper had earlier proffered a solution of its own:

> the combined effort of four or more dredgers employed temporarily at a favourable season of the year and kept incessantly at work until a deep channel has been cut across the Bar to be followed subsequently by constant dredging by a local dredger for keeping the channel cut, free of the accumulated washings.[22]

Hardly any dredging was done on the bar in the second half of 1910, owing to the rough weather during the rainy season, the disablement of the dredger *Sandgrouse* and the decking of a second dredger.[23] However, down to 1914 consistent dredging produced noticeable improvement in the bar draught. In August 1913, for example, Sir F. D. Lugard reported the 'unexpected maintenance for the past seven months of a sixteen feet draught over the Lagos Bar'. This, he noted, 'has created a new situation which demands immediate attention. Large ocean-going vessels are now entering the Port.'[24] In February 1914 the Woermann shipping line started a direct service from Hamburg. This event, Lugard contended, belied 'previous statements to the effect that shipping has so far derived no benefits from the improvements in the Lagos Bar'.[25] Other shipping lines also took advantage of the increasing depth of the entrance and ships were reported to have been 'entering the port direct from Europe'.[26] Improvements in the depth of the entrance, coupled with the extension of the railway and roads, redounded to the benefit of Lagos trade, as shown in table 3.

While these developments were taking place a considerable proportion of traffic was still being transhipped at Forcados. In the period from 9 January to 28 February 1914 total direct shipments in and out of Lagos amounted to 30,958 tons, as against a total of 30,262 carried by branch steamers.[27] This indicated that the depth of the entrance still required greater improvement. The *Nigerian Pioneer* noted that the 'low depth of water on the Bar is still exercising the minds of the Authorities and Shipping Companies, though we are yet far off from the old days of under 10 feet'.[28] Although the Harbour Department was reported in 1915 to be 'very busy of late in dredging the harbour' in anticipation of a post-war boom,[29] dredging operations during the war were constrained by the exigencies of wartime and lack of coal. None the less, steady improvements were recorded in the bar draught between 1907 and 1919, as shown in table 4.

Table 3. *Tonnage of cargo handled at Iddo Wharf, 1906–12*

Year	Imports			Exports	Total exports and imports
	Government	Public	Total		
1906	9,873	9,051	18,924	20,355	39,279
1907	20,940	13,401	34,341	34,901	69,302
1908	32,169	13,814	45,983	36,723	82,706
1909	36,637	14,495	51,132	46,756	97,888
1910	63,653	16,661	80,314	53,103	133,417
1911	30,975	23,096	54,071	57,275	111,346
1912	27,696	27,208	54,904	64,790	119,604

Source. N.A.I. CSO 1/32/2 Desp. 109 of 29 May 1913, Lugard to Harcourt.

Table 4. *Official bar draught in Lagos, 1907–19*

Year	Minimum	Maximum	Remarks
1907	9 ft	11 ft	*Egerton* arrived
1908	11 ft 6 in.	13 ft	East Mole begun
1909	12 ft	14 ft	*Sandgrouse* arrived
1910	13 ft	15 ft	*Sandgrouse* disabled and taken to England
1911	11 ft 6 in.	16 ft	*Sandgrouse* returned
1912	9 ft 6 in.	16 ft 6 in.	West Mole begun
1913	12 ft	18 ft	
1914	13 ft 6 in.	19 ft	East Mole stopped
1915	13 ft	17 ft	West Training Bank begun
1916	15 ft	19 ft 6 in.	
1917	19 ft 6 in.	20 ft	
1918	20 ft	21 ft	
1919	20 ft	20 ft	West Training Bank stopped

Source. CSO 1/32/49 1016 of 12 November 1919, Sir H. Clifford to Lord Milner, enc. Coode *et al.*, *Report on Lagos Harbour Works*, p. 5.

The development of the port of Lagos   67

A concomitant of dredging operations was the construction of moles to narrow and deepen the channel into Lagos harbour. As can be seen in table 4, work began on the East Mole in 1908, on the West Mole in 1912 and on the West Training Bank in 1915. At the end of 1918 the West Mole had attained a length of 4,090 ft, of which 412 ft were constructed that year. The Training Bank was extended to 2,516 ft, 490 ft of which was constructed in 1918 alone. The construction of the moles was an 'arduous and difficult task, for the Atlantic in those parts is as changeable and capricious as Paris used to be in the days of the Guises'.[30] Stone for the construction of the moles and other harbour works was obtained from the Aro quarry in Abeokuta. It was brought down by the railway and tipped as construction progressed. Table 5 gives the tonnage of stone used in the harbour between 1908 and 1918.

The provision of increased wharfage accommodation was the third facet of the physical development of the harbour during this period. This was a central issue of port policy before 1950 under a deliberate policy of concentrating investment at a few ports.[31] In the specific case of Lagos, the question of wharfage was part of the larger issue of whether development should be concentrated at Lagos or Apapa. The fundamental consideration was which site would be the outlet for rail-borne traffic. No definite decision was taken until 1913.

In a report of 11 July 1911, the consulting engineers had proposed that wharves should be erected along the margin of the harbour between Five Cowrie Creek and Wilmot Point. This would have entailed the construction of a railway between Iddo Island or the mainland and Lagos Island, together with railway connection across the latter island. To obviate what was considered the excessive cost of the attendant works, Lugard recommended in 1913 that the site of the wharves should be transferred to Apapa, to which the railway already had access. In that event, a deep-water channel would be dredged from the vicinity of Five Cowrie Creek to Apapa. This alternative was considered less costly than constructing and maintaining the bridge and railway to link Wilmot Point with Iddo or the mainland. The Apapa scheme was accordingly approved by the Secretary of State in October 1913. However, except for the erection of a wharf, 180 ft long and 26 ft deep at low water, and dredging in the approach channel, not much progress was achieved in implementing the scheme up to 1919. By that date wharves had been erected on Lagos Island, on Iddo and at Apapa. The one on Lagos Island had grown from the Customs pier of the 1860s, hence the reference to it as the Customs wharf.

The foregoing discussion has highlighted the pattern and problems of port development in Lagos up to the end of the First World War. In spite of the war and financial constraints, some progress was recorded in this endeavour. More remarkable changes, however, were to come.

Table 5. Tonnage of stone deposited annually in Lagos harbour, 1908–18

Year	East Mole		West Mole	West training Banke	Total tonnage deposited in mole works
	Mole proper	Northern extension			
1908	15,699	1,251	–		16,950
1909	39,878	14,546	–		54,424
1910	73,259	23,338	–		96,597
1911	111,501	–	–		111,501
1912	88,000	–	49,513		137,513
1913	84,709	–	101,095		185,804
1914	45,915	3,226	112,643	–	161,784
1915	12,884	1,892	85,320	23,664	123,760
1916	5,726	–	87,382	74,408	167,516
1917	6,412	–	58,537	74,161	139,110
1918	736	–	87,498	84,436	172,670
TOTALS	484,719	44,253	581,988	256,669	1,367,629

Note. a Figures for 1914–18.
Source. CSO 1/32/49 1016 of 12 November 1919 enc. op. cit., p. 13, appendix B.

Developments in the inter-war period

Dredging operations continued after the First World War and by 1923 the depth of the entrance to the harbour was as much as 25 ft. But, as was pointed out in the same year, the 'governing factor in navigating the entrance is not as many people suppose the depth of water, but the strength and direction of the tides'.[32] The tides were particularly strong during the rainy season, running as fast as five knots in the entrance. It was difficult in such circumstances to bring large vessels in. Pilots would then ask the incoming vessels to wait for a reduction in the speed of the currents. Against this background, it became superfluous to deepen the harbour beyond 25 ft. Hence when the Imperial Shipping Committee was asked to consider the question in its report on Nigerian harbours in 1928, it noted that shipping companies were not taking advantage of the existing depth of the entrance. For only a limited number of ships with a draught of more than 20 ft visited the port up to 1928.[33] By that date, therefore, the problem of a shallow entrance had ceased to be in itself a hindrance to shipping.

In the meantime, members of the commercial community in Britain were becoming impatient with the pace of work on harbour development in Nigeria. Specifically, they were critical of port policy and, therefore, desired to be actively involved in its formulation. Thus the Manchester Chamber of Commerce noted in correspondence with the Secretary of State that Lagos was 'the natural doorway to a vast hinterland' and that it was '*the port*' for northern and southern Nigeria. The chamber enjoined the government 'to come to a decision without delay respecting the development of Lagos Harbour and the lines upon which that development will take place'.[34]

The London Chamber of Commerce went a step further by demanding to *see* the plans of any proposed development of the port before any work was undertaken.[35] A more militant posture was adopted by the African Trade Section of the Liverpool Chamber of Commerce. Its chairman, Pickering Jones, deplored 'the waste of money . . . on abortive or over-expensive harbour schemes . . . on rival Governors' clashing railway policies and the setting up and abandonment of capitals'. He lamented that 'the old official attitude persists, that businessmen, the people chiefly concerned, who find the money and trade, must not be heard upon plans for public works till the money is gone and advice is useless'. He opined that in 'a commercial nation like ours this attitude is stupid. West African businessmen should give the Colonial Office no peace till that attitude is changed.'[36]

Eventually, in 1919, a definite decision was taken by government in respect of the crucial issue of the terminus of the railway. Speaking in the Nigerian Council in December 1919, Sir Kitoyi Ajasa,[37] a distinguished Lagosian of the time, expressed 'satisfaction [that] . . . the long delayed decision as to the provision of wharfage accommodation in connection with the main terminus of the railway has been taken in favour of Apapa'. The delay, he pointed out, had caused 'a great

Table 6. Total annual tonnages of imports and exports (including coal and railway materials) handled at the Iddo, Ijora and Apapa wharves, 1919–28/29

| | Exports | | | Imports | | | | | | | |
| | Iddo | Ijora | Apapa | Iddo | | | Ijora | | Apapa | | |
Year	Goods	Goods	Goods	Goods	Railway materials	Coal	Goods	Coal	Goods	Railway Materials	Coal
1919	85,688	–	3,049	32,696	35,582a	–	–	–	–	384	16,923
1920	88,136	–	16,318	30,183	45,939a	–	–	–	135	170	28,322
1921–22	89,527	–	11,899	28,489	52,849a	–	–	–	114	13,942	39,694
1922–23	87,040	–	11,436	34,489	42,428a	–	–	–	352	80	4,074
1923–24	111,258	–	17,125	32,825	80,051	62,418	–	–	58	–	5,236
1924–25	173,921	–	24,772	45,546	6,949	49,807	–	19,996	37	–	8,747
1925–26	182,609	–	55,786	55,454	7,167	–	2,362b	106,219	–	–	–
1926–27	87,180	–	127,241	62,006	4,121	–	7,886b	100,205	9,574	1,921	–
1927–28	–	–	178,128	1,005	–	–	3,571b	82,960	103,933	31,823	–
1928–29	–	417	201,307	–	–	–	11,457	74,144	111,470	14,134	–

Notes
a Railway materials and coal.
b Timber, kerosene, etc.
Source. CSO 1/32/97 702 of 25 June 1929, Baddeley to Webb, enc. 2.

deal of uneasiness. Today one heard that it was to be Wilmot Point and the next day it was Apapa.'[38]

The Lagos wharfage scheme, which entailed the dredging of channels in the inner harbour, the entrance to the Customs wharf and the Five Cowrie Creek to Apapa, was executed by the Harbour Department under the supervision of Coode & Partners. It had been practically completed by 1922 at a cost of £410,000 — £10,000 in excess of the original estimate. At Apapa work proceeded by stages concurrently with the deepening of the entrance to the harbour under the supervision of the consulting engineers. The early stages of the scheme were handled within the Harbour Department but later ones were contracted to Armstrong Whitworth & Co. Ltd. By 1924 a total of £3,344,137 had been expended on the Lagos, Apapa and Iddo schemes out of an estimate of £3,846,606.

By the mid-1920s the trade of Lagos was being handled at the wharves at Lagos, Apapa and Iddo (see table 6), each of which was associated with a particular type of trade. The Customs wharf on Lagos Island and the Iddo wharf handled the bulk of the import trade, the Customs wharf accounting for two-thirds of this traffic. The concentration of the import trade at Lagos in spite of the rapid developments at Apapa was due to the existence of extensive private warehouse accommodation on Lagos Island. It was observed, however, that 'sooner or later the conduct of the whole of the rail-borne traffic — apart from coal — must be concentrated at Apapa, although . . . the process may be gradual'.[39]

Up to 1925/26 the bulk of exports was handled over the Iddo wharf, but from 1926/27 the situation was reversed in favour of Apapa. Thus, while exports at Iddo in the two years were 182,609 and 87,180 tons respectively, the figures for Apapa were 55,786 and 127,241. The ascendancy of Apapa was confirmed when in the following two years it exported 178,128 and 201,307 tons while no figure was recorded for Iddo. The same trend was reflected in the import figures for the same period. The observation made in 1935 in respect of cargo handling at the wharves was true of the entire decade before the Second World War: 'The larger proportion of imports are landed on Lagos Island, exports handled at Apapa are greatly in excess of imports.'[40] Apapa's pre-eminence was due to the fact that the bulk of cargo for shipment was rail-borne and it was the only wharf which had railway connections. The pattern of trade at the Lagos wharves from 1929 to 1938 is indicated in table 7.

A number of deductions can be made from table 7. First, the tonnage of cargo handled on both sides of the harbour (Lagos and Apapa) was approximately equal. Indeed, the tonnage was shared equally in 1938. Second, lighterage was an important activity in the port, handling a quarter of the total traffic. The use of lighters was necessitated by the fact that ships which berthed on one side of the harbour (for example, Apapa, with its railway connections) also received cargoes from the other side (that is, Lagos, which was fed by the lagoon markets). The

Table 7. *Tonnage of cargo handled per annum in the port of Lagos,*
1929–38 inclusive

	Imports		Exports		Totals		Area total	
Handled at	Tonnage	%	Tonnage	%	Tonnage	%	Tonnage	%
Customs wharf, Lagos	138,990	65	–	–	138,990	23	Lagos	
By lighterage	2,500	1	152,196	40	154,696	25	293,686	48
Apapa quay	34,140	16	225,402	57	259,542	43	Apapa	
Other Apapa wharves	39,041	18	14,539	3	53,580	9	313,122	52
Totals	214,671	100	392,137	100	606,808	100	606,808	100

Source. N.A.I. CSO 26 34307 vol. II 'Port Services . . .', enc. Report on Co-ordination . . ., para. 16.

importance of lighterage is attested by the statistics: the total tonnage handled at Apapa rose from 314,909 in 1929 to 499,061 in 1938 (a 79 per cent increase) whereas the respective figures for lighterage were 103,265 and 205,319 tons (an increase of 99 per cent).[41] The statistics served to justify the plan to make Apapa the centre of port operations in Lagos.

Port policy in Nigeria during this period favoured the concentration of activity at a few ports. With specific reference to Lagos, this meant the concentration of efforts on the development of Apapa. A memorandum which expressed the official attitude on the issue stated in 1937 that:

it is already clear that the capacity of the Lagos Island waterfront to deal with a rapidly increasing trade will soon be reached. Augmented trade and the prospects of a far greater development of the immense resources of Nigeria now make it imperative . . . for a positive scheme of development for the Port of Lagos to be shaped and for the first steps towards its accomplishment to be taken without delay. Failure to do this must result in further piecemeal contriving on the Lagos side of the harbour with eventual chaos due to trade overtaking port development.[42]

The Lagos side of the harbour was facing severe congestion because of the rapid increase in the population occupying the small area of land on the island. The situation was compounded by the fact that the island was served by only one form of inland transport and the lack of land on the waterfront was impeding further development. Hence, it was stated, 'freeing the streets of vehicles standing to load and unload is already a live issue increasing in intensity'.[43] The fate of the island was sealed by the Port Engineer's report that the Customs wharf located there had a maximum life span of another twelve years.

The development of the port of Lagos   73

Against this background, Governor Bernard Bourdillon declared in the Legislative Council in March 1937 that there was need for a 'definite trend of port development for the future . . . It appears almost certain that any extension of activities must take place on the Apapa side . . .'[44] He asked the Port Advisory Board to put forward proposals in this regard.

When the board met on 5 May 1937 its chairman opined that, from a purely shipping point of view, it was desirable to have only one deep-water wharf in Lagos harbour. This, he explained, would save vessels the trouble of moving from one side of the harbour to the other. While the shipping members of the board — H. S. Feggetter of Elder Dempster Lines[45] and Captain C. C. Roberts of the Barber West Africa Line — agreed that this was the case, the trading members were not as enthusiastic over the prospect of abandoning the Lagos side of the harbour.

The attitude of the merchants was informed by self-interest, for they had been too well entrenched on that side of the harbour. As late as 1946, when the issue was still being considered, the Lagos Chamber of Commerce expressed its 'concern at the future prospect of closing Lagos [Island] as a port since, in a large number of cases, it was found by local commercial concerns, that it was more convenient [to handle cargo] . . . at Lagos rather than Apapa'.[46] The chamber argued that clearance from wharf to store was achieved with greater despatch at the Customs wharf. Moreover, warehousing facilities and administrative supervision were available only at Lagos.

After all was said and done, the Port Advisory Board made some recommendations in respect of port development in Lagos.[47] The first was that the consulting engineers should submit draft plans and estimates for a two and three-berth southward extension of Apapa quay, equipped alternatively with single and double-storeyed transit sheds. Second, all further extensions of the Apapa quay should be designed to give equal access to road and rail vehicles. Third, a road should be constructed from the Iddo end of Carter bridge via Ijora to Apapa. The consulting engineers would then make recommendations in respect of a bridge across the Ebute–Metta creek which the proposed road rendered necessary. Finally, the mainland coastline from Apapa quay towards Iddo should be reclaimed.

The consulting engineers submitted a plan dated 15 November 1937 in respect of the extension of the Apapa wharf. They recommended that the wharf should be extended 1,500 ft southwards. However, until the post-war period no progress was made in this respect. It required fresh recommendations from the Port Advisory Board in 1946 before the plan of the consulting engineers was endorsed.[48] Thus the board requested that the first extension of the Apapa wharf should be in the range of 2,500 ft. This figure was based on the calculation that the Customs wharves had a total length of 1,200 ft and were designed to take three ships each of which was less than 400 ft long. But as shipowners were building

larger and longer vessels (of an average length of 450 ft), three such vessels would
need a minimum wharfage of 1,500 ft. A thousand feet was added to this figure in
anticipation of increased tonnage.[49] Although the total of 2,500 ft fell far short of
the 6,000 ft recommended by the consulting engineers in 1937, it was considered
sufficient for a first instalment. In any case, it was envisaged that the provision
of modern mechanical appliances, which ensured quicker turn-round of ships,
would compensate for any insufficiency of wharfage and berthage.

The reference to shipping turn-round leads us to an examination of port
operations in Lagos during this period. The following discussion shows how
attempts were made to overcome problems of port working which delayed
shipping and thus hampered business in the port.

Port operations and shipping turn-round

For a clear perception of the problems of port working in Lagos, it is necessary
to describe the approach to, and system of port operations in, the harbour.[50] A
five-mile fairway, which separated the wharves from the bar, followed at first
the eastern side of the harbour and then divided at the Five Cowrie Point.
One channel continued up the eastern side of the Customs wharf on Lagos
Island while the other crossed diagonally to the railway wharves at Apapa on
the western or mainland side. The normal routine was for vessels to proceed
first to the Customs wharf, where they discharged most of their cargo into the
warehouses of the Lagos merchants for distribution to the inland markets in
small quantities. The vessels would then go to the Apapa wharves to discharge
railway materials and other goods for transport by railway into the hinterland.
For the return journey the vessels loaded in reverse order.

This arrangement was not as smooth in practice, for slow turn-round —
delays in loading and off-loading — characterised the working of the port. In
December 1919, for instance, the managing director of Elder Dempster Lines
complained about 'the poor despatch our steamers are getting at Lagos'.[51] He
cited instances to buttress the point: the *Gaboon* had spent four days and nineteen
hours discharging 760 tons; the *Shonga* arrived in Lagos on 17 November with
1,390 tons which she spent thirteen days discharging, while the *Benin* lost two and
half days in November 1919 owing to congestion in Lagos. The Lagos agent of
the company provided further examples of delays while speaking in the Nigerian
Council in 1919.[52] The particulars were as follows:

Steamer	Tonnage discharged	Time taken	Average per hour
Baro	982 tons	Eight days	15 tons
Iddo	892 tons	Nine days	12 tons
Uromi	681 tons	Eight days	10 tons

Although information is lacking on the period up to 1929, there are indications that the problem of slow turn-round persisted. In February 1929 the issue was raised in a meeting of the Lagos Chamber of Commerce.[53] Mr F. Bateman Jones of Elder Dempster Lines testified that two of his firm's vessels were held up during the month: SS *Bakana* (five days) and SS *Jebba* (three days). He calculated that the average daily discharge per vessel at Apapa was approximately 600 tons for 'fine goods' despite the use of electric cranes, whereas at the Customs wharf, and in Port Harcourt and Calabar, where no delay was experienced and double-decked stores were used, ships worked an average discharge of 1,100 tons of cargo per day.

The debate by the chamber of commerce revealed a number of possible causes of delay in Lagos. First, the electric crane at Apapa was said to have been defective during the previous season. Second, time was wasted in slinging cargo from the cranes into the doorways of the top storey of the Apapa sheds. Third, the direct loading of goods into railway wagons was believed to have been done too slowly, while shunting caused long delays. Moreover, delays were caused by frequent shortages of wagons. Finally, imports of large quantities of construction materials during the busy season at Apapa had compounded the situation at the wharf.

The Lagos Chamber of Commerce therefore suggested means of remedying the situation. The use of a large number of reliable electric cranes was recommended. Second, an adequate supply of spare parts and accessories should be retained to prevent cranes being out of action for three or four months on end. Third, the ledge of the top storey of the sheds should be widened so that cargo could be landed on it and labourers could remove it under safe conditions. This would abolish the practice of swinging cargo into the doors for labourers to catch — a dangerous and time-wasting practice. It was also recommended that storage facilities should be improved so that vessels could tie up alongside the particular shed they wished to use in discharging or loading cargo. Government was also enjoined to ensure that imports of its construction materials did not coincide with the busy season at Apapa.

Official reactions to these suggestions are unknown for the records are silent on the issue of port turn-round after 1929. This could be interpreted as suggesting that certain changes were effected in line with the recommendations of the business community. It could also mean that the merchants resigned themselves to enduring what seemed to be an intractable problem.

Conclusion

The foregoing discussion has dwelt on the process and problems of the physical development of the port of Lagos in the period between 1892 and 1946. Dredging operations were carried on in the harbour to deepen its entrance, while moles were constructed to narrow and deepen the approach channel. Wharves were also constructed to facilitate port working. These developments obviated the need to tranship Lagos cargo at Forcados and permitted the entry of vessels of deeper draught. From the end of the First World War developments were concentrated at Apapa, where wharves were provided to keep pace with the increase in trade.

The functional development of the port was, however, complemented by changes in its hinterland: the construction of roads and railway lines.[54] These developments redounded to the benefit of Lagos, which was able to live up to its reputation as the 'Liverpool' of West Africa. The increase in trade none the less put pressure on port facilities — which were generally inadequate for the volume of trade — resulting in slow shipping turn-round.

On the whole, the problems of site and situation were not peculiar to Lagos. They were characteristic of most West African ports. The situation in Lagos was, however, ameliorated by the commitment of capital and human resources on the part of the colonial state and expatriate firms. Consequently, by 1950 the functional development of the port of Lagos had established it as Nigeria's chief port, handling 70 per cent of the country's imports and over 50 per cent of her export trade.

Notes

1 D. Hilling and B. S. Hoyle, 'Seaports and the economic development of tropical Africa', in D. Hilling and B. S. Hoyle (eds), *Seaports and Development in Africa*, (1970), p. 1.

2 Standard works on African ports include: G. F. Deasy, 'Harbours of Africa', *Economic Geography*, 18 (1942), pp. 325–42; R. G. Albion, *Seaports South of the Sahara* (New York, 1959); H. P. White, 'The Ports of West Africa: some geographical considerations', *Tijdschrift voor Economische en Sociale Geografie*, 50 (1959), pp. 1–8; D. Hilling, 'The evolution of the major ports of West Africa', *Geographical Journal*, 135 (1969), pp. 365–77.

3 See, for example: B. W. Hodder, 'The growth of trade at Lagos (Nigeria)', *Tijdschrift . . .*, 50 (1959), pp. 197–202; B. O. Ogundana, 'Lagos, Nigeria's premier port', *Nigerian Geographical Journal (N.G.J.)*, 4 (1961), pp. 26–40; *id.* 'The fluctuating significance of Nigerian seaports before 1914', *ODU: A Journal of West African Studies*, 3 (1967), pp. 44–71; *id.*, 'Patterns and problems of seaport evolution in Nigeria', in Hilling and Hoyle, *Seaports*, pp. 167–82; and *id.*, 'The location factor in changing seaport significance in Nigeria', *N.G.J.*, 14 (1971), pp. 71–88.

4 Ogundana, 'Lagos . . .', *op. cit.*

5 Political and commercial relations between the British colony in Lagos and the hinterland states are examined in A. B. Aderibigbe, 'Trade and British expansion in the Lagos area in the second half of the nineteenth century', *Nigerian Journal of Economic and Social Studies*, 4 (1962), pp. 188–95, and Ayodeji Olukoju, 'The politics of free trade between Lagos and the hinterland, 1861–1907', in

Ade Adefuye, Babatunde Agiri and Jide Osuntokun (eds), *History of the Peoples of Lagos State* (Lagos, 1987), pp. 85–103.

6 For a detailed study of these developments see A. G. Hopkins, 'An Economic History of Lagos, 1880–1914', Ph.D. thesis, University of London, 1964.

7 *Ibid.*, p. 240.

8 *Ibid.*, p. 380.

9 *Lagos Weekly Record* (L.W.R.), 6 April 1910, 'Lagos through foreign eyes'.

10 Colonial port policy is studied in B. Ogundana, 'Seaport development in colonial Nigeria', in I. A. Akinjogbin and S. O. Osoba (eds), *Topics on Nigerian Economic and Social History* (Ile-Ife, 1980), pp. 159–81. The discussion in Ogundana's work does not, however, incorporate the themes examined in this article.

11 Ogundana, 'The location factor . . .', *op. cit.*.

12 Hodder, 'The growth of trade . . .', p. 199.

13 National Archives Ibadan (NAI) CSO 1/1/15 Desp. 185 of 7 October 1895, G. Denton to J. Chamberlain.

14 *Ibid.*

15 NAI CSO 1/19/37 Desp. 60 of 7 February 1911, W. Egerton to L. Harcourt, enc. Report on Progress of Harbour Works.

16 *West Africa*, 6 July 1918, p. 376, culled from the *Lagos Standard*.

17 NAI CSO 1/19/12 Desp. 435 of 9 July 1908, Egerton to Earl of Crewe, enc. Southern Nigeria Trade Report, 1907.

18 *Ibid.*

19 NAI CSO 1/19/37 Desp. 90 of 15 February 1911, Egerton to Harcourt, enc. Report on . . . Lagos Harbour, 28 January 1911.

20 NAI CSO 1/19/27 Desp. 165 of 24 March 1910, Egerton to Crewe.

21 *L.W.R.*, 5 November 1910.

22 *L.W.R.*, 8 October 1910.

23 NAI CSO 1/19/37 Desp. 60 of 7 February 1911, *op. cit.*

24 NAI CSO 1/19/59 Desp. 380 of 18 August 1913, F. D. Lugard to Harcourt.

25 NAI CSO 1/32/5 Desp. 141 of 11 February 1914, Lugard to Harcourt.

26 NAI CSO 1/32/6 Desp. 286 of 25 March 1914, Lugard to Harcourt.

27 NAI CSO 1/32/7 Desp. 325 of 1 April 1914, Lugard to Harcourt.

28 *Nigerian Pioneer (N.P.)*, 31 July 1914.

29 *N.P.*, 10 September 1915, 'Random notes and news'.

30 *West Africa*, 24 February 1917, p. 63.

31 Babafemi Ogundana, 'Ports and external trade', in J. S. Oguntoyinbo, O. Areola and M. Filani (eds), *A Geography of Nigerian Development* (Ibadan, 1978), p. 338.

32 NAI AR.5/M1 Nigeria: Annual Report on the Marine Department for the year 1923, p. 2.

33 NAI MTA 1/1 T.0328 'Imperial Shipping Committee: Appointments, Reports etc.', *Report on the Harbours of Nigeria*, September 1928, p. 101.

34 NAI CSO 20/5 NC 57/17 'Scheme for making Apapa the main terminus of the Nigerian Railway . . .', Walter Speakman, Secretary, Manchester Chamber of Commerce, to Walter Long, 20 December 1916.

35 *West Africa*, 27 April 1918, p. 196.

36 *West Africa*, 12 October 1918, p. 613.

37 Sir Kitoyi Ajasa, OBE, was a successful lawyer and one of the colonial governor's African nominees in the Legislative Council. He was the proprietor of the *Nigerian Pioneer*, which published his pro-government and pro-business views. As legal retainer to the European firms, Sir Kitoyi was naturally interested in port development and commercial growth in Lagos. There is no biography of this eminent Lagosian but there are references to him in some texts. See P. D. Cole, *Modern and Traditional Elites in the Politics of Lagos* (1975), p. 236 n. 162 and p. 250 n. 37, for sketches of his biography.

38 NAI CSO 19/7 N2683/1919 'Nigerian Council, 1919', Proceedings of the Sixth Meeting of the Nigerian Council, 29 December 1919, p. 7.

39 NAI CSO 26/1 09896 vol. III 'Lagos Island Wharfage', Extracts from Nigeria — Lagos Harbour: Entrance . . ., para. 74, enc. in Resident Engineer, Harbour Works, to Chief Secretary to Government, 29 March 1926.

40 NAI CSO 1/32/128 Desp. 879 of 21 November 1935, Maybin to MacDonald.

41 NAI CSO 26 34307 vol. II 'Port Services', enc. Report on Co-ordination of Port Services, para. 18.

42 NAI CSO 26/1 09860/S.7 vol. I 'Lagos Port Advisory Board: Agenda and Proceedings 1936–38', Memo, for PAB meeting of 5 May 1937, para. 4.

43 *Ibid.*, para. 5.

44 *Ibid.*, f. 18; Minutes of the Second Meeting of the LPAB, 5 May 1937, citing Governor's speech.

45 An authoritative study of the firm is in P. N. Davies, *The Trade Makers: Elder Dempster in West Africa* (1973).

46 NAI CSO 26/1 09860/S.7A 'Lagos Port Advisory Board . . . 1946', Cassleton Elliot & Co., Secretaries, Lagos Chamber of Commerce, to Chairman, LPAB, 7 October 1946.

47 NAI CSO 26/1 09860/S.7 vol. I, *op. cit.*, f. 25.

48 NAI CSO 26/1 09860/S.7A, *op. cit.*, Meeting of the LPAB, 18 February 1946.

49 The growth of Lagos trade in the 1940s justified such projections. Thus the tonnage of palm oil exports rose from 5,216 in 1940 to 12,731 in 1945 and 27,280 in 1949. Figures for groundnuts for these years were 129,469, 198,303 and 260,204 respectively. See *Nigeria: Trade Reports*, 1940, 1945, 1949.

50 This paragraph is based on MTA 1/1 T.0328 . . ., *op. cit.*, *Report* . . ., pp. 11–12, paras 20–1.

51 NAI CSO 19/7 N325/19 'Exports received at and shipped from Iddo . . . 1919', J. H. Sharrock to Central Secretary, Lagos, 27 December 1919.

52 NAI CSO 19/7 N2683/1919 'Nigerian Council, 1919', *op. cit.*, p. 9.

53 NAI CSO 26 09756 vol. III 'Chambers of Commerce, Lagos, Minutes of Meetings', Meeting of 15 May 1919.

54 For railway construction see T. N. Tamuno, 'Genesis of the Nigerian Railway', Parts I and II, *Nigeria Magazine*, 83 (1964), pp. 272–92 and 84 (1965), pp. 31–43; Wale Oyemakinde, 'Railway construction and operation in Nigeria, 1895–1911: labour problems and socio-economic impact', *Journal of the Historical Society of Nigeria*, III (1974), pp. 303–24. For road transport see A. M. Hay, 'The development of road transport in Nigeria, 1900–1940', *Journal of Transport History*, n.s., I (1971), pp. 95–107.

Acknowledgements

This article is a product of research into the growth of the maritime trade of Lagos. It was inspired by G. G. Weigend's earlier study of Hamburg. I acknowledge the financial support of the Central Research Committee of the University of Lagos and the helpful comments of the anonymous reader of an earlier draft of the article.

10 From coal to oil in British shipping

MAX E. FLETCHER

INTRODUCTION

THE shipping and shipbuilding industries of Great Britain, during the late nineteenth and early twentieth centuries, proved to have more vitality than the other major sectors of the British economy. Iron and steel, hardwares, textiles – these and other industries were unable to hold their own against aggressive competition from abroad. But in shipping and shipbuilding Britain reigned supreme well into the twentieth century. In the period just before the First World War, one-third of the world's merchant fleet was owned in Britain, British ships carried around one-half of the seaborne trade of the world, and British shipyards supplied about two-thirds of all new ships launched.[1]

Partly this was a matter of mere good fortune. A strong American challenge, for example, based on a clear-cut competitive advantage in the building of wooden sailing ships, faded into insignificance with the outbreak of the Civil War. Renewal of the challenge after the war was forestalled by the shift to iron and steel ships propelled by steam and the opening of the Suez Canal in 1869, the latter virtually guaranteeing a near-monopoly of the crucial Eastern trade to improved British steamers.[2] But, of far greater importance, it was the ability of the British to capitalize on their unique resource endowments, capital, and skills that assured their continued predominance. Easily accessible coal and iron ore deposits furthered the development of the iron and steel industry; relatively cheap, high-grade iron and steel, coupled with available marine engineering skills, promoted the growth and transformation of shipbuilding; and British coal-fired ships, assured of abundant supplies of high-grade fuel and of an outbound cargo in the form of export coal, carried British goods economically to all parts of the world and brought back in exchange the foods and raw materials so necessary to British economy. The importance of coal in this sequence is evident. It is the purpose of this paper to examine the process of change and consequences when oil replaced coal as fuel for the world's ocean-going fleet.

THE AGE OF COAL

The decades preceding the beginning of the First World War have been labelled, with reason, Great Britain's 'Age of Coal'.[3] Coal had played a role in Britain for centuries, partly as an export commodity, but mainly as a domestic fuel. It did not begin to exert a profound influence on the British economy until it was made the basis of many of the major developments of the Industrial Revolution. During the nineteenth century, the coal resources of Great Britain were developed further than those of any other country, and on the basis of abundant supplies of this high-quality, cheap fuel the British textile and metallurgical industries were able to flood the world with their mass-produced products. The assessment of coal and the coal-mining industry by the Royal Commission on the Coal Industry in 1925 would have been even more true of pre-war conditions:

> The paramount importance of the coal mining industry in the economic and social life of this country is a commonplace.... With the exception of agriculture, to which it is a close second, the industry employs more men than any other; not less than one-twelfth of our population is directly dependent on it. It is the foundation of our iron and steel, shipbuilding and engineering trades, and, indeed, of our whole industrial life.[4]

This sums up the case for assigning a high rank to coal for its role in the British domestic economy. In the maritime and foreign trades, coal had an equally if not more important role to play. Between 1850 and 1900, while the quantity of coal produced in the United Kingdom and retained for home consumption more than trebled, the quantity exported, including coal shipped for the use of steamers engaged in foreign trade, grew 15-fold.[5] During this period, down to the beginning of the First World War, coal came to the fore as one of Britain's staple exports. The 16 million tons exported annually in 1871–5 (including foreign bunkers) accounted for only 13·22 per cent of British coal output and for only 4·3 per cent of the value of Britain's total exports; the 98 million exported in 1913 were 24 per cent of total tonnage raised and 10·43 per cent of Britain's exports.[6] Since all of Britain's exports and re-exports in 1913 other than coal and coal products amounted to less than 17 million tons,[7] coal made up over 85 per cent of the total volume of exports.[8]

The British foreign coal trade was based on an abundant and seemingly inexhaustible supply of good coal, situated to best possible advantage for the export trade. With the exception of a small part of the Midlands all the British coalfields have easy access to the sea. The combination of abundant coal supplies, a short overland haul, and cheap ocean transportation enabled British exporters to land coal in the ports of foreign countries very cheaply – often at prices lower than if supplied from the countries' own coalfields. When the industrial demands for coal increased during the later part of the nineteenth century, therefore, it was naturally towards Great Britain that the nations of western Europe turned to supplement their inadequate coal supplies. In the five-year period immediately preceding the First World War, 1909–13, Britain supplied France with an annual average of 10·6 million tons of coal, Germany with 9 million tons, and Italy with 9·2 million tons.[9]

Growing industrial demands on the Continent, however, only partly explain the growth in the export of British coal. The other part of the explanation is tied up with the transition from sail to steam in ocean shipping. When steam took the place of sail the importance of British coal was vastly magnified. It became necessary to establish special stations where steamers could obtain coal and effect repairs on long ocean routes. As the greatest maritime power and the leader in the swing from sail to steam, Great Britain naturally took the lead in establishing coaling stations. By the end of the First World War she had established a total of 181 stations, strategically distributed throughout the world.[10] In addition, many of the non–British stations were dependent on British coal for their existence. This unique system of coaling stations, of course, could not have been built up by a nation not fortunate enough to be in possession of colonies on every continent. It was estimated that, previous to the First World War, Britain supplied 60 million of the 80 million tons of bunkers consumed annually, and the British colonies supplied another 5 million.[11] So a sizeable portion of the millions of tons of coal shown in the export columns of the British trade returns was nothing more than shipments destined for overseas bunker stations, to be consumed for the most part by British ships.

TABLE I

Quantity of Coal Leaving United Kingdom Ports during Selected Years, 1850–1913

(millions of tons)

Year	Exported as cargo	Shipped as bunker fuel in ships engaged in foreign trade	Total
1850	3·2	—	—
1860	7·1	—	—
1870	10·2	3·2 (1873)	—
1880	17·9	4·9	22·8
1890	28·7	8·1	36.8
1900	44·1	11·8	55·9
1913	73·4	21·0	94·4

Source: Erich W. Zimmermann, *Zimmermann on Ocean Shipping* (New York, 1923), 226.

Another large part of British annual coal production left the country as bunker fuel in the holds of steamships headed for foreign stations, as table 1 shows. If these bunker shipments are added to the total cargo shipments to overseas bunker stations it is easy to see that a very large part of British coal exports was destined for the use of steamships, primarily British steamships. One estimate is that at the turn of the century over half the British coal exports were ultimately used for purposes of navigation.[12]

Although coal was well down the list of leading exports in 1913 in order of value, ranking after textiles, iron and steel manufactures, and machinery, it was nonetheless the cornerstone of British maritime supremacy, the key to the British carrying trade. As British ships increased in number during the later part of the nineteenth century to handle the increasing demands for foodstuffs and industrial raw materials, shipowners needed an outbound cargo that would move in volume and supplement exports of high-value, low-tonnage manufactured goods, thereby helping to balance the volume moving in both directions. In the years just before the First World War, Britain drew from abroad all the raw cotton needed by her textile mills, over half the iron ore used in domestic iron and steel production,[13] and three-quarters of the wheat required to feed her population.[14] England could afford to purchase these low-value, bulky imports only if freight rates were low, but low inbound rates were contingent on the availability of outbound cargoes; shipowners could offer such rates only when their vessels carried pay loads on both legs of their voyages. British coal was practically the only bulk commodity which moved in large and regular volume from north-western Europe to overseas ports; the one commodity which tramp steamers bringing raw materials and foodstuffs to north-western Europe could take out. The importance of coal, then, lay in the fact that with each cubic foot of cargo space filled in both directions and earning returns, it was possible for English shippers to charge lower freight rates than could their competitors who had insufficient outgoing or return cargoes.[15]

The First World War was a turning point in the development of the British coal export trade. Whereas British coal exports had climbed steadily upwards, decade by decade, during the second half of the nineteenth century, until they reached a peak of 73·4 million tons (exclusive of bunkers) in 1913, the post-war years witnessed a shrinking export market: 60·27 million tons in relatively prosperous 1929; 39·66 millions in less prosperous 1934.[16]

The reasons for the decline in British coal exports were numerous and varied, but among the more important were increased utilization of hydro-electric power by Britain's former customers; greater efficiency in the utilization of coal; the increase of foreign output of coal, especially in Germany (largely as the result of re-equipment during the inflation); and above all the much more rapid improvement in coal-mining efficiency abroad than in Britain. In 1913 coal output per manshift in Great Britain had been 21·5 cwts, which was exceeded in Europe only by Upper Silesia.[17] Between 1913 and 1936 British coal mines increased their output per manshift by 10 per cent, but the increase during this period was 117 per cent in Holland, 80 per cent in the Ruhr, 73 per cent in Poland, 50 per cent in Belgium, and over 22 per cent in France.[18] By 1936 British output per manshift was substantially lower than that of several Continental coal-mining regions.[19] The improvements in efficiency on the Continent were mainly the result of much greater progress in mechanization, and they resulted in wage costs per ton of output often much below the British level. Although fuel and diesel oil made some inroads in the British coal export markets on the Continent, the use of petroleum and its products in the industrial nations of Europe during the inter-war period tended to be complementary to coal rather than competitive. It was not until after the Second World War that oil began to compete seriously with coal in the European market.

Parallel to the decline in the export of coal as cargo went a decline in the bunker trade in coal. The quantity of British coal used as bunker fuel by vessels engaged in the foreign trade had averaged 19·6 million tons annually in the immediate pre-First World War period; in 1924 it was down to 17·5 million tons, in 1929 to 16·39 million, and in 1934 to 13·49 million.[20] This decrease can be attributed partly to the general fall in the British foreign coal trade, since about 270,000 tons of coal were needed as bunkers by transporting ships for every million tons of coal sold abroad.[21] The decline in the bunker trade resulted in part also from advances made during this period in marine engineering. By increasing the average speed of shipping by several knots and simultaneously reducing fuel consumption per sea mile, the marine engineers considerably lessened the dependence of the world's merchant marine on the services of coal bunkering stations. This effect was cumulative, of course, since not merely was less coal required from the bunkering stations, but also less coal was needed for fuelling ships that carried coal to the bunkering stations. The primary reason for the decline in Britain's bunker coal trade, however, was that it was in the shipping industry that the Age of Coal first encountered head-on the Age of Oil.

FROM COAL TO OIL

When the petroleum industry was still in its infancy ships were already being propelled with fuel oil instead of coal. The economies to be gained in space and fuel consumption through the use of oil in place of coal were recognized very early, despite certain technical problems. Efforts of British shipbuilders to construct a workable oil-propelled steamer were rewarded in 1886, when the steamer *Himalaya* came down the slipway. When placed in operation on the Brazilian run, the *Himalaya* called for only about one-eighth of the space for her oil fuel as would have been the case had she been burning coal, and on a weight basis consumed only one-third as much fuel.[22] Two difficulties, however, had to be surmounted before oil could replace coal to any large extent in maritime uses: distribution at suitable depots and price. British coal was excellent for marine use, relatively cheap, and, because of the number of widely-distributed bunker stations, nearly ubiquitous. Oil, on the other hand, was still relatively expensive, largely controlled by foreigners, and available at only a small number of depots. Most of the early experiments in substituting oil for coal for steam-raising purposes, therefore, were restricted to installing oil-fed burners in ships trading to and from the East, where the new wells in Borneo guaranteed a supply of fuel.[23]

In addition to developing a method of utilizing oil instead of coal for steam-raising purposes, successful efforts were also made before the First World War to get away from steam entirely and power ships with internal combustion (diesel) engines utilizing oil as fuel. This provided an even smaller fuel consumption for the development of equal power of output, as well as cutting the weight of machinery, bunkers, and boiler water, all of which meant an increase of useful load. In 1909 the Royal Dutch/Shell Group ordered the building of the world's first ocean-going motor vessel, a 1,179-ton tanker called the *Vulcanus*.[24]

The shift from coal to oil in merchant ship propulsion, however, had not progressed very far by the time the First World War broke out, as figures taken originally from *Lloyd's Register of Shipping* indicate.

TABLE 2
Motive Power of World's Total Merchant Fleet, June 1914

Type of motive power	Percentage of total gross tonnage
Sail power only	7·95
Oil, etc., in internal combustion engines	0·47
Oil fuel for steam boilers	2·62
Coal	88·96
	100·00

Source: *Parliamentary Papers*, Committee on Industry and Trade, *Survey of Metal Industries* (1928), ch. iv, 'The Shipbuilding Industry', 387.

Little more than 3 per cent of the total gross tonnage of the world's merchant fleet was equipped to burn oil. Even so, sufficient experience had been gained to remove the 'bugs' from oil propulsion and to prove the advantages of this source of power over coal: reduction of bunker space (and consequent increase in cargo-carrying capacity) because of oil's greater efficiency and lighter weight; cleaner stoke rooms; smaller stokehold staffs; quicker, cleaner, more convenient bunkering; more rapid steam raising; and extension of cruising radius.[25] From this point onward, conversion of the world's merchant fleet from coal to oil was to be purely a matter of availability and relative costs of the two fuels. For the moment the picture regarding the latter was extremely hazy. At prices prevailing immediately before the war, oil had a clear advantage, but what was the future of oil? For every person who asserted that the future would provide abundant supplies of low-priced oil, there were several to announce either that the world's supplies of oil would shortly give out, or that the 'trusts' controlling its distribution would never allow the using public the advantage of low prices. The First World War and the actions of public authorities effectively disposed of these uncertainties.

Financial considerations were of smaller concern to the fighting navies of the world, so the clear-cut technical advantages of oil (especially the ability to gain full power in a short time and maintain that power over a long period) led to an early swing to oil.

Italy was apparently the earliest to investigate the use of oil fuel on warships and to solve the problems associated with its use. Very shortly after the turn of the century she equipped her vessels with oil as an auxiliary to coal for emergency uses in getting up steam and in maintaining full speeds for extended periods.[26] Russia followed suit, and went to war in 1904 with several liquid-fuelled capital ships in her fleet.[27] Germany at this time was also extending the use of oil in her navy. The French navy shortly came to recognize the advantages of oil and by 1911 was sufficiently committed to its use that action was taken to install oil storage tanks at naval bases and supply these directly from Rumania by naval tank steamer.[28] Before the beginning of the First World War, the United States provided for oil burners exclusively in its new battle-ships, and in the last two years before the war, the Royal Navy specified oil fuel "over almost the whole field of the new construction programme".[29] By 1913 the stake of the Admiralty in oil-burning ships had become so important that it was considered absolutely essential that it have the certainty of being able to buy "a steady supply of oil at a steady price".[30] It was only a short step from the announced policy that Britain "must become the owners, or at any rate, the controllers at the source of at least a proportion of the supply of natural oil which we require"[31] to government purchase of oil holdings in Persia – with its profound long-run consequences.

As might have been expected of a great oil-producing nation, the United States led the world in the movement to shift from coal to oil for merchant marine propulsion. The major part of the transition took place during the First World War and was induced by war-time conditions. Because of a shortage of maritime labourers, it was necessary to limit the number of men employed in the operation of the merchant fleet. The use of oil in place of coal permitted a material reduction in the size of engine-room and fire-room crews. Even more important, the war-time Shipping Board became convinced of the necessity to emancipate American shipping from reliance on British coal bunkering stations. During the early stages of the war Great Britain put into effect a system of bunker licences (warrants) as a military measure. The officials of the American government and shipping men realized that the situation could arise after the war where Britain would use such bunker restrictions to the disadvantage of American ships calling at British bunker stations. When the United States was called upon to build millions of tons of ships during the war, then, oil burners were constructed in preference to coal burners, with the result that at the end of the war around 80 per cent of American sea-going ships burned oil.[32]

As the following table indicates, shipbuilders of other nations readily followed the lead of the United States when they found coal prices soaring during and following the war while oil was becoming more abundant through the expansion of production and the extension of the world's oil-bunkering system. By the middle of 1922 one-fourth of the world's mercantile marine was equipped to burn oil; five years later the proportion had climbed to 35 per cent. The latter figure indicates that the decline in coal prices during this period did little to stem the tide of shift away from coal in marine propulsion. The advantages of oil over coal had become widely recognized. Coal-burners continued to be built, of course, down through the Second World War, but for some types of ships – naval warships, tankers, passenger liners – oil quickly displaced coal almost completely. The 'Queens of the Atlantic', for example, were converted to oil burning in the early 1920s and all of the 18 new ships included in Cunard's building programme after the war called for oil burners.[33] Passenger lines operating on other routes also shifted to oil during this same period.[34] The days of the 'Hairy Ape' were clearly numbered with no particular regrets by anyone concerned.[35] Some shipping operators hedged their bets by constructing steamers equipped to burn either coal or oil alternatively and turned from one to the other as comparative prices changed,[36] but the motor vessel – strictly an oil burner – secured an increasing number of adherents, especially for use as passenger ships, tank ships, and in the coastal trades.

TABLE 3

*Percentages of World's Total Merchant Fleet (exclusive of Sailing Ships)
using the Specified Form of Motive Power*

Year	Coal	Oil fuel under boilers	Internal combustion (diesel) engines
1914	96·6	2·9	0·5
1922	74·1	23·4	2·5
1924	68·9	27·9	3·2
1927	63·9	29·3	6·8
1929	60·8	29·2	10·0
1935	51·0	31·2	17·8

Sources: Adapted from *Parliamentary Papers*, Committee on Industry and Trade, *Survey of Metal Industries* (1928), 387, and P.E.P. (Political and Economic Planning), *Report on the British Coal Industry* 1936), 116.

The advocates of the continued use of coal in ocean shipping refused to give in without one major last-ditch effort to make coal – this time in pulverized form – an effective competitor for oil. Pulverized coal had been used for years for stationary plants on land because of its superiority to lump coal in terms of efficiency, saving of labour, and steady steaming conditions. Its use at sea had been precluded, however, by the size of the burner required. In the late 1920s the Peabody Engineering Corporation of New York developed a new smaller burner permitting the use of pulverized coal at sea, and the U.S. Shipping Board thought sufficiently highly of its possibilities to convert an oil-burning freighter into a coal user by installing the new burner. The *Mercer* performed reasonably successfully during its trial runs in 1928, but several drawbacks were disclosed: minor mechanical problems, ashes settling on the deck from the smoke generated, and, most important, the necessity for the ship to carry pulverizing equipment and convert lump coal into powdered form just prior to use because of the danger of spontaneous combustion in pulverized coal stored in bunkers. Failure to resolve this latter problem put the 'wishful thinking' label on the articles in British journals which saw the new fuel as a revivifying agent for the British coal industry.[37]

It was clear, then, that nothing would halt the swing from coal to oil in world shipping, with all its attendant consequences for the British coal industry. But the adverse impact on British shipbuilding was not so apparent. Vested interests in coal as fuel and as cargo were jeopardized, it is true, but were not new opportunities being created by rising demands for oil-fired ships? The answer is in the affirmative, but it must be qualified.

The increasing use of fuel oil did not entirely provide a fresh demand on the shipbuilding industry for new construction. Many vessels were simply converted from coal to oil burning – a relatively simple operation, requiring primarily the installation of oil burners and the stiffening and tightening of the coal bunkers and some of the double bottoms to carry oil. A coal-burning vessel, however, could not be converted into a motor vessel (diesel), so here was a new area opened for exploitation. As it turned out, the opportunities created in the construction of motor vessels were not adequately exploited by British firms.

TABLE 4
Percentage of Fleet using Diesel Propulsion

Country	1923 %	1929 %	1939 %
Norway	8·3	29·9	62·2
Denmark	16·0	29·2	52·2
Sweden	16·1	27·1	46·6
Holland	2·9	13·2	45·5
Japan	0·8	5·4	27·2
Germany	4·2	14·4	26·2
Great Britain	2·0	9·5	25·6
Italy	3·1	14·4	20·8
World	2·6	9·7	24·4

Source: S. G. Sturmey, *British Shipping and World Competition* (1962), 84. Based on figures in *Lloyd's Register*.

The shippers of the world were quick to realize the advantages of the diesel ship: while over 63 per cent of the ships on the world's register in 1927 (exclusive of sailing ships) were coal burners, almost half of the ships under construction in March of that year were being built as motor ships.[38] But in the United Kingdom, motor ships made up only 38 per cent of new construction.[39] Recognizing that fuel is the largest single item of internationally variable costs, making up at that time around one-fifth to one-fourth of total costs,[40] the Scandinavian countries not only pioneered in the development of the motor ship but also converted their shipyards over to the production of motor ships as early as the First World War. Scandinavian shipowners, sold on the advantages of the motor ship, favoured their yards with substantial orders for new ships of that type (in turn disposing of many of their old steamers to German shippers as replacements for ships lost under the terms of the Versailles Treaty). In addition to providing an important export commodity, the result, as the following table shows, was that the Scandinavian countries built up fleets made up in large proportion of the efficient, economical diesel-propelled ships.

Firmly wedded to the steam engine, British shipbuilders had left the adaptation of the diesel motor to marine propulsion to others and largely continued to do what they had proved they could do so well – build steamers. And with some reason. Over the years the tramp steamer – the backbone of British shipping – had been improved to the point where it was efficient, reliable, and economical. The early diesel, on the other hand, while providing significant economies as compared with steam under the best conditions, had a pronounced tendency to break down under other than ideal conditions.[41] The First World War came along to divert the energies of British shippers and shipbuilders just as the most active period of development of the diesel motor got under way. The staggering amount of British shipping lost during the war was replaced by the early 1920s, but with conventional steamers, not motor vessels. In order to take advantage of high post-war freight rates, British shippers took the ships most readily available: those built during the war by the British government, ceded German ships, those placed on the market by foreign owners, and new ships turned out by British builders.[42] Since few British builders had taken much interest in the new diesel motors, and since British shippers were more interested in lower first cost than in longer-run economies of operation,[43] few of the new ships were diesel burners. Added to this was the fact that "the combination of a group structure and the conference system had resulted in an industry heavily biased towards maintaining the *status quo* and ill-adapted to showing flexibility to meet the enormous changes of the inter-war period."[44] During the 1920s, after the question of oil availability had been resolved and the diesel engine had proved itself, British shipowners found themselves locked into a steamer fleet, for which they had made commitments to pay exorbitant prices. The difficulty of raising additional capital, then, partly explains why "British owners...showed a lack of initiative and a general reluctance to keep abreast of modern developments in marine engineering."[45] And when a British shipper was found who championed the motor vessel, his efforts were frustrated. Both in his leadership of the Royal Mail group and in the exercise of his authority as chairman of Harland and Wolff – the sole licence-holders for probably the best British diesel engines – Lord Kylsant promoted the motor ship. When the Royal Mail group foundered in 1932, this vigorous force for modernization of the British fleet came to a halt. Which of the various elements described should be given greatest weight is still a matter of dispute, but the unquestionable reluctance or inability of British shipping and shipbuilding to innovate, thereby allowing the business to fall into other hands, has been given as the major reason for the relative decline in British shipbuilding.[46]

Evidence for this view is of two sorts: the rising proportion of diesel-propelled ships in the world's fleets, and the failure of British shipbuilders to keep pace with shipyards specializing in the production of such ships. The ratio of gross tonnage of motorships in the world's merchant navy to steamships (oil and coal combined) rose from about 1 to 14 in 1927 and to around 1 to 3 in 1950.[47] This reduction in the ratio was achieved by an extraordinary rise in motorship tonnage (4·3 to 21·0 million), accompanied by virtual stagnation in steamship building (59 million to 63·5 million tons).[48] Since Britain was concentrating on building steamers and the Scandinavian countries were building diesel ships, it necessarily follows that the relative proportions of shipping tonnage built by Great Britain, as compared with the smaller European countries (the most important of which, for present purposes, are the Scandinavian countries), fell steadily during this period: seven to one before the First World War, around three to one in the 1920s, two to one in the 1930s, and as little as three to two in the immediate post-Second World War years.[49] If further evidence of the weakened British position is needed, it is provided by the decline in British shipbuilding exports. Just before the First World War Britain supplied slightly more than one-fourth of the tonnage requirements of the non-British world; in the period just before the Second World War she built less than one-eighth of this tonnage.[50] In view of the foregoing, the judgment of one recent writer on the failure of the world's leading shipbuilding nation to capitalize on this basic new opportunity appears reasonable: "With this passing of technical genius in the shipbuilding world to another country there went something of the brilliance, adaptability and experimental attack of the industry which had come to the fore when, with steam and steel in the ascendancy, shipbuilding centered itself in the industrial centers of the north."[51]

This loss of business for British yards and shipping was watched with dismay in Britain, but was not watched idly. Convinced that the large amount of idle shipbuilding capacity increased unit building costs, the British shipbuilding industry in 1930 launched a program to scrap 1¼ million tons of construction capacity. A new private corporation, National Shipbuilders Security Ltd, was formed and succeeded in buying and dismantling berths sufficient to reduce costs of production by 1939 by an estimated 5 per cent.[52] The British government also provided help. Tramp shipping was provided with an operating subsidy in 1935, to vary with the level of freights. And to encourage shippers to modernize their fleets, providing employment thereby for British yards, a 'scrap-and-build' programme was promulgated. Low-interest loans were made available for the building of new ships, provided that two tons were scrapped for every ton built. This accelerated the shift from coal to oil propulsion, because it could be taken for granted that the ships scrapped would be coal burners. The activity stimulated by the program, however, was not extraordinary: only 50 vessels, aggregating less than 200,000 tons, were built under the scheme – and many of these would have been built without the aid of the programme. And many of the ships scrapped came from abroad, having been bought in the open market instead of being taken from the shipping firms' own fleets.[53]

As well as a new method of propulsion, the shift to oil created a demand for an entirely new type of carrier – the oil tanker. Just where and when the first oil tanker was built and came into use is impossible to say with certainty, because of the difficulty of defining the term 'tanker'. Most of the earliest experiments with the carriage of petroleum in bulk were made in vessels designed for other purposes but equipped to carry bulk oil cargoes through the ironplating of holds, the installation of tanks in holds, or the building of double walls, sealed with felt and cement, between holds. The steel sailing vessel *Atlantic* sailed along the American coast as early as 1863, carrying bulk oil in her holds which had been divided into compartments.[54]

In the early 1870s three ships were built at Jarrow-on-Tyne, with the primary purpose of transporting passengers but also equipped to transport oil in bulk. Oil had such a reputation as a dangerous cargo at the time, however, that the passengers were never informed that the vessels carried oil. In fact, so carefully was the secret of the 'dangerous' cargo kept that it is doubtful that the ships ever carried oil at all.[55] Robert and Ludwig Nobel, brothers of Alfred Nobel of explosives fame, are credited with having had the first real tanker built, based on the principle that the skin of the vessel was at the same time the wall of the cargo tanks. Their *Zoroaster*, a 250-ton oil burner as well as bulk oil carrier, came out of a Swedish yard in 1878 and went to work transporting petroleum products from Baku over the Caspian Sea to the mouth of the Volga. Within four years of the delivery of the *Zoroaster* the Nobel brothers' fleet grew to include a dozen tank steamers.[56]

The success of the Baltic tankers undoubtedly contributed to the introduction of the tank ship into the Atlantic trade. Once the pioneer voyage was completed by the *Glück Auf* in July 1886 the advantages of the Atlantic trade appeared so obvious that by 1891 between 80 and 90 tank steamers were operating on the Atlantic alone.[57]

Interestingly, the Suez Canal – which in the twentieth century has carried millions of tons of oil – was introduced late to the tanker. In the 1890s there was an extensive carriage of petroleum through the canal, but the passage was from north to south, not the reverse as it was later, and the petroleum took the form not of crude oil but of kerosene – "oil for the lamps of China". The kerosene was packed and transported in the 'American fashion' – put up in five gallon tins can and shipped from Batum to the Far East via Suez in ordinary cargo ships. There it competed against Standard Oil Company kerosene which had been similarly packed and carried by sailing ships around Cape Horn. When Marcus Samuel, founder of the 'Shell' Transport and Trade Co. of London, asked permission of the Suez Canal Company to send his tanker *Murex* through the canal with bulk kerosene his request touched off a furore of opposition. Welsh makers of tin-plates envisioned a drastic decline in demand for their product, cargo shipowners feared the loss of their trade to tankers, and the Standard Oil Company foresaw the loss of its competitive advantage in the Far East. Petitions flooded the offices of the British government, demanding that the government use its influence to induce the Suez Canal Company to keep the canal forever closed to bulk tankers. Experts were hired to prove that the passage of tank steamers through the canal would result in disastrous explosions and uncontrollable fires. The British government refused to intercede, however, and the Suez Canal Company finally, and after thorough investigation, gave permission for passage of the *Murex*.[58] The *Murex* was shortly followed by other tankers, mainly Shell or Royal Dutch. By the beginning of the First World War the two companies, now allied, were moving around half-a-million tons of oil through the canal each year. The First World War reversed the flow of oil through the Suez Canal. Access to the oil-producing fields of Russia – chief source of supply for eastward-bound petroleum – was denied to non-Russian distributors following the Revolution. The loss was not as serious as it might have been, however, because of the increasing exploitation of oil resources elsewhere, especially in the Far and Middle East. Ultimately the westbound traffic via Suez (or via the Cape of Good Hope when the canal was closed) reached gigantic proportions.

As with diesel propulsion the opportunities created in the carriage of oil were not fully utilized by British builders. Although some of the pioneering work in the development of the tanker had been carried out in British yards, British shipbuilders steadily lost ground to the builders of other nations, as table 5 shows. In part the reason for British backwardness was the same as with the diesel – failure to keep

TABLE 5
Dry-Cargo and Tanker Fleets, 1913 to 1938
(*Ships of over 100 tons gross*)

Year	World fleet (million tons)			British fleet (million tons)			British percentage of world fleet		
	Tanker	Dry cargo	Total	Tanker	Dry cargo	Total	Tanker	Dry cargo	Total
1913	1·4	45·4	46·9	0·7	18·0	18·7	50·0	39·6	39·8
1923	5·2	60·0	65·2	1·7	17·6	19·3	32·7	29·3	29·6
1928	6·6	60·4	67·0	2·1	17·8	19·9	31·8	29·4	29·7
1933	8·9	59·0	67·9	2·3	16·4	18·7	25·8	27·8	27·5
1938	10·7	57·1	67·8	2·7	15·1	17·8	25·2	26·4	26·2

Source: S. G. Sturmey, *British Shipping and World Competition* (1962), 75. Based on figures in *Lloyd's Register*.

abreast of changing technology as a result of over-fondness for steam propulsion. But there were additional factors involved: (1) Profit margins were skimpy under the sale and lease-back arrangements then in effect. (2) Until 1932 there were no international load-line rules for tankers, but British owners were subject to stringent Board of Trade rules dating from 1906. (3) In order to conserve their own capital for exploration British oil interests preferred to lease foreign-owned tonnage rather than build their own ships. (4) Liner owners did not see tankers as an obvious venture, and besides they needed their capital for replacement and improvement of liner fleets. (5) And the tramp owners, faced with operating high-cost post-war ships in a period of depressed freight rates, had little margin for speculation, especially when they were at a competitive disadvantage in bargaining with their main customers, the large oil companies.[59] But perhaps it is also true, as Sturmey insists, that "British shipowners scarcely thought of tankers, which they regarded as hardly being ships at all, much as the American sailing shipowners in the nineteenth century turned their backs on steamships which they regarded as floating kettles not worthy of their consideration."[60] Whatever the reason, the simple fact is that the British were offered another opportunity – one which their past history suggests they should have seized eagerly – but they failed to take full advantage of it.

By the 1950s the shift from coal to oil in ocean shipping was virtually complete. The Second World War accelerated a process already well advanced when the war broke out, and the immediate post-war years saw the consummation of the process. Not only had the construction of coal-burning ships been given up by 1955, but practically all coal-burners had been replaced by ships using oil as their source of power.[61] All that remained was the reckoning.

CONCLUSION

The most apparent consequence of the shift from coal to oil was the loss of Britain's coal bunkering trade. Because Europe was rather slow to replace coal with oil for uses other than marine propulsion,[62] there was still some market for British coal on the Continent – 4·2 million tons as late as 1958.[63] But by that year bunker coal shipments had fallen to well under one million tons.[64] Although the volume of exports other than coal had grown during the previous half-century (from 16·9 million tons in 1913 to 24·3 million in 1958),[65] the growth had by no means matched the increase in the volume of imports (from 56·0 million tons in 1931 to 104·2 million in 1958) – a substantial part of which was the import of petroleum (47·3 million tons in 1958).[66] Whereas, thanks to coal, shippers earlier had had an abundance of outbound cargo (roughly two tons for each ton of inbound freight), the situation was exactly reversed by 1958, when each ton of imports was matched by less than one-third of a ton of export cargo. No longer, it is apparent, did British shippers enjoy the competitive advantage of an earlier era, when an outbound voyage in ballast was a rarity. The result was a rise in inbound freights, as had long been predicted should coal exports decline. To give one example, freight figures published by the *Statist* show that while coal freights from Cardiff to the River Plate fell from 14s. (70p) on 30 July 1914 to 9s. 3d. (46p) on 2 August 1934, in response to increased competition for outbound payloads, return rates for grain rose from 12s. 6d. (62½p) on 30 July 1914 to 17s. 6d. (87½p) on 2 August 1934, as shippers tried to recoup their outbound losses.[67] A more general example is provided by the *Economist* Index of Freight Rates, extracts from which are given in table 6. The bonus provided the British consumer and manufacturer in the form of low import freight rates as result of the availability of large-volume exports of coal was largely a thing of the past. Shippers made a constant search for ways to increase their round-trip load factor – including the building of 'half-breed' ships, part dry cargo carrier, part oil tanker – but these availed little. Britain had finally to face up to the fact that she would henceforth have the unfavourable freight balance that highly-industrialized countries tend always to have because imports of foods and raw materials outweigh exports of manufactured goods. Arrangements were made whereby a few of the British tankers which came home with crude oil went out with fuel oils for bunkering stations lying on their return routes, but this was a far cry from 'wheat inwards, coal outwards' of tramp shipping days.

TABLE 6

Route	Index of Freight Rates (1898–1913 = 100)			
	February 1936	May 1936	August 1936	November 1936
Total all routes, inbound and outbound	90·6	88·8	97·5	96·6
Mediterranean:				
outwards	81·3	80·3	85·3	93·1
homewards	88·4	89·2	99·7	124·9
South America:				
outwards	61·9	61·3	60·8	68·8
homewards	108·4	109·1	118·2	137·0
India:				
outwards	84·2	77·2	80·0	88·4
homewards	115·2	107·7	125·3	123·1

Source: Adapted from the *Economist* Index of Freight Rates, published in the issues of 21 March (p. 641), 20 June (p. 670), 12 September (p. 470), and 12 December 1936 (pp. 517–18).

In fact, the replacement of coal by oil went far to destroy Britain's tramp shipping business. The tramp is the drudge of the seas, carrying the dirty and bulky cargoes which have great weight or size in proportion to value – which meant pre-eminently coal. British tramp shipping, built up to a large extent on the long-distance coal trade, was seriously weakened by losses during the First World War and the terms on which replacements were built after the war. Then came the post-war decline in the coal trade, which served to undermine the economic basis of the tramp shipping business. In the days of coal, a tramp could count on an outbound cargo and could almost always pick up a cargo of coal to pay its way from port to port. But tramps could not carry oil, and a substantial part of the dry cargo other than coal could easily be carried by ships operating on a regular schedule. In consequence, British tramps declined in number and tonnage by over 50 per cent from 1913 to 1933.[68] Part of this decline was more apparent than real, since British liners took over some traffic that had previously been handled by tramps. But another part was indeed real. Increasingly, as table 7 shows, British shippers fell back on the ties of empire for continued business, leaving to foreign ships the carriage of goods from foreign country to foreign country. In fact, British ships, having lost their competitive edge, were unable to hold the home trade against foreign competition, as table 8 indicates.

TABLE 7
Geographical Distribution of British Carrying Trade

Trade	Proportion by value of goods carried in each trade		
	1912 %	1931 %	1936 %
Inter-Imperial			
United Kingdom–Empire	23·5	29·0	36·0
Empire–Empire	3·5	4·0	5·0
Total	27·0	33·0	41·0
Empire–Foreign			
United Kingdom–Foreign	40·0	37·0	29·5
Empire–Foreign	11·5	14·0	15·5
Total	51·5	51·0	45·0
Total trade of Empire	78·5	84·0	86·0
Foreign–Foreign	21·5	16·0	14·0
Total	100·0	100·0	100·0

Source: Adapted from H. Leak, 'The Carrying Trade of British Shipping', *Journal of the Royal Statistical Society*, CII (1939), 254.

In ocean shipping, substantial benefits were offered nations able to capitalize on the opportunities presented in the shift from coal to oil. But the British, as has been shown, were unable or unwilling to take full advantage of the situation. The consequences are well known: a drastic decline in Britain's role as world shipper and world ship-builder.

In place of coal exports, of course, Great Britain now has an important oil refining industry which provides employment for a large fleet of tankers, serves as a basis for the manufacture and export of oil-well drilling machinery and petroleum refining equipment, and contributes substantial amounts of refined petroleum products for export as well. But for these Britain must stand ready to lay out millions of pounds sterling annually for imports of crude petroleum and refined petroleum products she produces in insufficient amounts for her own needs. The net drain on her balance of payments is substantial, and it is vain to hope that oil can ever attain the position in the balance of payments that coal had achieved at the turn of the century, when coal exports and their carriage contributed something like £60 million toward payment of imports.[69] The supersession of coal by oil created opportunities, but for the British economy it is clear that the benefits by no means matched the losses.

TABLE 8

Proportion by value of British Imports and Exports Carried in British Ships

Trade with	Imports		Exports	
	1913	1937	1913	1937
	%	%	%	%
British countries	97	92·4	99	98·7
Foreign countries	66	51·6	64	58·5

Source: Adapted from H. Leak, 'The Carrying Trade of British Shipping',
Journal of the Royal Statistical Society, CII (1939), 226.

Perhaps the most important long-run consideration is non-economic: Britain has placed herself in the position where her fleets, merchant and naval, are almost entirely dependent on foreign fuel supplies. Any curtailment of oil supplies means a threat to her maritime position and economic well-being – as the Arab oil embargo of 1973 demonstrated.

NOTES

For helpful suggestions, special thanks are due to the Editorial board.

1. D. H. Aldcroft, 'The Mercantile Marine,' in D. H. Aldcroft (ed.), *The Development of British Industry and Foreign Competition*, 1875–1914 (1968) 328.
2. See Max E. Fletcher, 'The Suez Canal and World Shipping, 1869–1914', *Journal of Economic History*, XVIII (December 1958).
3. W. Stanley Jevons, *The Coal Question* (1865), vii.
4. *Parliamentary Papers*, 1926, xiv, 3.
5. D. A. Thomas, 'The Growth and Direction of Our Foreign Trade in Coal During the Last Half Century', *Journal of the Royal Statistical Society*, LXVI (1903), 440.
6. G. P. Jones and A. G. Pool, *A Hundred Years of Economic Development in Great Britain* (1940), 188.
7. *Economist*, 21 February 1925, 338.
8. This statement does something less than justice to the remaining 15 per cent of the volume of exports since coal was largely carried by tramp ships and the important part of other heavy or bulky exports, such as iron and steel, machinery, and textiles, was carried by liners. The liners therefore depended on these latter products for export cargoes much as the tramps depended on coal.
9. P.E.P. (Political and Economic Planning), *Report on the British Coal Industry* (1936), 152.
10. Robert E. Annin, *Ocean Shipping* (New York, 1920), 89.
11. *Ibid.*, 90.
12. Thomas, *op. cit.*, 469.
13. Witt Bowden, Michael Karpovich, and Abbott Payson Usher, *An Economic History of Europe since 1750* (New York, 1937), 386–7.
14. R. S. Sayers, *A History of Economic Change in England, 1880–1939* (1967), 108.

15. The close relationship between inbound and outbound freight rates during this period has been demonstrated many times. Erich W. Zimmermann, for example, in *Zimmermann on Ocean Shipping* (New York, 1923), p. 240, provides figures showing coal freight rates from Cardiff to La Plata and return wheat freight rates from La Plata to Europe in 1910. In July both rates stood at about 13s. (65p). From that point to the end of the year coal freight rates fell steadily, reaching 7s. 6d. (37½p) on 18 December – and on that date wheat rates from La Plata were quoted at 18s. 6d. (92½p).

16. P.E.P., *op. cit.*, 97.

17. *Ibid.*, 11.

18. W. H. B. Court, 'Problems of the British Coal Industry Between the Wars', *Economic History Review*, XV (1945), 21.

19. Recent analysis has suggested that Britain's coal industry problems were the predictable results of a carry-over of unsatisfactory conditions and developments of the pre-war and wartime periods. On the basis of seemingly unlimited demands for coal, Britain had built up a high wage, labour-intensive industry before the war, giving insufficient thought to problems of effective management and organization of the industry in the face of the rapidly diminishing returns resulting from the necessity to mine deeper, thinner seams. The war aggravated this situation by forcing dilution of the skilled labour force, overworking of the more productive seams, and retardation of long-term development work. See A. J. Taylor, 'The Coal Industry', in D. H. Aldcroft (ed.), *op. cit.*, esp. 68–70, and Sidney J. Pollard, *The Development of the British Economy*, 1914–1967 (2nd edn, New York, 1969), 4–5.

20. *Parliamentary Papers, Report of the Royal Commission on the Coal Industry* (1925), 1926, 13; P E.P., *op. cit.*, 97. The decline in the bunker trade was actually more severe than these figures indicate, since the figures refer only to coal shipped by vessels refuelling at ports of the United Kingdom. They do not represent the total amount of British coal consumed by the world's shipping. In years past, as previously mentioned, considerable quantities of British coal were shipped to such places as Gibraltar, Malta, Port Said, etc., and figured in the trade returns as 'exports', although in fact they represented, to a large extent, supplies for replenishment of bunkering stations at these places. It is impossible to know exactly, but perhaps as much as one-third of the British coal exports were used ultimately as steamer fuel, which means that around one-half of all coal shipped from ports in the United Kingdom ended up in steamer stokeholds.

21. *Ibid.*

22. 'Angier Brothers' Freight and Steam Shipping Review', 31 December 1886, in E. A. V. Angier, *Fifty Years' Freights: 1869–1919* (1920), 67.

23. 'Angier Brothers' Steam Shipping Report, 1898', in Angier, *op. cit.*, 96.

24. *The Royal Dutch Petroleum Company (N.V. Koninklijke Nederlandshe Petroleum Maatschappij)* (The Hague, 1950), 130. This gives the Dutch credit for the first ocean-going motor vessel, but the claim has been vigorously disputed. The Danes, the Swedes, and even the Italians have all made cases for their own ships. See Knut Berg, 'Early Scandinavian Motor Vessels', in Craig J. M. Carter (ed.), *Ships Annual* (1958), 49, and S. C. Gilfillan, *Inventing the Ship* (Chicago, 1935), 203.

25. These were sufficient, it was estimated, to reduce operating costs other than for the fuel itself (wages, victualling, repairs to furnace tools, stokehold plates, lamps, etc.) from 2s.–2s. 6d. (10–12½p) per ton of coal to 7½d.–9d. (3–4p) per ton of oil in the case of moderate-sized cargo steamers, and to as low as 4d. (1½p) per ton of oil in large liners. And far less oil than coal was burned per ton-mile. See Andrew Laing, 'Oil Fuel on Shipboard', *Engineering Magazine*, XXXVI (January 1909), 695. It is obvious that oil could be considerably more expensive than coal on a per-ton basis and still be the cheaper fuel.

26. George Melville, 'Liquid Fuel for Naval and Marine Uses,' *Scientific American*, S61 (17 February 1906), 25183.

27. *Ibid.*

28. 'Crude Oil Fuel in the French Navy', *Scientific American*, S71, (24 June 1911), 391.

29. *Parliamentary Debates*, House of Commons, 5th ser., LV (1913), 1469.

30. *Ibid.*, 1474.

31. *Ibid.*, 1475.

32. Zimmermann, *op. cit.*, 177.

33. Cunard Steam Ship Co., Ltd, *Over Eighty Years of Trans-Atlantic Travel* (n.d.), no page numbers.

34. See Francis E. Hyde, *Liverpool and the Mersey: An Economic History of a Port, 1700–1970* (Newton Abbot, 1971), esp. 150, 153.

35. William McFee, 'Oil and the Hairy Ape', *Fortnightly Review*, CXXXVII (May 1932), 565–79.

36. The rule of thumb at the time in the British merchant marine was that oil was priced out of the marine propulsion market whenever its price exceeded about twice that of coal. At that point, steamers which had been converted to oil burners were simply converted back to coal-fired furnaces. See 'Oil-III,' *Economist*, 26 May 1923, 1183.

37. F. D. McHugh, 'Pulverized Coal Goes to Sea', *Scientific American*, CXXXVIII (May 1928), pp. 434f.

38. *Parliamentary Papers*, Committee on Industry and Trade, *op. cit.*, 388.

39. *Ibid.*

40. R. O. Roberts, 'Comparative Shipping and Shipbuilding Costs', *Economica*, N.S. XIV (November 1947), 297.

41. McFee, *op. cit.*, 571.

42. S. G. Sturmey, *British Shipping and World Competition* (1962), 58–60.

43. S. B. Saul, 'The Engineering Industry', in D. H. Aldcroft (ed.), *op. cit.*, 218–19.

44. Sturmey, *op. cit.*, 397.

45. Leslie Jones, *Shipbuilding in Britain* (1957), 83. Jones is here referring to widely-held views, not necessarily his own.

46. Ingvar Svennilson, *Growth and Stagnation in the European Economy* (Geneva, 1954), 155.

47. *Ibid.*

48. *Ibid.*

49. *Ibid.*

50. Jones, *op. cit.*, 62.

51. John R. Parkinson, *The Economics of Shipbuilding in the United Kingdom* (1960), 7.

52. *Ibid.*, 140.

53. *Ibid.*, 152f.

54. *The Royal Dutch Petroleum Company*, *op. cit.*, 122.

55. *Ibid.*

56. Laurence Dunn, *The World's Tankers* (1956), 22.

57. *Ibid.*

58. The full story of this episode is contained in *Parliamentary Papers, Correspondence Respecting the Passage of Petroleum in Bulk through the Suez Canal* (1892), lxxi.

59. These from Sturmey, *op. cit.*, 77.

60. *Ibid.*, 78–9.

61. O.E.E.C., Oil Committee, *Oil: The Outlook for Europe* (Paris, 1956), 15.

62. Oil supplied only 15 per cent of total energy requirements in Europe in 1955, compared with 37 per cent for the world as a whole. *Ibid.*, 13.

63. *Parliamentary Papers, Statistical Abstract of the United Kingdom.*

64. *Ibid.*

65. Parkinson, *op. cit.*, 59.

66. *Ibid.*

67. *Statist*, 4 August, 1934, 180.

68. Jones, *op. cit.*, 52.

69. Thomas, *op. cit.*, 455.

11 The development of Japan's post-war shipping policy

TOMOHEI CHIDA

The development of Japan's post-war shipping industry

When World War II ended in August 1945 Japanese-owned tonnage totalled a mere 1·34 million gross tons (g.t.). In view of the fact that Japan had owned 6·32 million g.t. at the outbreak of war in 1941, and that an additional 3·97 million g.t. was built during the war, the volume of tonnage lost during the war becomes immediately apparent. Of the 1·34 million tonnage remaining at the end of the war, most was too obsolete to be operated; among the 500,000 g.t. that could be operated, only five or six vessels could be put on to the ocean-going service. In effect, then, Japan's shipping industry had by the end of the war been virtually extinguished.[1]

By 1980, however, Japan had become the second largest maritime nation in the world, owning a total of 34·24 million g.t. Her shipping industry had developed very rapidly in the intervening thirty years. That figure, however, represents only a part of her total shipping industry. In the same year Japan chartered many foreign vessels, to a total of 22·49 million g.t. Many of these were vessels owned by Japanese shipping companies but registered under foreign flags. Taking these into consideration, the actual scale of shipping operations was even more extensive than at first appears.[2] At the same time, the structure of Japan's shipping industry underwent considerable change. Let me compare it with the pre-war structure.

Between the two world wars, the industry consisted roughly of three groups of companies:

1. Two large-scale liner companies. NYK (Nippon Yusen Kaisha) and OSK (Osaka Shosen Kaisha) fell into this group. They were subsidised by the government, and were generally called 'Sha-sen'.
2. Tramp 'operators'. Yamashita Line, Kawasaki Line, Daido Line, the shipping division of Mitsui Bussan KK (which developed into Mitsui Line during the war), and others fell into this group. They were generally called 'Shagai-sen'. These companies differed in their establishment, but resembled one another in the way

they operated tramps on a large scale, both their own vessels, whose tonnage was generally very small, and many vessels chartered, on a time charter basis, from the next, 'owner', group. The top managements of these companies were enterprising, and it was, I think, their managerial skill that helped the country's shipping industry to develop in the depressed world market between the wars. Gradually they started operating liners and expanded their business.

3. 'Owners'. These were small companies, some of which owned only one vessel. There were many of them, and they were generally called 'owners'. They had no intention, nor were they capable, of operating the vessels they owned. They owned them simply to charter them out.

Since 1945, shipping companies which started operating liners have increased. The companies in group 1 continued their liner operations and those in group 2 also expanded their business in this field. On top of this, many new companies were established and joined them. In the 1960s many concerns in groups 1 and 2, and newly established ones, started operating tankers and other specialised vessels. One after another they diversified their business to their utmost possible extent. Group 3 companies, on the other hand, worked closely with specific operators and modified their function in the changing post-war shipping market.

In the first half of the 1960s the world shipping industry was stagnant for a long period. The industry was greatly depressed in Japan in particular, and many felt that the situation was hopeless. The main reason for such acute depression was the growth in the number of shipping companies and the keen competition between them. The government offered subsidies to help them recover from the depression and, in exchange, instructed them to reorganise themselves independently into groups. On 1 April 1964 ninety-five companies engaged in ocean-going shipping were reorganised into six groups. The tonnage owned by these ninety-five totalled about 90 per cent of the Japanese ocean-going fleet. This demonstrates how significant a reorganisation it was. Following the success of this reorganisation and a favourable upswing of the shipping market, most of the companies were able to pay dividends by March 1968. This grouping has been maintained up to the present, and it was this basic structure which enabled Japan's shipping industry to develop during the period.

The causes of growth

Immediately after the war the Allied forces imposed restrictions on Japan's shipping industry as a part of the process of demilitarising and democratising the country's economy. These restrictions had to be removed before the industry could develop. Foremost among them was a limit on the tonnage the industry could own. Initially this was so severe that the permitted tonnage was equal to that of 1903. Subsequently several missions were sent from the United States to discuss what tonnage

Japan should own. Each time the restriction was relaxed. In May 1948 the Draper mission published the Johnston report, which advised against retaining any restriction, but rather encouraged a larger ownership. It also proposed an expansion of shipbuilding facilities. The US government made a decision based on this view in September 1949. It is said that tension between East and West caused the relaxation and eventual lifting of the restrictions. In fact in June 1950 the Korean war broke out.

A second set of restrictions were imposed upon the economic activities of the major shipping companies by the anti-trust policy of the Allies. These restrictions, too, were removed in 1948. And thirdly, for some time after the war, shipping companies could not manage nor operate their own vessels. During the war, in 1942, a controlling agency called Sempaku Uneikai had been established. It alone controlled and operated Japanese merchant vessels hired on a bare charter basis. After the war all vessels were put under Allied control, but the Sempaku Uneikai retained their actual management and operation. The owners of the vessels merely owned them. Gradually this restriction was lifted. In April 1950 the owners regained full control of the management and operation of their own vessels. This was called 'return of management to ship owners'. Crews as well as vessels were restored to the owners' control. Numbering some 65,000 at the end of the war, crew members had been employees of Sempaku Uneikai; now they returned to the employment of their former companies. Since then Japanese merchant vessels have been allowed to fly the national flag.

'Return of management to ship owners', however, did not permit the shipping companies complete freedom to put their vessels into international trade. This was part of the third restriction. In October 1945 Japanese vessels began shipping goods to Korea for the first time. For some time thereafter they had to obtain closed clearance from the trade partner for each voyage. Gradually, as Japan expanded her trade, some countries began to allow Japanese vessels to call at their ports by an open clearance, and such countries increased in number. However, it was not until the peace treaty of 1952 that Japan gained almost full right to unrestricted voyages.

In addition to these changes in the structure of the industry and the operational climate governing Japanese shipping, I believe the rapid growth noted above was facilitated by a number of other considerations, particularly the enactment of various maritime laws based upon a new concept.

The vital energy of the companies. Enterprising managers and hard-working shore staff and crew were the source of the industry's vitality. As mentioned above, it was commonly believed at the end of the war that Japan's shipping industry was virtually ruined. However, I do not believe this to have been true. Certainly the industry possessed neither vessels nor capital, having lost most of its fleet during the war and received no compensation from the government. In this respect, the industry could be said to have been completely destroyed. However, the experienced seamen, shore staff and the managers who reconstructed the industry later were the legacy of the pre-war era. The top management of the war period were purged by the Allies, and left their companies. However, their successors had also been employed in shipping before the war and had possessed the necessary industrial know-how. With all the top management gone, they became the new company managers at an exceptionally early age by Japanese standards.

Human energy and resources explain the revival of the Japanese shipping industry over the last thirty years — for example, keen competition between companies, which led to the reorganisation of 1964, and the introduction of advanced technology. Rivalry, for example, between NYK and MOL (Mitsui OSK Line) has been another factor: since the later 1970s they have become the 'big two' and are consolidating their positions. They co-operate with each other in some instances, but in others they are in strong competition. This competition has penetrated into every level of their organisations, from top management down to the rank-and-file crew members. Internal competition of this kind has been the major source of energy and the driving force behind the revival of Japanese shipping.

The attitude of the union. The Seamen's Union in Japan embraces every type of vocation, unlike seamen's unions in other countries. As an industry-wide union, it differs also from other Japanese unions. Established first after the war, it organises all the crew of ocean-going vessels except for a few radio operators. The union's strike record has not been good, compared, for example, with that of Great Britain, a fact which has annoyed ship owners.

Several other issues have divided employers and employees, but as far as rationalisation on board ship is concerned, the union has, at least since 1961, responded flexibly to the companies. I believe that such flexibility derives from the fact that the union is organised by crew who are employed for life by their company. Despite some occasional disputes, therefore, the union's attitude has made it possible to introduce new technology from the 1960s, and to maintain the international competitiveness of Japanese vessels in spite of rising labour costs.

The remarkable growth of the Japanese economy. The Japanese economy started its rapid growth in the 1960s. Since economic growth depended on exports and imports of goods, the shipping industry expanded at the same pace. Japan's economic growth depended on a changing industrial structure: the share of heavy industry and chemicals increased. The introduction of new technologies wrought a similar transformation in her merchant fleet. This successful adjustment can, I believe, be attributed to the vitality of the shipping companies and the flexibility of the union in accepting technological change.

The significance of post-war shipping policy: the government-sponsored 'Programmed Shipbuilding Scheme' and its effect. A shipping policy implies government measures for the national shipping industry and covers an extremely wide range. The important element, however, is a protective policy for the development or maintenance of the national shipping industry. In post-war Japan, the government-sponsored 'Programmed Shipbuilding Scheme' (Keikaku Zosen) and the 'Interest Subsidy for Shipping Finance' were the important protective measures. Under the latter programme the government would give a shipping company a subsidy to lighten the burden of interest payments on shipbuilding capital obtained on loan, mainly from private banks. If a company made a profit above a certain level, however, the subsidy had to be returned. This programme was put into effect spasmodically, to supplement the shipbuilding scheme. The government-sponsored Programmed Shipbuilding Scheme was the more significant.

This scheme is very simple. The government decides the tonnage to be built every year and loans the public fund on favourable terms to those companies that wish to build the appropriate ships. The amount of the loan varies according to the financial condition of the fund, the types of vessel the scheme is intended to promote, and so on.

The loan must be properly repaid and the amount does not cover the full cost of the vessel. The company, therefore, must absorb the balance itself. Shipping companies have also often built vessels using only funds they have raised themselves. The programme was introduced in 1947 and has been applied continuously to the present. It has contributed to the development of the merchant fleet, despite being less advantageous than government aid to shipping in foreign countries. I think it was because the scheme not only supplied capital but also allocated it in such a way as to determine the shape of Japan's shipping industry. Had it been merely a capital-supplying programme, its effect would have been very much less. Because of its flexibility, the scheme could be operated to take account of the changing economic environment in which the industry operated. The scheme has undergone many changes in its thirty-year history. One of the important reasons for them has been the need to encourage the industry to adapt to its changing environment. From time to time it has failed, but on the whole it successfully established the appropriate restructuring. The changes in the environment which have most affected the industry have been the rapid technological progress of ships, changes in the world shipping market, and the growth and structural change of the Japanese economy which is the industry's major market.

The following describes the role of the Programmed Shipbuilding Scheme in shaping the development and structure of Japan's merchant fleet over the last thirty years by citing important examples.[3]

It was after 1949, immediately before the 'Return of management to the ship owners', that the scheme was introduced to supply funds for ocean-going vessels. At the time many of the Allied restrictions had been removed, and Japanese vessels were engaged in ocean-going transport. My theme is especially concerned with the policy on ocean-going transport, and I will therefore elaborate on that further.

I have stated that the Programmed Shipbuilding Scheme has been applied flexibly. The first thing to notice here is that its final objective changed gradually in accordance with the change in the economy as a whole. The direct aim of the scheme was to promote the building of vessels: however, in practice it often also served as a policy to maintain the shipbuilding industry or as a labour policy to secure the employment of Japanese seamen.

In 1949 the construction of ocean-going vessels was started with the aid of the scheme. At that time Japanese vessels were not able to engage in ocean-going transport freely; their services were limited to the transport of goods indispensable to the Japanese people. Since the shipping industry had been cut off from the war indemnity, it could not build vessels with funds of its own. Hence, the scheme adopted as a priority the construction of vessels to transport goods indispensable to the Japanese people. The Korean war, which broke out in 1950, played a role as a springboard for the economy to stand on its own feet. After Japan became independent politically following the peace treaty in 1951, she made strides towards economic independence. At that time the main bottleneck in the economy was an unfavourable balance of international payments. This became very evident following the adoption in 1960 of an economic strategy aimed at doubling the national income in ten years, and it became a major constraint on economic growth. This condition lasted into the mid-1960s. The expansion of the ocean-going fleet under the scheme was initiated in order to improve the deficit in the balance of payments by minimising freight charges paid in foreign currency to overseas shipping companies.

Until the first closure of the Suez Canal in 1956, the scheme worked also as a shipbuilding policy. During this period Japanese orders for new vessels under the scheme created employment for Japanese shipbuilding yards. Lacking in international competitiveness, Japanese yards were confined to the home market, financed by funds supplied through the scheme. In this way they secured a larger tonnage for construction and could maintain a higher level of operation. By this means they caught up with foreign competitors technologically, and by 1956 they were constructing the largest tonnage in the world. At the same time, after 1955 the volume of tonnage exported exceeded that built for domestic use. After the closure of the Suez Canal, large orders were obtained at higher prices from overseas and their competitive position was enhanced. They then successfully developed economical large-type vessels. Along with other measures to lower the costs, such as their unique system of inventory management or process management, this formed the basis of the growth of the Japanese shipbuilding industry.

Since the mid-1960s, Japan's economy has grown as exports have increased. It became policy to develop the heavy and chemical industries, and their international competitive power increased. With this rapid growth of exports, Japan's international balance of payments remained favourable. The objective of the Programmed Shipbuilding Scheme was then shifted to accommodate this change, viz. from improving the balance of payments to securing enough tonnage to import the raw materials (mainly oil and iron ore) necessary for economic growth. The object was to protect economic growth from fluctuations in freight rates or in the availability of shipping by ensuring a ready supply of domestic vessels. This objective has been pursued up to the present day.

Secondly, the types of vessels built under the scheme and the tonnage of each type have quite flexibly changed, keeping pace with shifts in the overall objective of the scheme. In the same way vessels incorporating advanced technology, such as specialised vessels, large vessels and labour-saving vessels, have been built rapidly since the end of the 1950s. By means of the scheme, it was possible to plan not only the total tonnage to be built but also the proportion of types of vessels, and to provide the necessary finance. More finance has been allocated to the types of vessel the scheme wished to promote.

Thus by the mid-1960s the scheme placed priority on the construction of liners; the planned tonnage, the allotment of finance and the loan ratio were all adjusted. To expand the number of liners was the only way, in terms of shipping, to solve the country's unfavourable balance of payments. However, since the mid-1960s importance has also been placed on building tankers and ore carriers as well as liners, which were being replaced by container vessels.

As time went by, more priority was given to building tankers, especially those of the larger type. Construction of tankers under the scheme started in 1949. Since 1964 the planned tonnage has increased greatly, the loan ratio has risen and more priority has been given to the construction of larger tankers such as VLCCs. In 1969 a tanker of 130,000 g.t. was launched under the scheme. However, tonnage decreased greatly after the oil crisis of 1973. Ore carrier construction under the scheme was also started in 1958. Since the mid-1960s the planned tonnage has increased and its size has become larger.

So far I have broadly argued that varying the types of vessel built under the scheme was an important factor in determining the composition of Japan's merchant fleet. Since that has been achieved by actively introducing advanced technology in vessels, it has also served to modernise the fleet.

The Programmed Shipbuilding Scheme has also played an important role in the structuring of the Japanese shipping industry. Although it has made some mistakes in its thirty years' existence, they have been corrected.

Over this period, at least by the first oil crisis in 1973, most shipping companies have wished to build ships under the scheme. It has not been easy to select the companies or to determine the type and number of vessels to be built. Especially up to about 1963, long established shipping companies which had lost capital because of the war and newly established ones with limited finance rushed for the chance to expand their business by receiving loans under the scheme. In this situation the government made it a general rule to supply capital for one vessel to each chosen company each year. Even the large, long established companies received finance for no more than two vessels. The reason for pursuing this rule was not clear. The result was that, between 1947 and 1952, 161 vessels were allotted to more than sixty companies, and by 1963 a total of 434 vessels had been allotted to fifty-nine companies,[4] despite a reduction in the number of companies by way of amalgamation. Since all the companies were engaged in the transport of import and export goods, keen competition inevitably arose among them. This reflects the vitality and energy that these companies possessed. However, this keen competition did the industry considerable harm, particularly during the depression in world shipping which began to be felt about 1962. It seemed that it could scarcely recover. Evidently the structure of the industry created through the Programmed Shipbuilding Scheme had gone awry.

To rectify the problem, a drastic reorganisation of the shipping industry was undertaken on 1 April 1964, in which the scheme again played a significant role. Companies which had already been gradually amalgamated into a smaller number were further integrated into six groups. Ninety-five companies which owned about 90 per cent of the tonnage of Japan's ocean-going vessels were involved. In the context of world maritime history this reorganisation was unusual in its scope and in that it was undertaken at a stroke after only nine months' preparation. By comparison with the reorganisation of liner companies in Great Britain at the beginning of the 1900s, which took almost twenty years to accomplish, it was accomplished in an amazingly short period. The depression was so severe that it was the only way for the companies to survive.

The initiative of the government also made the reorganisation attainable. The government imposed no compulsion upon the companies; any company was free to participate or not, and it was left to their discretion as to how they should group themselves. It simply gave support to a group which met a set of requirements. The major part of its support was to approve the construction of vessels under the scheme. Here again, the allocation of finance under the scheme served to influence the structuring of the industry. It was another example of the scheme's flexibility.

The reorganisation was a success. In an extremely short period, Japanese shipping recovered from the depression, because the reorganisation had removed the excessive competition. Also, in the following period, the reformed organisations were unexpectedly able to raise huge capital sums, enabling them to afford the risks which accompanied containerisation and the construction of a large tonnage of large-type vessels, including tankers.

Conclusion

So far I have emphasised that Japan's post-war shipping policy developed with the government-sponsored Programmed Shipbuilding Scheme playing a leading role. The scheme has been previously interpreted only as a means of supplying government finance at a lower rate of interest. Along with that I have emphasised the significance of its flexible application, resulting in the formation of vessel types which were nicely adapted to economic change and the advance in shipping technology.[5] Nobody has paid attention to the point, but it was this flexibility that made the financing effective and promoted the development of the industry. However, such a performance would not have been achieved without the vital power of the industry.

I have previously given a few examples to show the vitality of the industry. Generally speaking, it is seen up to the present in its entry into new fields of business where it can expect more profits, while not being afraid of competition. In the shipping market an innovation by one company is not generally permitted to be monopolised by it for more than a short period. This applies to the development of new markets, new methods of management and especially in the introduction of vessels with high technology. These innovations would soon be imitated by the followers.[6]

After the war Japan's shipping companies were faced by many opportunities for innovation. The rapid progress in the technology of ship construction was one example. The most important factor, however, was the growth and structural change of the Japanese economy, which enabled the shipping industry to handle an increased volume of imports and exports. The industry showed the ability and vigour to exploit these opportunities fully. It owed a great deal especially to the flexible attitude of the union, allowing vessels which incorporated advanced technology to be introduced without any serious problems. Because of this vigour, however, many companies rushed to expand their business activities, which in turn led to an excessive competition.

Notes

1 There are various statistics of the tonnage at the end of the war, each of which shows a different figure. The figures here are taken from Ministry of Transport, *The Current Situation of Japanese Shipping* (1951).

2 The figure for 1980 is taken from Ministry of Transport, *The Current Situation of Japanese Shipping* (1982).

3 The financing of the government-sponsored Programmed Shipbuilding Scheme has changed in the course of time. From 1953 it was furnished by the Development Bank, which was established in 1951 as a government financial agency for the recovery of the economy and the development of industry. It relies for its funds on postal savings and social insurance premiums.

4 Y. Hirai and R. Furuta, *A Short History of Japanese Merchant Shipping* (Tokyo, 1967), pp. 152–3.

5 The situation has been gradually changing since the oil crisis of 1973. As noted earlier, Japan's shipping industry has relied increasingly on vessels chartered from overseas. Among them are many which are Japanese-owned but registered under foreign flags. They are of course built on the owners' initiative and not under the Programmed Shipbuilding Scheme. The scheme's influence on the structure of the industry and of the merchant fleet has to that extent declined. Increasingly the industry has to determine that structure itself. At the same time the changing situation tends to weaken the monopolistic power of the union in the labour market because the crews of chartered vessels are not under its control.

6 T. Chida, *The Economics of the Shipping Industry* (1978), Part 2, chapter 2.

For Product Safety Concerns and Information please contact our EU
representative GPSR@taylorandfrancis.com Taylor & Francis Verlag GmbH,
Kaufingerstraße 24, 80331 München, Germany

Printed and bound by CPI Group (UK) Ltd, Croydon, CR0 4YY
01/05/2025
01858383-0001